AN INTRODUCTION
TO DEVIANCE

The disability of blindness is a learned social role. The various attitudes and patterns of behavior that characterize people who are blind are not inherent in their condition but rather are acquired through ordinary processes of social learning. Thus, there is nothing inherent in the condition of blindness that requires a person to be docile, dependent, melancholy, or helpless; nor is there anything about it that should lead him to become independent or assertive. Blind men are made, and by the same processes of socialization that have made us all.

————Robert A. Scott, *The Making of a Blind Man*

AN INTRODUCTION TO DEVIANCE
Readings in the Process of Making Deviants

edited by
WILLIAM J. FILSTEAD
Associate Director of Research and Education
Rehabilitation Center
Lutheran General Hospital, Park Ridge, Illinois

MARKHAM PUBLISHING COMPANY / Chicago

MARKHAM SOCIOLOGY SERIES
Robert W. Hodge, Editor

To my wife, Diane

Preface

One question is of prime importance in the sociological study of deviant behavior: How are the actions of an individual labeled deviant? The labeling approach to deviance suggests that an actor is assigned a deviant status through social differentiation. It is unfortunate that very little attention has been directed at specifying the process of social differentiation. In short, there is little knowledge about the production of deviance.

This reader presents a collection of articles that articulate the production of deviance in terms of interpersonal and institutional processes. The selections show clearly how deviants are produced through the everyday processes of socialization that make us all.

I would like to thank Jerry Suttles for his comments on the reader. The discussions with Jean Rossi and other members of the Rehab Staff of Lutheran General Hospital provided a source of stimulation in the formulation of the reader. My fellow graduate students at Northwestern, especially Shelly Goldenberg and Jack Katz, added invaluably to the ideas in this reader. I owe special thanks to John Kitsuse for his encouragement and intellectual stimulation.

Finally, in between everything else, my secretary Nancy Scovill made sure everything was done when it had to be. To her and Team Four many thanks.

October, 1971

W. J. F.
Park Ridge, Illinois

Contents

General Theoretical Framework: An Introduction

WILLIAM J. FILSTEAD

Within the field of deviant behavior, the labeling perspective has gained prominence as a major approach to understanding the nature of deviance. The labeling perspective considers the question of how social actors become defined and treated as deviant rather than traditional etiological question of what makes social actors commit deviant acts. This switch in emphasis expands the study of deviance to include not only the alleged deviant, but also the reactions of others and especially the reactions of agencies of social control established to deal with the deviance. In short, the context surrounding the social actor becomes the primary focus of research.

MAIN ASSUMPTIONS OF THE LABELING PERSPECTIVE

More than twenty years have passed since Lemert formulated some of the major assumptions of the labeling perspective. Since that formulation and subsequent refinements of the perspective, a substantial body of theoretical and empirical evidence has been accumulated in support of its main tenets.[1] This has imputed to the labeling perspective a level of respectability that may impede a thorough assessment of its assumptions and implications. Rather than directly address the exchange between the critics and adherents of the labeling point of view,[2] I shall simply present some of the key assumptions of this approach and then suggest directions future investigations might pursue. The time is ripe for sociologists to critically evaluate this approach to deviance.

A fundamental position of the labeling perspective is that the reactions of others produce awareness of deviant behavior. This places deviance in a framework external to the actor, situation, or event and subject to the process of identification and reaction by others. Closely related to "others' reactions" is a second assumption eschewing the notion that certain behaviors by their very nature are deviant.

> From this point of view, deviance is *not* a quality of an act a person commits, but rather a consequence of the application by others of rules and sanctions to an 'offender.' The deviant is one to whom that label has been successfully applied; deviant behavior is behavior that people so label (Becker, 1963: 9).

> Forms of behavior *per se* do not differentiate deviants from non-deviants; it is the response of conventional and conforming members of society who identify and interpret behavior as deviant which sociologically transforms people into deviants (Kitsuse, 1962: 253).

Conceptualization of deviance as a "reaction process" on the part of others leads to a third assumption that posits that the distinction between conventional and unconventional behavior is very ambiguous. According to the labeling approach, acceptable and unacceptable behavior is relative. There are inherent ambiguities involved in the distinction of whether an action is deviant or nondeviant. The investigations of paranoia and stuttering by Lemert (1962a, b) and of blindness by Scott (1970) are excellent analyses of how a social actor, through social differentiation, is assigned a deviant status.

Finally, a fourth assumption essential to the labeling perspective is the conceptualization of deviant behavior in an interactionist framework.[3] The interactionist framework is a general perspective of society that emphasizes the collective nature of social action, the dynamics of interaction between self and others, the processual nature of human interaction, and the importance of seeing reality from the point of view of those engaged in the action. This particular assumption integrates the preceding points into a framework for understanding not only deviance, but behavior in general.

Having briefly discussed the assumptions of the labeling approach, which in itself represents a new departure from the traditional explanations of deviance, the remainder of the article will suggest areas in need of development, gaps in present understanding, and current limitations of the labeling approach. These areas are in need of explanation in order to further elaborate this fruitful approach to the understanding of deviance. The space limitations preclude an indepth discussion of the following points; however, the direction will be clear enough to enable future investigations to pick up on their implications.

ISSUES TO CONSIDER IN THE LABELING APPROACH TO DEVIANCE

An understanding of the rules by which social actors make judgments concerning the appropriateness or inappropriateness of an act are of fundamental importance to an understanding of deviance. Although the labeling approach emphasizes the ambiguity surrounding the process of labeling an actor, act or situation as deviant, there has been little systematic investigation of the prior process of constructing labels. To say that an individual is an "alcoholic" is not to explain the process by which that label was deemed appropriate instead of another, such as "heavy drinker." There has been a lack of effort directed toward developing a description of the labeling process.[4] Rather, investigators have assumed the process has occurred, and traditionally have engaged in analysis of the consequences of having been labeled.

The conceptualization of the nature of interaction is closely tied to the labeling process. The labeling approach views the nature of interaction as problematic, rather than conforming to a more or less coherent system of shared norms. Throughout the writings of Becker, Lemert, Scheff, Kitsuse, Douglas, and others, phrases such as "emergent definitions," "social construction of reality," "evolving social meaning," and "retrospective reconstructions," imply that the nature of the social order is problematic, in flux, and continually being negotiated.[5] This problem of making sense out of reality is vitally important in the process of attaching social meanings to actions, and deserves more serious attention than it has received up to date by the labeling approach. It is one thing to postulate the problematic nature of social interaction; it is quite another to systematically investigate this complex process that is coterminous with social action.

With the switch in emphasis from the study of deviance in isolation to the study of the context in which behavior is identified as deviant, the labeling approach expanded the area of investigation to include the reactions of others, and the influence of legally mandated agencies of social control. While providing new insights into the understanding of deviance, this shift has also produced some blind spots that need to be reexamined. Two of these blind spots immediately present themselves for clarification. First, there is a tendency to oversimplify and reify the social determinacy implications of the labeling approach. This is quite clear in Lemert's description of the sequence of interaction leading to secondary deviation (1951: 77). One of the paradoxes of the labeling perspective is that investigators assume the problematic and interpretive nature of interaction and then suggest that once a social actor's behavior is labeled deviant, these same rules become rigid and inflexible. That a social actor is labeled by others and by social agencies of control as deviant in no way freezes the problematic and interpretive nature of interaction and rule making. Numerous examples in the real world reject this social determinacy, such as the "alcoholic" who has undergone treatment many times and who still may be seen as a "heavy drinker" by himself, family, friends, and even agencies of social control all of whom have conflicting ideological frameworks regarding the nature of alcoholism.

The second blind spot concerns the reactions of others. According to the interaction perspective, it is through the collective action of individuals that shared meanings arise, develop, and change. Because the labeling approach strongly emphasizes the importance of others' reactions in the production of deviance, the approach might reasonably be expected to develop a theory of the reaction process.[6] Such a theory would concern itself with the various strategies employed by social actors to make sense out of their worlds. The work of Scott and Lyman (1968), Glaser and Strauss (1964), Matza (1970), Douglas (1970) represents an attempt in this direction. The thrust of investigations should be directed at depicting the moves and countermoves in the exchange process between self and others. For example, one possible area of research could deal with the "process of denial" on the part of those refusing to accept the label of deviant.[7]

Traditionally, the labeling approach has been concerned with the kind of behavior referred to as secondary or public forms of deviance. This focus has led to a concentration on agencies of social control and the social determinancy implied in the labeling process. If a full understanding of the process of labeling is to be achieved, future research will have to analyze everyday violations of the social order and thus obtain an awareness of the process of developing shared social meanings. Norman K. Denzin (1970: 121) recently emphasized the need to shift the study of deviance into secret or normal deviance by stating:

> . . . I will propose a refocus in labeling theory such that daily forms of interaction are given central attention. I will delineate the variety of rules that play upon daily conduct, treat the nature of social worlds and social relationships, and indicate under what circumstances we feel a public or private deviant will be created.

Finally, the labeling approach uses the concept career as a key term to characterize deviant behavior as a process. Career conveys the processual nature of the contingencies in interaction. A clear depiction of this processual nature is embodied in the concept of a status passage. This appears true for two important reasons. First, status passages allow one to conceptualize process as a series of interlocking positions, the availability of which are subject to the exigencies of social interaction. Second, whereas the term career carries the connotation of a fizzed and inevitable process, status passage conveys the ambiguous nature of the context surrounding collective action. Status passage, a more abstract concept, allows for greater flexibility in the conceptualization of the process of producing deviants.

In summary, the intent of this introductory article is to delineate the main assumptions of the labeling approach and to point to areas of future work. The continued fruitfulness of the labeling perspective is contingent on the ability of sociologists to meet the challenges of its limitations. The following readings represent an attempt to meet one of these challenges by articulating the nature of the production of deviance.

NOTES

[1] See Lemert (1951, 1967), Becker (1963, 1964), Kitsuse (1962), Scheff (1964), Schur (1965), and Sudnow (1965).

[2] See Gibbs (1966), Bordua (1967), Matza (1969), Douglas (1970), Rains and Kitsuse (1970), and Becker (1971).

[3] For an understanding of the interactionist framework see Mead (1934), Blumer (1969), and Rubington and Weinberg (1968).

[4] One exception can be found in Blum (1970).

[5] For more detail on this issue, see Kitsuse in this volume.

[6] This point is made by Kitsuse in his work in this volume.

[7] See Davis (1961) and Matza (1970) for examples of efforts in this direction.

REFERENCES

Becker, H. S.
  1963   Outsiders. Glencoe, Ill.: Free Press.
  1971   "Labeling theory revisited." Paper presented at the British Psychological Association Meeting, April, 1971.
Becker, H. S., ed.
  1964   The Other Side: Perspectives on Deviance. New York: Free Press.
Blum, A.
  1970   "The Sociology of mental illness." In Jack Douglas, ed., Deviance and Respectability. New York: Basic Books. Pp. 35-60.
Blumer, H.
  1969   Symbolic Interactionism: Perspective and Method. Englewood Cliffs, N.J.: Prentice-Hall.
Bordua, D.
  1967   "Recent trends: Deviant behavior and social control." The Annals of the American Academy of Political and Social Science 369: 149-163.
Davis, F.
  1961   "Deviance disavowal: The management of strained interaction by the visibly handicapped." Social Problems 9: 120-132. Reprinted as chapter 9 of this volume.

Denzin, N. K.
  1970   "Rules of conduct and the study of deviant behavior: Some notes on
         the social relationship." In T. Shibutani, ed., Human Nature and
         Collective Behavior. Englewood Cliffs, N.J.: Prentice-Hall. Pp.
         120–139.
Douglas, J., ed.
  1970   Deviance and Respectability. New York: Basic Books.
Gibbs, J.
  1966   "Conceptions of deviant behavior: The old and the new." Pacific
         Sociological Review 9: 9–14. Reprinted as chapter 14 of this volume.
Glaser, B. G., and Strauss, A. L.
  1964   "Awareness contexts and social interaction." American Sociological
         Review 29: 669–679. Reprinted as chapter 2 of this volume.
Kitsuse, J.
  1962   "Societal reaction to deviant behavior: Problems of theory and
         method." Social Problems 9: 247–256.
Kitsuse, J.
  1972   "Deviance, deviant behavior, and deviants: Some conceptual
         issues." Published as Chapter 14 of this volume.
Lemert, E.
  1951   Social Pathology. New York: McGraw-Hill.
  1962a "Paranoia and the dynamics of exclusion." Sociometry 25: 2–25.
  1962b "Stuttering and social structure in two Pacific island societies."
         Journal of Speech and Hearing Disorders 27: 3–10.
  1967   Human Deviance, Social problems, and Social Control. Englewood
         Cliffs, N.J.: Prentice-Hall.
Matza, D.
  1970   Becoming Deviant. Englewood Cliffs, N.J.: Prentice-Hall.
Mead, G. H.
  1934   Mind, Self and Society. Chicago: University of Chicago Press.
Rains, P., and Kistuse, J.
  1970   "Comments on the labeling approach to deviance." Unpublished
         paper.
Rubington, E., and Weinberg, M.
  1968   Deviance: The Interactionist Perspective. New York: Macmillan.
Scheff, T.
  1966   Being Mentally Ill. Chicago: Aldine.
Schur, E.
  1965   Crimes Without Victims. Englewood Cliffs, N.J.: Prentice-Hall.
Scott, M., and Lyman, S.
  1968   "Accounts." American Sociological Review 33: 44–62. Reprinted as
         Chapter 3 of this volume.
Scott, R. A.
  1970   The Making of Blind Men. New York: Basic Books.
Strauss, A.
  1970   "Discovering new theory from previous theory." In T. Shibutani,
         ed., Human Nature and Collective Behavior. Englewood Cliffs,
         N.J.: Prentice-Hall. Pp. 46–53.
Sudnow, D.
  1965   "Normal crimes: Sociological features of the penal code in a public
         defender office." Social Problems 12: 255–276.

Part I

THE CONSTRUCTION
OF SOCIAL REALITY

2

Awareness Contexts and Social Interaction

BARNEY G. GLASER
ANSELM L. STRAUSS

When men confront each other, each cannot always be certain—even when given seemingly trustworthy guarantees—that he knows either the other's identity or his own identity in the eyes of the other. An honest citizen may be taken in by a confidence man, a government official by a foreign spy passing as his secretary, or a dying patient by his doctor. But the confidence man's mark may actually be from the local detective squad; the official, suspecting undercover play, may be pretending innocence while slipping the secretary false documents; and the dying patient may suspect his true condition but not reveal his suspicion to the physician. Thus, who is really being "taken in" is a matter of the awareness of both parties to the situation.

The phenomenon of awareness—which is central to the study of interaction—can be quite complex for at least two reasons. First, interaction may involve not merely two persons, but a third or quite a few

Reprinted from *American Sociological Review,* 29 (1964), pp. 669–679, by permission of the American Sociological Association.

Many of the examples used in this paper are taken from the authors' study of Hospital Personnel, Nursing Care and Dying Patients, supported by National Institutes of Health, Grant GN9077. For a full discussion of awareness contexts related to social interaction in the hospital dying situation, see Glaser and Strauss, *Awareness of Dying: A Study of Social Interaction* (Chicago: Aldine, 1965). Jeanne Quint, a member of our project team, has worked closely with us on these data. We are indebted to Howard S. Becker, Fred Davis, Erving Goffman, Sheldon Messinger, and Melvin Sabshin for their helpful comments on this paper.

more. For instance, when a homosexual flashes cues to another homosexual in the presence of many straight people, some may not notice and others may misread the cues, while others might be aware of their intended meaning. The identity of the homosexual is, therefore, unknown or suspect to some straights and known to still others. Conversely, a homosexual cannot always be certain who suspects or who is or is not aware of his true identity. Second, each person involved may be the representative of a system with specific requirements for, and perhaps a high stake in, how the person manages his own and the other's identity. Spies and counterspies are linked to such systems as often as are doctors and nurses.

These considerations highlight important features of the relation between interaction and awareness. To establish our basic notions, however, we shall content ourselves in this paper with the least complex situation: two interactants (whether persons or groups) who face the dual problem of being certain about both their identity in the other's eyes and the other's identity.

CONTEXTS OF AWARENESS

By the term *awareness context* we mean the total combination of what each interactant in a situation knows about the identity of the other and his own identity in the eyes of the other.[1] This total awareness is the context within which are guided successive interactions between the two persons over periods of time—long or short. Empirically the question of true identity may focus only on that of one of the two persons (the dying patient) or on that of both persons (spy and counterspy).

We have singled out four types of awareness context for special consideration since they have proved useful in accounting for different types of interaction. An *open* awareness context obtains when each interactant is aware of the other's true identity and his own identity in the eyes of the other. A *closed* awareness context obtains when one interactant does not know either the other's identity or the other's view of his identity. A *suspicion* awareness context is a modification of the closed one: one interactant suspects the true identity of the other or the other's view of his own identity, or both. A *pretense* awareness context is a modification of the open one: both interactants are fully aware but pretend not to be.

These types illustrate how the sociologist's total picture may differ from that held by each interactant, no matter how well informed or expert. For example, a doctor may state that a patient does not yet know that he is dying (his identity in the eyes of the doctor) while the patient may very well suspect the physician's definition. Thus, the doctor believes that closed awareness obtains when actually there is a suspicion context within which the patient is testing his suspicions. If the doctor recognizes those suspicions he may attempt to parry them. If the doctor believes himself sucessful, he may only report to the sociologist that as yet the patient is unaware, neglecting to mention the patient's suspicions. Therefore, delimiting an awareness context requires always that the sociologist ascertain independently the awareness of each interactant. The safest method is to obtain data, through observation or interview, from each interactant on his own state of awareness. To accept the word of only one informant is risky, even perhaps for the open awareness context.

The successive interactions occurring within each type of context tend to transform the context. As yet it is an empirical question as to the direction in which a change in one context will lead, or what are some patterns of successive transformations. Thus, a closed context can be shattered by arousing suspicions; but if suspicions are quelled, the closed context is reinstituted. If suspicions are validated, the context may change to either pretense or open awareness. With a change in identity of one interactant in the eyes of the other, an open context can easily become either closed or pretense. For instance, the government official who suspects that his secretary is a spy must now check his suspicions. If he discovers that she is a spy but does not reveal his knowledge, then she in turn misreads his view of her identity. Thus, a closed context now obtains! If she in turn surreptitiously learns of his new view of her but says nothing, the context is again closed. But if he unmasks her spying, then the context now becomes open, since each now fully acknowledges the other's true identity.

How long each context will last before it is transformed is also an empirical question. In the abstract none is inherently less stable than another; although within a given substantive area, differential degrees of stability may become apparent. For dying patients, a suspicion context is probably the least stable, becoming resolved by successive interactions with staff which confirm the patient's suspicions.

A PARADIGM FOR THE STUDY
OF AWARENESS CONTEXTS

To organize a study of interaction within different awareness contexts, we have developed a paradigm or set of directives. These directives focus on the study of developmental interaction process—interaction that changes as it continues—as distinct from the relatively static study of the rules that govern interaction.[2]

The component parts of the paradigm are as follows: (1) a description of the given type of awareness context; (2) the structural conditions under which the awareness context exists;[3] (3) the consequent interaction; (4) changes of interaction that occasion transformations of context, along with the structural conditions for the transforma-tions; (5) the tactics of various interactants as they attempt to man-age changes of awareness context; and (6) some consequences of the initial awareness context, its transformation and associated interac-tions—for interactants and for the organizations or institutions notably affected.

To illustrate the use of this paradigm, we briefly sketch the closed awareness context surrounding dying patients.

(1) Hospitalized patients frequently do not recognize their im-pending death while staff does.[4] Thus interaction between staff and patient occurs within a closed awareness context about the patient's true identity.

(2) At least four major structural conditions determine this closed awareness context. First, most patients are not especially ex-perienced at recognizing the signs of impending death. Second, the hospital is magnificently organized, both by accident and design, for hiding the medical truth from the patient. Records are kept out of reach. Staff is skilled at withholding information from him. Medical talk about him occurs generally in far-removed places. Also, the staff is trained or accustomed to act collusively around patients so as not to disclose medical secrets. Third, physicians are supported in their withholding of information by professional rationales: "Why deny them all hope by telling them they are dying?" Fourth, ordinarily the patient has no allies who can help him discover the staff's secret: even his family or other patients will withhold such information if privy to it.

(3) To prevent the patient's comprehension of the truth, the per-sonnel utilize a number of "situation as normal" interaction tactics. They seek to act in his presence as if he were not dying but only ill. They talk to him as if he were going to live. They converse about his future, thus enhancing his belief that he will regain his health. They tell him stories about others (including themselves) who have re-covered from similar or worse illnesses. By such indirect signaling they offer him a false biography. Of course, they may directly assure him that he will live, lying with a clear purpose.

To supplement these tactics the staff members use additional ones to guard against disclosure. They carefully guard against the patient's overhearing any conversation about his real condition. They engage also in careful management of expressions, controlling their facial and other gestures so as not to give the show away:[5] they must control the expression of any sadness they experience over the patient's approach-ing death. Almost inevitably they attempt, not always consciously, to reduce the number of potentially disclosing cues by reducing time spent with the patient or by restricting their conversations with him.

(4) In such collusive games, the teamwork can be phenomenal but the dangers of disclosure to the patient are very great. Unless the

patient dies quickly or becomes permanently comatose, the patient tends to suspect or even clearly understand how others identify him. Patients do overhear occasional conversations about themselves. Personnel unwittingly may flash cues or make conversational errors, which arouse the patient's suspicions. Day and night staff may give him contradictory information or divergent clues. The frequent practice of rotating personnel through the hospital services, or adding new personnel, may add to the danger of disclosure. The patient himself may become more knowledgeable about what is going on around him after some days in the hospital, or after repeated hospitalizations. Eventually he may also understand that the hospital is organized not to give him all the information about his condition but rather to withhold most information. He therefore takes what is told him with a grain of salt and some distrust of its accuracy. In short, the original structural conditions that sustain closed awareness begin to disappear, or are counteracted by new structural conditions that make for suspicion or open awareness. This is true even when the patient's symptoms do not badly worsen, but when he does turn worse this may cause him to ask new questions about his illness, which staff members need to handle cannily to keep from his their knowledge that he is dying.

(5) Some interactants may wish to move him along into other types of awareness contexts. If so, they can employ certain interactional tactics which are, for the most part, merely the opposites of the nondisclosure tactics. Intentionally, a staff member may give the show away wholly or partly, by improper management of face, by carefully oblique phrasing of words, by merely failing to reassure the patient sufficiently about a hopeful prognosis, by changing all talk about the future into concentration upon the present, or by increasing avoidance both of conversation and the patient himself. Of course, personnel occasionally may just plain tell him that he is dying.

(6) The closed awareness that "surrounds" the dying patient has many significant consequences for patient and staff. The patient, unaware of the other's view of his identity, cannot act as if he were aware of dying. Thus, he cannot talk to close kin about his fate. He cannot assuage their grief. Nor can he act toward himself as if he were dying, by facing his expected death gracefully—or with panic and hysteria.

The kinsmen and hospital personnel are saved from certain stressful scenes that accompany open awareness about death, but they are also blocked from participating in various satisfying rituals of passage to death. Wives cannot openly take farewells of husbands; personnel cannot share the patient's sometimes ennobling acceptance of death. A profound consequence for the hospital itself, as well as for staff, of the closed awareness context is an interesting division of labor wherein nurses carry the brunt of stressful verbal interaction during which dying and death talk must be avoided. The physicians escape much of this stress since only brief visits are required for patients seemingly on the mend, hence talk is held to a minimum. Moreover, the climate of certain hospital services would be quite different (usually less oppressive) if closed awareness contexts were completely absent—as they are on certain special types of hospital wards.[6]

PREVIOUS ANALYSES OF INTERACTION

The notion of awareness context is useful for understanding other theoretical approaches to awareness as it relates to social interaction. Our paradigm for the study of interaction within awareness contexts may be used to locate, in a single scheme, the diverse aspects of awareness and social interaction attended to in sociological writings. To illustrate this application of both concept and paradigm, we shall discuss the theoretical work of George H. Mead and Erving Goffman as well as the researches of Donald Roy and Fred Davis. Rather than assess their work *per se,* we shall discuss the writings of these men as good examples of the current state of theory and research about social interaction.

George H. Mead: Mead's concern with social interaction was secondary to a lifetime preoccupation with the problems of social order and its orderly change. We interpret his analysis of interaction—also his writing about communication and thought—as bearing principally on an open awareness context. In a well known passage he wrote that: "In short, the conscious or significant conversation of gestures is a much more adequate and effective mechanism of mutual adjustment within the social act—involving, as it does, the taking, by each of the individuals carrying it on, the attitudes of the others toward himself—than is the unconscious or non-significant conversation of gestures."[7] For Mead, "awareness" was essentially an *accurate* awareness of how one's own gesture (vocal or otherwise) was being defined by others, followed by further action based on that awareness. Thus: "That process . . . of responding to one's self as another responds to it, taking part in one's own conversations with others, being aware of what one is saying and using that awareness of what one is saying to determine what one is going to say thereafter—that is a process with which we are all familiar" (p. 217). This perceptive social philosopher gave his readers a rich but highly generalized analysis of that universal situation in which men genuinely and openly communicate.

Mead was not always consistently concerned with shared communication but—as the preceding quotations suggest—also with how one guesses the other's perception of his behavior so as further to direct that behavior oneself. Whether on the basis of these guesses one then misleads the other or plays the game honestly is left ambiguous. Presumably Mead meant the ensuing interaction to be genuinely open and cooperative.[8] The full force of our commentary on this aspect of his work is best demonstrated by an unusual passage wherein Mead raises and dismisses those aspects of interaction that do not involve shared symbolization. He remarks:

> There is, of course, a great deal in one's conversation with others that does not arouse in one's self the same response it arouses in others. That is particularly true in the case of emotional attitudes. One tries to bully somebody else; he is not trying to bully himself. . . . We do at times act and consider just what the effect of our attitude is going to be, and we may deliberately use a certain tone of voice to bring about a certain result. Such a tone arouses the same response in ourselves that we want to arouse in somebody else. But a very large part of what goes on in speech has not this . . . status.

> It is the task not only of the actor but of the artist as well to find the sort of expression that will arouse in others what is going on in himself . . . the stimulus calls out in the artist that which it calls out on the other, but this is not the natural function of language. . . ." (pp. 224–226).

And what is the natural function of language? "What is essential to communication is that the symbol should arouse in one's self what it arouses in the other individual." Mead seems here to touch on interaction based on something different from open awareness and genuine communication. In deliberate bullying, for example, one's activity may frighten the other but does not frighten oneself. In writing poetry, one finds the means to arouse responses in others what one finds in himself (and Mead remarks that Wordsworth took some years to turn those immediate responses into poetry). And in this same passage, Mead notes that "we do not assume that the person who is angry is calling out the fear in himself that he is calling out in someone else;" that is, in this spontaneous expression of feeling, actor and audience do not respond identically. We should not be surprised to find, sandwiched within this passage, Mead's laconic comment that though we can act—quite like the actor does—"It is not a natural situation; one is not an actor all of the time." Of course no one is! But what about the times when we do act?

Mead's analysis is especially pertinent to this paper because it emphasizes a property of interaction so often absent in other men's work: the developmental properties of interaction. In Mead's writing the concept of significant symbol not only underscores the consensual character of social order but also shows how social order is changed— how social objects are formed and transformed during the course of constructed acts. In current reading of Mead, this developmental aspect tends to be overlooked; so does his processual, rather than substantial, treatment of the self. The self as process insures that interaction is usually not static or merely repetitive. In Mead's world, acts are open-ended, frequently surprising to the actors themselves. And in some of his finest writings Mead emphasizes how even past events are reconstructed, powerfully influencing the directions taken by present events. In short, interaction always tends to go somewhere, but exactly where is not always known for certain by the interactants.

Erving Goffman: Erving Goffman's work is probably the most influential among current theoretical analyses of interaction. If he does not stand at an opposite pole from Mead, he surely stands far removed—in style, temperament, theoretical perspective, and above all in his focus on the interplay of people. In his first book, *The Presentation of Self in Everyday Life,*[9] one can easily follow his detailed, central analysis of interaction.

From the beginning, Goffman emphasizes an audience's need to define an individual's identity. "When an individual enters the presence of others, they commonly seek to acquire information about him or to bring into play information about him already possessed" (p. 2). Whether or not an actor wishes, his actions yield impressions of him to his audiences. Therefore, people most frequently "devote their efforts to the creation of desired impressions" rather than act completely without guile or contrivance. "Engineering a convincing impression" is an inescapable fact (p. 162). It is a way for each interactant "to control the conduct of others" (p. 2).

Because of such impression management, "events may occur within the interaction which contradict, discredit, or otherwise throw doubt upon the actor's projection of himself." Much of Goffman's book turns around the confusion or embarrassment that occurs when interaction is thus disrupted. He analyzes extensively the "preventive practices" consequent upon disruptions: "defensively by the actor himself, and protectively when the audience strives to save the definition of the situation projected by another" (p. 7).

In all of this, Goffman focuses on closed awareness. He has a section on "team collusion" (pp. 112–120), and another on the maintenance of expressive control" (pp. 33–37). Second, he explicitly treats pretense awareness contexts. For instance, "each team tends to suppress its candid view of itself and of the other team, projecting a conception of self and a conception of other that is relatively acceptable to the other. And to insure that communication will follow established, narrow channels, each team is prepared to assist the other team, tacitly and tactfully, in maintaining the impression it is attempting to foster" (page 107).[10] In general, Goffman, at least in this volume, is uninterested in open awareness contexts; and though he touches on contexts where audiences are suspicious of the actor's projected definition, he does not go into the ways in which the suspicion gradually grows and then is validated.

But whether pretense or closed awareness is at issue, Goffman's principal focus is on how the interaction is kept going, or if disrupted, how interactants manage to get it going again. He has little interest in awareness contexts that are transformed through the deliberate operations of the interactants or through the continued course of the interaction itself. Indeed, his analysis is geared to episodic or repeated interactions rather than to sustained interplay. Consistently with this non-developmental focus, his dramaturgical model refers to the *team* of stage actors who night after night seek to create an acceptable illusion, rather than to the *drama* itself, with its plot line and evolving, relatively unpredictable, sequence of transactions.[11] Particularly it is worth underscoring that the identity of Goffman's actor is rarely problematical to himself, but only and always to his audience.[12]

In this book Goffman tends to leave implicit the structural conditions imposed by the larger social unit. Rather, he focuses mainly on situational conditions such as setting and front and back regions. Of course, most interaction in *The Presentation of Self* occurs in establishments containing service personnel and clients, insiders and outsiders; that is, persons who are either relatively unknown to each other or respectively withhold significant aspects of their private lives from each other. Goffman leaves to his readers the task of considering what kinds of structural conditions might lead to interactions quite different from those described. For example, his discussions of impression management might have been very different had he studied neighborhood blocks, small towns, or families, where participants are relatively well known to each other. Similarly, he is not much concerned with systematically tracing various consequences of the interaction (especially for larger social units); although for interactants, of course, consequences are noted in terms of specific linkages with the disruption or smooth continuance of encounters.

Aside from its restricted range of awareness contexts, Goffman's world of interaction is nondevelopmental and rather static. In other writings, he is concerned with interaction of considerable duration, but characteristically his interest is in the rules that govern that interaction. Often interaction proceeds to its termination almost as inexorably as a Greek tragedy.[13] For these aspects, however, his analysis is a considerable advance beyond those of his predecessors.

Next we reexamine two useful papers, our aim being first, to locate the reported research within our awareness paradigm; second, to assess its contribution to interactional analysis; and third, to suggest what might be added to that analysis if one were now to undertake such research.

Donald Roy: In his "Efficiency and 'The Fix': Informal Inter-group Relations in a Piecework Machine Shop,"[14] Roy is interested in demonstrating "that the interaction of two groups in an industrial organization takes place within and is conditioned by a larger intergroup network of reciprocal influences." The interaction is a contest between management and the workers. The latter adroitly scheme, connive, and invent methods for attaining quotas set by management; while management attempts to minimize the success of these "black arts of 'making out.' " These arts "were not only responses to challenge from management but also stimulations, in circular interaction, to the development of more effective countermagic in the timing process" established by management's time-checkers. An important segment of Roy's discussion deals with "intergroup collusion" among workers from other departments, who become allies in this unending contest with management.

Where shall we locate Roy's research in our awareness context paradigm? From Roy's discription, the awareness contexts are not entirely clear since we do not always know the extent to which management was aware of what was going on among the workers. But in general, workers' attempts to keep closed awareness about their specific collusive games seem to have alternated with management's periodic awareness of such games. Whether this periodic awareness of management transformed the closed context temporarily into pretense or open awareness is difficult to determine. Roy does, however, clearly give the structural conditions that permit both the closed awareness context and its periodic, temporary transformation to pretense or open before the workers reinstitute the closed context with a new collusive game.

Roy describes in great detail the interactional tactics of both sets of players which maintain, transform and reinstate closed awareness. Teamwork on the worker's side is exceptionally well sketched. Managerial tactics, however, are described principally from "below," for two reasons. First, Roy was doing field work as an industrial worker, and could scarcely be privy to management's specific perspectives and decisions. Second, he did not need to scrutinize management's views because his research was designed to explore how workers organized their work.

In spite of the fact that Roy describes the phases through which the contest, and hence the awareness context, oscillates, true temporal development is lacking. This is because he conceives of the interaction as unendingly the same. Apparently the limits of the interaction were set by the time period devoted to the research itself. As Roy himself notes in passing: "How far the beginning of the series [of new rules] antedated the writer's arrival is not known. Oldtimers spoke of a 'Golden Age' enjoyed before the installation of the 'Booth System' of production control." An interest in interactional process must raise these questions: from what situation did the interaction phases develop, where did they end, and what happened if someone attempted to bring the collusive interaction out into the open?

The consequences of the interaction are noted sporadically—mainly in terms of work blockages and cumulative inefficiency—but again we might wish to know much more, especially about diverse consequences for the functioning of the organization at large.

Fred Davis: A very different presentation of interaction is Fred Davis's "Deviance Disavowal: The Management of Strained Interaction by the Visibly Handicapped."[15] The sub-title accurately describes what this paper is all about. The visible stigma of the handicapped person presents a threat to sociability which "is, at minimum, fourfold: its tendency to become an exclusive focal point of the interaction, its potential for inundating expressive boundaries, its discordance with other attributes of the person and, finally, its ambiguity as a predicator of joint activity." These are "contextual emergents which, depending on the particular situation, serve singly or in combination to strain the framework of normative rules and assumptions in which sociability develops."

After a discussion of these various emergents, which constitute a grave threat to interaction, we are shown "how socially adept handicapped persons cope with it so as to either keep it at bay, dissipate it, or lessen its impact upon the interaction." The analysis is aimed at delineating "in transactional terms the stages through which a social relationship with a normal typically passes." The stages are: (1) fictional acceptance, (2) "breaking through" or facilitating normalized role-taking, and (3) institutionalization of the normalized relationship. From the viewpoint of the handicapped person, the "unfolding" of the stages represents deviance disavowal; from that of the normal person it is normalization. For each stage in the process, a certain number of interactional tactics are noted, though David is more interested in interactional stages than in the "tremendous variety of specific approaches, ploys and strategems that the visibly handicapped employ in social situations."

This research deals with the transformation of pretense awareness ("fictional acceptance") to open awareness ("institutionalization of the normalized relationship"), chiefly but not solely under the control of transforming operations by the handicapped. As Davis describes it, the handicapped person attempts first to keep interaction in the fictional mode (both interactants mutually aware of his stigma but neither acting as though it existed); then, gradually, the handicapped person engineers matters to a final phase where it is openly "fitting and safe to admit to certain incidental capacities, limits, and needs"—that is, where both parties may openly refer to the stigma of the handicapped person.

Davis' discussion is additionally rich because he makes some very explicit remarks about how difficult the open awareness (normalization) phase is for either party to maintain. For instance: "to integrate effectively a major claim to 'normalcy' with numerous minor waivers of the same claim is a tricky feat and one which exposes the relationship to the many situational and psychic hazards of apparent duplicity. . . ." By implication, this relationship between the two parties has a future: because it is difficult to maintain, it cannot remain at a standstill. We say "by implication" because Davis is content to carry the story only to where something like normal sociability can take place. Said another way, Davis actually is analyzing a developmental—not merely as engineered—interaction situation. "As against the simplistic model of a compulsive deviant and a futile normalizer we would propose one in which it is postulated that both are likely to become engaged in making corrective interactional efforts toward healing the breach." Precisely because *both* are likely to make those correctional efforts, this is a developmental relationship. Our paradigm helps raise the questions of where the relationship is going and what further transformations, under what conditions, may occur.

Our paradigm also suggests focusing on both parties to the interplay even when it is relatively adeptly controlled by one, since our understanding of the relationship's developmental aspects necessarily requires knowledge of the actions and awareness of both parties. Thus, how does the normal interactant see the handicapped, and the interaction, at various phases of the interaction—and what is he doing, or deciding to do, about it? What will his tactics be, whether occasional or continual? Davis also assumes that the handicapped person has often been through this type of interaction—hence has evolved tactics for handling it—while the normal person is a novice. This may be so, but in actual life both players may have had similar experiences.

Lastly, Davis attempts to specify one class of structural conditions that permit the handicapped person to manage strained interaction. He beings his paper by referring to "that genre of everyday intercourse" which is characteristically face-to-face, not too prolonged but not too fleeting either, with a certain degree of intimacy, and "ritualized to the extent that all know in general what to expect but not so ritualized as to preclude spontaneity and the slightly novel turn of events." This explicit detailing is not a mere backdrop but an intrinsic part of the analysis of interaction in the presence of physical stigma. The consequences of interaction (e.g., the satisfaction of both parties and the possibility of a continuing relationship) are left mainly implicit.

GENERAL IMPLICATIONS OF PARADIGM

Our examination of these four writers indicates that future research and theory on interactional problems should encompass a far broader

range of phenomena than heretofore. Of course, one need not do everything demanded by the paradigm. But it guides the researcher in ex-
ploring and perhaps extending the limits of his data, and in stating
clearly what was done and left undone, perhaps adding why and why
not. The paradigm helps the theorist achieve greater clarity, integration, and depth of analysis by encouraging reflection upon what he has
chosen *not* to make explicit. It also raises questions about development and structure that a straight factor approach to the study of
interaction typically does not:[16] how does one type of context lead to
another; what are the structural conditions—including rules—in the
relevant institutions that facilitate or impede existence of a context,
and changes in it; what are the effects of a changing awareness context
on the identity of a participant; why does one party wish to change a
context while another wishes to maintain it or reinstate it; what are
the various interactional tactics used to maintain or reinstate change;
and what are the consequences for each party, as well as for sustaining
institutional conditions?

This developmental focus helps to eliminate the static quality and
restricted boundaries for analysis that are characteristic of the factor
approach. The factor approach is useful only when the analyst is conscious of the location of his conceptual boundaries within a larger
developmental, substantive scheme, and can thereby explain their
relevance to his readers, rather than implicitly declaring all other substantive factors out of bounds. Only then is it sensible to leave out so
much that other sociologists, in the light of present theory and knowledge, recognize as relevant to the area under consideration.

The focus on structural conditions increases the likelihood that
the microscopic analysis of interaction will take into account the nature of the larger social structure within which it occurs. The usual
structural approach in sociology tends to neglect microscopic analysis
of interaction and also inhibits attention to its developmental character. Our paradigm encompasses in one developmental scheme the twin,
but often divorced, sociological concerns with social structure and
social interaction. Neither need be slighted, or forgotten for a focus
on the other.

Our discussion has touched on only four possible types of awareness contexts: open, closed, pretense, and suspicion. These four types
are generated by the substantively relevant combinations of four variables found in our study of the literature and in our data on awareness
of identity and interaction. We have considered two variables as di-
chotomous—*two interactants; acknowledgment of awareness* (pretense or
no pretense)—and two as trichotomous—*degree of awareness* (aware,
suspicious and unaware); and *identity* (other's identity, own identity,
and own identity in the eyes of the other). Logical combination of
these variables would yield 36 possible types, but to start research
with all the logical combinations of these variables would be an un-
necessarily complex task, considering that many or most types are

empirically non-existent. Therefore, the procedure used to develop awareness context types related to interaction was first, to search data for relevant types; second, to logically substruct the variables involved; and third, on the basis of these variables to judge whether other possible types would be useful or necessary for handling the data.

Presumably, more empirically relevant types can be found by scrutinizing the sociological literature, one's own data, and one's own life.[17] Another implication of the present analysis is that increasingly complex types of awareness contexts and their distinctive consequences should be systematically sought. We recommend our procedure for evolving types, as opposed to starting out with the full set of logical combinations, each of which must then be screened for empirical relevance.

We suggested, at the beginning of the paper, two factors that further complicate awareness contexts: additional people, and people representing organized systems with a stake in certain types of awareness context. Certain types of social phenomena are probably strategic for extending our knowledge of awareness contexts: for example, research discoveries in science and in industry, spy systems, deviant communities whose actions may be visible to "squares," types of bargaining before audiences, such as occurs in diplomatic negotiations, and unofficial reward systems like those depicted by Melville Dalton[18] and Alvin Gouldner.[19]

NOTES

[1]The concept of awareness context is a structural unit, not a property of one of the standard structural units such as group, organization, community, role, position, etc. By "context" we mean it is a structural unit of an encompassing order larger than the other unit under focus: interaction. Thus, an awareness context surrounds and affects the interaction. Much as one might say that the interaction of staff with dying patients occurs within the context of a cancer ward or a veteran's hospital, one can also say that this interaction occurs within a type of awareness context. Note that ward or hospital are concrete, conventional social units, while awareness context is an analytic social unit, constructed to account for similarities in interaction in many diverse conventional units.

A more general definition of awareness context is the total combination of what specific people, groups, organizations, communities or nations know what about a specific issue. Thus, this structural concept can be used for the study of virtually any problem entailing awareness at any structural level of analysis.

[2]See Erving Goffman, *Behavior in Public Places*, New York: Free Press, 1963.

[3]We use the phrase "structural conditions" to emphasize that the conditions are conceived of as properties of social structural units. These units may vary from the smallest (such as role, status, or relationship) to the largest (such as organization, community, nation or society) and may be either larger or smaller than the unit of discussion. Usually they are larger contextual units. Structural conditions are the tools-in-trade of most sociologists, this footnote is not meant for them. The structural conditions under which interaction takes place, however, are not typically included in the work of social psychologists, especially those trained in departments of psychology.

[4]We shall assume that the staff members all share the same awareness and that the staff's definition of a patient's identity (dying) is correct.

[5]Erving Goffman, *The Presentation of Self in Everyday Life*, Edinburgh, Scotland: University of Edinburgh, 1956; see also the Anchor edition.

[6]See Renée Fox, *Experiment Perilous*, Glencoe, Ill.: Free Press, 1959.

[7]Anselm Strauss (ed.), *The Social Psychology of George Herbert Mead*, Chicago: University of Chicago Press, 1956, p. 173. All references are to this volume.

[8]Herbert Blumer, in pointing to the great value of Mead's approach, has also emphasized concerted action, whether accomplished or developed. See Blumer's "Society as Symbolic Interaction" in Arnold Rose, (ed.), *Human Behavior and Social Processes*, Boston: Houghton Mifflin, 1962, esp. pp. 187–188.

[9]All references are to the original Edinburgh edition.

[10]This passage is a pretty fair description of the situation in which a dying patient and his nurses both engage in pretense by delicately avoiding talk about the patient's impending death.

[11]Many readers seemed to have missed this point. Compare a similar comment in Sheldon Messinger, Harold Sampson and Robert Towne, "Life as Theater: Some Notes on the Dramaturgic Approach to Social Reality," *Sociometry*, 25 (March, 1962), p. 108.

[12]To Goffman, surprise means potential disruption of interaction—as compared with Mead's notion of the creative and surprising impulsivity of the "I."

[13]See Messinger, et al., "Life as Theater."

[14]*American Journal of Sociology*, 60 (November, 1954), pp. 255–266.

[15]*Social Problems*, 9 (Winter, 1961), pp. 120–132.

[16]The factor approach is a standard one in sociology; it is legitimated by the notion that one can only consider so much at one time with precision and clarity, and therefore boundaries must be chosen, usually according to one's interests, provided they are theoretically relevant. For a discussion of "simultaneous *versus* sequential" factor models, see Howard S. Becker, *Outsiders: Studies in the Sociology of Deviance*, New York: Free Press, 1963, pp. 22–25.

[17]We are working with the "unawareness" context, in which neither party knows the identity of the other or his identity in the others eyes. This is illustrated by strangers meeting or passing each other on a dark street. If they stop to talk, the first task they are likely to engage in is to transform the "unawareness" context to facilitate interaction.

[18]Melville Dalton, *Men Who Manage*, New York: Wiley, 1959.

[19]Alvin Gouldner, *Patterns of Industrial Bureaucracy: A Case Study of Modern Factory Administration*, Glencoe, Ill.: Free Press, 1954.

3

Accounts

MARVIN B. SCOTT
STANFORD M. LYMAN

From time to time sociologists might well pause from their ongoing pursuits to inquire whether their research interests contribute in any way to the fundamental question of sociology, namely, the Hobbesian question: How is society possible? Attempts to answer this question could serve to unite a discipline that may not yet have forgotten why it was founded.

Our purpose here is not to review the various answers to the Hobbesian question,[1] but rather to suggest that an answer to this macro-sociological problem might be fruitfully explored in the analysis of the slightest of interpersonal rituals and the very stuff of which most of those rituals are composed—talk.

Talk, we hold, is the fundamental material of human relations. and though sociologists have not entirely neglected the subject,[2] the sociology of talk has scarcely been developed. Our concern here is with one feature of talk: Its ability to shore up the timbers of fractured sociation, its ability to throw bridges between the promised and the performed, its ability to repair the broken and restore the estranged. This feature of talk involves the giving and receiving of what we shall call *accounts*.

An account is a linguistic device employed whenever an action is subjected to valuative inquiry.[3] Such devices are a crucial element in the social order since they prevent conflicts from arising by verbally bridging the gap between action and expectation.[4] Moreover, accounts are "situated" according to the statuses of the interactants, and are standardized within cultures so that certain accounts are terminolog-

Reprinted from *American Sociological Review*, 33 (1963), pp. 46–62, by permission of the American Sociological Association.

ically stabilized and routinely expected when activity falls outside the domain of expectations.

By an account, then, we mean a statement made by a social actor to explain unanticipated or untoward behavior—whether that behavior is his own or that of others, and whether the proximate cause for the statement arises from the actor himself or from someone else.[5] An account is not called for when people engage in routine, common sense behavior in a cultural environment that recognizes that behavior as such. Thus in American society we do not ordinarily ask why married people engage in sexual intercourse, or why they maintain a home with their children, although the latter question might well be asked if such behavior occurred among the Nayars of Malabar.[6] These questions are not asked because they have been settled in advance in our culture and are indicated by the language itself. We learn the meaning of a married couple by indicating that they are two people of opposite sex who have a legitimate right to engage in sexual intercourse and maintain their own children in their own household. When such taken-for-granted phenomena are called into question, the inquirer (if a member of the same culture group) is regarded as "just fooling around," or perhaps as being sick.[7]

To specify our concerns more sharply we should at this point distinguish accounts from the related phenomenon of "explanations." The latter refers to statements about events where untoward action is not an issue and does not have critical implications for a relationship. Much of what is true about accounts will also hold for explanations, but our concern is primarily with linguistic forms that are offered for untoward action. With this qualification to our concern, we may now specify further the nature and types of accounts.

TYPES OF ACCOUNTS

There are in general two types of accounts: *excuses* and *justifications*.[8] Either or both are likely to be invoked when a person is accused of having done something that is "bad, wrong, inept, unwelcome, or in some other of the numerous possible ways, untoward."[9] Justifications are accounts in which one accepts responsibility for the act in question, but denies the pejorative quality associated with it. Thus a soldier in combat may admit that he has killed other men, but deny that he did an immoral act since those he killed were members of an enemy group and hence "deserved" their fate. Excuses are accounts in which one admits that the act in question is bad, wrong, or inappropriate but denies full responsibility. Thus our combat soldier could admit the wrongfulness of killing but claim that his acts are not entirely undertaken by volition: he is "under orders" and must obey. With these introductory remarks, we now turn our focus to a more detailed examination of types of justifications and excuses.

Excuses are socially approved vocabularies for mitigating or relieving responsibility when conduct is questioned. We may distinguish initially four modal forms by which excuses are typically formulated:[10] *appeal to accident, appeal to defeasibility, appeal to biological drives,* and *scapegoating.*

Excuses claiming *accident* as the source of conduct or its consequences mitigate (if not relieve) responsibility by pointing to the generally recognized hazards in the environment, the understandable inefficiency of the body, and the human incapacity to control all motor responses. The excuse of accident is acceptable precisely because of the irregularity and infrequency of accidents occurring to any single actor. Thus while hazards are numerous and ubiquitous, a particular person is not expected ordinarily to experience the same accident often. In other words, social actors employ a lay version of statistical curves whereby they interpret certain acts as occurring or not occurring by chance alone. When a person conducts himself so that the same type of accident befalls him frequently, he is apt to earn a label—such as "clumsy"—which will operate to stigmatize him and to warn others not to put him and themselves or their property in jeopardy by creating the environment in which he regularly has accidents. When the excuse is rooted in an accident that is unobservable or unable to be investigated—such as blaming one's lateness to work on the heaviness of traffic—frequent pleas of it are likely to be discredited. Excuses based on accidents are thus most likely to be honored precisely because they do not occur all the time or for the most part to the actor in question.[11]

Appeals to *defeasibility*[12] are available as a form of excuse because of the widespread agreement that all actions contain some "mental element." The components of the mental element are "knowledge" and "will." One defense against an accusation is that a person was not fully informed or that his "will" was not completely "free." Thus an individual might excuse himself from responsibility by claiming that certain information was not available to him, which, if it had been, would have altered his behavior. Further, an individual might claim to have acted in a certain way because of misinformation arising from intentional or innocent misrepresentation of the facts by others. An excuse based on interference with the "free will" of an individual might invoke duress or undue influence. Finally both will and knowledge can be impaired under certain conditions, the invocation of which ordinarily constitutes an adequate mitigation of responsibility—intoxication (whether from alcohol or drugs) and lunacy (whether temporary or permanent) being examples.

In ordinary affairs and in law a person's actions are usually distinguished according to their intent. Further, a person's intentions are distinguished from the consequences of his actions. Under a situation where an action is questioned an actor may claim a lack of intent or a failure to foresee the consequences of his act, or both. If the action in question involves a motor response—such as knocking over a vase—the situation is not very different from that subsumed under the term accident. When actions going beyond motor responses are at issue, the actor's intentions and foresight can be questioned. "Why did you make her cry?" asks the accuser. The presentational strategies in reply to this question allow several modes of defeating the central claim implied in the question, namely, that the actor intended with full knowledge to make the lady weep. The accused may simply deny any intention on his part to have caused the admittedly unfortunate consequence. However, men ordinarily impute to one another some measure of foresight for their actions, so that a simple denial of intent may not be believed if it appears that the consequence of the action in question was indeed what another person might expect and therefore what the actor intended.

In addition to his denial of intent an actor may also deny his knowledge of the consequence. The simplest denial is the cognitive disclaimer: "I did not *know* that I would make her cry by what I did." But this complete denial of cognition is often not honored, especially when the interactants know one another well and are expected to have a more complete imagery of the consequences of their acts to guide them. A more complex denial—the gravity disclaimer—includes admitting to the possibility of the outcome in question but suggesting that its probability was incalculable: "I knew matters were serious, but I did not know that telling her would make her weep."

Still another type of excuse invokes biological drives. This invocation is part of a larger category of fatalistic forces which in various cultures are deemed in greater or lesser degree to be controlling of some or all events. Cultures dominated by universalist-achievement orientations[13] tend to give scant and ambiguous support to fatalistic interpretations of events, but rarely disavow them entirely. To account for the whole of one's life in such terms, or to account for events which are conceived by others to be controlled by the actor's conscience, will, and abilities is to lay oneself open to the charge of mental illness or personality disorganization.[14] On the other hand, recent studies have emphasized the situational element in predisposing certain persons and groups in American society to what might be regarded as a "normalized" fatalistic view of their condition. Thus, for example, Negroes[15] and adolescent delinquents[16] are regarded and tend to regard themselves as less in control of the forces that shape their lives than whites or middle-class adults.

Among the fatalistic items most likely to be invoked as an excuse are the biological drives. Despite the emphasis in Occidental culture since the late nineteenth century on personality and social environment as causal elements in human action, there is still a popular belief in and varied commitment to the efficacy of the body and biological factors in determining human behavior. Such commonplaces as "men are like that" are shorthand phrases invoking belief in sex-linked traits that allegedly govern behavior beyond the will of the actor. Precisely because the body and its biological behavior are always present but not always accounted for in science or society, invocation of the body and its processes is available as an excuse. The body and its inner workings enjoy something of the status of the sociological stranger as conceived by Simmel, namely, they are ever with us but mysterious. Hence, biological drives may be credited with influencing or causing at least some of the behavior for which actors wish to relieve themselves of full responsibility.

The invocation of biological drives is most commonly an appeal to natural but uncontrollable sexual appetite. Among first- and second-generation Italians in America the recognition and fear of biologically induced sexual intercourse serves men as both an excuse for pre- and extramarital sexual relations and a justification for not being alone with women ineligible for coitus. Thus one student of Italian-American culture observes:

> What the men fear is their own ability at self-control. This attitude, strongest among young unmarried people, often carries over into adulthood. The traditional Italian belief—that sexual intercourse is unavoidable when a man and a woman are by themselves—is maintained intact among second-generation Italians, and continues even when sexual interest itself is on the wane. For example, I was told of an older woman whose apartment was adjacent to that of an unmarried male relative. Although they had lived in the same building for almost twenty years and saw each other every day, she had never once been in his apartment because of this belief.[17]

Biological drive may be an expected excuse in some cultures, so that the failure to invoke it, and the use of some other excuse, constitutes an improper account when the appropriate one is available. Oscar Lewis provides such an example in his ethnography of a Mexican family. A cuckolded wife angrily rejects her wayward husband's explanation that the red stains on his shirt are due to paint rubbed off during the course of his work. She strongly suggests, in her retelling of the incident, that she would have accepted an excuse appealing to her husband's basic sex drives:

> And he had me almost believing it was red paint! It was not that I am jealous. I realize a man can never be satisfied with just one woman, but I cannot stand being made a fool of.[18]

Homosexuals frequently account for their deviant sexual desires by invoking the principle of basic biological nature. As one homosexual put it:

> It's part of nature. You can't alter it, no matter how many injections and pills they give you.[19]

Another of the biological elements that can be utilized as an excuse is the shape of the body itself. Body types are not only defined in purely anatomical terms, but also, and perhaps more importantly, in terms of their shared social meanings. Hence fat people can excuse their excessive laughter by appealing to the widely accepted proverb that fat men are jolly. Similarly persons bearing features considered to be stereotypically criminal[20] may be exonerated for their impoliteness or small larcenies on the grounds that their looks proved their intentions and thus their victims ought to have been on guard. The phrase, "he looks crooked to me," serves as a warning to others to carefully appraise the character and intentions of the person so designated, since his features bespeak an illegal intent.

The final type of excuse we shall mention is *scapegoating*. Scapegoating is derived from another form of fatalistic reasoning. Using this form a person will allege that his questioned behavior is a response to the behavior or attitudes of another. Certain psychological theory treats this phenomenon as indicative of personality disorder, and, if found in conjunction with certain other characteristic traits, a signal of authoritarian personality.[21] Our treatment bypasses such clinical and pathological concerns in order to deal with the "normal" situation in which individuals slough off the burden of responsibility for their actions and shift it on to another. In Mexican working-class society, for example, women hold a distinctly secondary position relative to men. Marriage causes a loss of status to the latter, and sexual intercourse is regarded ambivalently as healthy and natural, but also as a necessary evil.[22] Such a set of orientations predisposes both men and women to attribute many of their shortcomings to women. An example is found in the autobiography of a Mexican girl:

> I was always getting into fights because some girls are vipers; they get jealous, tell lies about each other, and start trouble.[23]

Similarly, a Mexican youth who tried unsuccessfully to meet a girl by showing off on a bicycle explains:

> She got me into trouble with my father by lying about me. She said I tried to run her down with my bike and that all I did was hang around spying on her.[24]

In another instance the same youth attributes his waywardness to the fact that the girl he truly loved was his half-sister and thus unavailable to him for coitus or marriage:

> So, because of Antonia, I began to stay away from home. It was one of the main reasons I started to go on the bum, looking for trouble.[25]

Like excuses, *justifications* are socially approved vocabularies that neutralize an act or its consequences when one or both are called into question. But here is the crucial difference: to *justify* an act is to assert its positive value in the face of a claim to the contrary. Justifications recognize a general sense in which the act in question is impermissible, but claim that the particular occasion permits or requires the very act. The laws governing the taking of life are a case in point. American and English jurisprudence are by no means united on definitions or even on the nature of the acts in question, but in general a man may justify taking the life of another by claiming that he acted in self-defense, in defense of others' lives or property, or in action against a declared enemy of the state.

For a tentative list of types of justifications we may turn to what has been called "techniques of neutralization."[26] Although these techniques have been discussed with respect to accounts offered by juvenile delinquents for untoward action, their wider use has yet to be explored. Relevant to our discussion of justification are the techniques of "denial of injury," "denial of victim," "condemnation of condemners," and "appeal to loyalties."[27]

In *denial of injury* the actor acknowledges that he did a particular act but asserts that it was permissible to do that act since no one was injured by it, or since no one about whom the community need be concerned with was involved, or finally since the act resulted in consequences that were trifling. Note that this justification device can be invoked with respect to both persons and objects. The denial of injury to *persons* suggests that they be viewed as "deserving" in a special sense: that they are oversupplied with the valued things of the world, or that they are "private" persons ("my friends," "my enemies") who have no standing to claim injury in the public, or to be noticed as injured. Denial of injury to *objects* involves redefining the act as not injurious to it but only sing it, e.g., car "borrowing" is not theft.

In *denial of the victim* the actor expresses the position that the action was permissible since the victim deserved the injury. Four categories of persons are frequently perceived as deserving injury. First, there are proximate foes, i.e., those who have directly injured the actor; second, incumbents of normatively discrepant roles, e.g., homosexuals, whores, pimps; third, groups with tribal stigmas, e.g., racial and ethnic minorities; and finally, distant foes, that is, incumbents of roles held to be dubious or hurtful, e.g., "Whitey," the "Reds," "politicians." Besides categories of persons, there are categories of objects perceived as deserving of injury. To begin with, the property of any of the above mentioned categories of persons may become a focus of attack, especially if that property is symbolic of the attacked persons's status. Thus the clothing of the whore is torn, the gavel of the politician is smashed, and so on. Secondly, there are objects that have a neutral or ambiguous identity with respect to ownership, e.g., a park bench. A final focus of attacked objects are those having a low or polluted value, e.g., junk, or kirsch.

Using the device of *condemnation of the condemners,* the actor admits performing an untoward act but asserts its irrelevancy because others commit these and worse acts, and these others are either not caught, not punished, not condemned, unnoticed, or even praised.

Still another neutralization technique is *appeal to loyalties.* Here the actor asserts that his action was permissible or even right since it served the interests of another to whom he owes an unbreakable allegiance or affection.[28]

Besides these "techniques of neutralization," two other sorts of justification may be mentioned: *"sad tales,"* and *"self-fulfillment."* The *sad tale* is a selected (often distorted) arrangement of facts that highlight an extremely dismal past, and thus "explain" the individual's present state.[29] For example, a mental patient relates:

> I was going to night school to get an M.A. degree, and holding down a job in addition, and the load got too much for me.[30]

And a homosexual accounts for his present deviance with this sad tale:

> I was in a very sophisticated queer circle at the university. It was queer in a sense that we all camped like mad with "my dear" at the beginning of every sentence, but there was practically no sex, and in my case there was none at all. The break came when I went to a party and flirted with a merchant seaman who took me seriously and cornered me in a bedroom. There was I, the great sophisticate, who, when it came to the point, was quite raw, completely inexperienced; and I might tell you that seaman gave me quite a shock. I can't say I enjoyed it very much but it wasn't long after before I started to dive into bed with anyone.[31]

Finally, we may mention a peculiarly modern type of justification, namely, *self-fulfillment.* Interviewing LSD users and homosexuals in the Haight-Ashbury district of San Francisco, we are struck by the prominence of self-fulfillment as the grounds for these activities. Thus, an "acid head" relates:

The whole purpose in taking the stuff is self-development. Acid expands consciousness. Mine eyes have seen the glory —can you say that? I never knew what capacities I had until I went on acid.[32]

And a Lesbian:

Everyone has the right to happiness and love. I was married once. It was hell. But now I feel I have fulfilled myself as a person and as a woman.[33]

We might also note that the drug users and homosexuals interviewed (in San Francisco) who invoked the justification of self-fulfillment did not appear to find anything wrong with their behavior. They indicated either a desire to be left alone or to enlighten what they considered to be the unenlightened establishment.

HONORING ACCOUNTS, AND BACKGROUND EXPECTATIONS

Accounts may be honored or not honored. If an account is honored, we may say that it was efficacious and equilibrium is thereby restored in a relationship. The most common situation in which accounts are routinely honored is encounters interrupted by incidents—slips, boners, or gaffes which introduce information deleterious to the otherwise smooth conduct of the interactants.[34] Often a simple excuse will suffice, or the other interactants will employ covering devices to restore the *status quo ante*. A related situation is that in which an individual senses that some incident or event has cast doubt on that image of himself which he seeks to present. "At such times," the authority on impression management writes, "'the individual is likely to try to integrate the incongruous events by means of apologies, little excuses for self, and disclaimers; through the same acts, incidentally, he also tries to save his face."[35]

One variable governing the honoring of an account is the character of the social circle in which it is introduced. As we pointed out earlier, vocabularies of accounts are likely to be routinized within cultures, subcultures and groups, and some are likely to be exclusive to the circle in which they are employed. A drug addict may be able to justify his conduct to a bohemian world, but not to the courts. Similarly kin and friends may accept excuses in situations in which strangers would refuse to do so. Finally, while ignorance of the consequences of an act or of its prohibition may exculpate an individual in many different circles, the law explicitly rejects this notion: "Ignorance of the law excuses no man; not that all men know the law but because 'tis an excuse every man will plead, and no man can tell how to confute him."[36]

Both the account offered by *ego* and the honoring or nonhonoring of the account on the part of *alter* will ultimately depend on the *background expectancies* of the interactants. By background expectancies we refer to those sets of taken-for-granted ideas that permit the interactants to interpret remarks as accounts in the first place.[37] Asked why he is listless and depressed, a person may reply, "I have family troubles." The remark will be taken as an account, and indeed an account that will probably be honored, because "everyone knows" that "family problems" are a cause of depression.

This last illustration suggests that certain accounts can fit a variety of situations. Thus in response to a wide range of questions— Why don't you get married? Why are you in a fit of depression? Why are you drinking so heavily?—the individual can respond with "I'm having family problems." The person offering such an account may not himself regard it as a true one, but invoking it has certain interactional payoffs: since people cannot say they don't understand it— they are accounts that are part of our socially distributed knowledge of what everyone knows—the inquiry can be cut short.

Clearly, then, a single account will stand for a wide collection of events, and the efficacy of such accounts depend upon a set of shared background expectations.

In interacting with others, the socialized person learns a repertoire of background expectations that are appropriate for a variety of others. Hence the "normal" individual will change his account for different role others. A wife may respond sympathetically to her depressed husband because his favorite football team lost a championship game, but such an account for depression will appear bizarre when offered to one's inquiring boss. Thus background expectancies are the means not only for the honoring, but also for the nonhonoring of accounts. When the millionaire accounts for his depression by saying he is a failure, others will be puzzled since "everyone knows" that millionaires are not failures. The incapacity to invoke situationally appropriate accounts, i.e., accounts that are anchored to the background expectations of the situation, will often be taken as a sign of mental illness.[38] There are grounds then for conceptualizing normal individuals as "not stupid" rather than "not ill."[39] The person who is labeled ill has been behaving "stupidly" in terms of his culture and society: he offers accounts not situationally appropriate according to culturally defined background expectations.[40]

Often an account can be discredited by the appearance of the person offering an account. When a girl accounts for her late return from a date by saying the movie was overlong—that no untoward event occurred and that she still retains virgin status—her mother may discredit the account by noting the daughter's flushed appearance. Since

individuals are aware that appearances may serve to credit or discredit accounts, efforts are understandably made to control these appearances through a vast repertoire of *impression management* activities.[41]

When an account is not honored it will be regarded as either *illegitimate* or *unreasonable*. An account is treated as *illegitimate* when
the gravity of the event exceeds that of the account or when it is offered in a circle where its vocabulary of motives is unacceptable. As
illustration of the former we may note that accidentally allowing a pet
turtle to drown may be forgiven, but accidentally allowing the baby
to drown with the same degree of oversight may not so easily be excused. As illustration of the latter, male prostitutes may successfully
demonstrate their masculinity within the subculture of persons who
regularly resort to homosexual acts by insisting that they are never
fellators, but such a defense is not likely in heterosexual circles to lift
from them the label of "queer."[42]

An account is deemed *unreasonable* when the stated grounds for
action cannot be normalized in terms of the background expectancies
of what everybody knows. Hence when a secretary explained that she
placed her arm in a lighted oven because voices had commanded her
to do so in punishment for her evil nature, the account was held to be
grounds for commitment to an asylum.[43] In general those who persist
in giving unreasonable accounts for questioned actions are likely to be
labelled as mentally ill. Or, to put this point another way, unreasonable accounts are one of the sure indices by which the mentally ill are
apprehended. Conversely, those persons labeled as mentally ill may
relieve themselves of the worst consequences of that label by recognizing before their psychiatrists the truth value of the label, by reconstructing their past to explain how they came to deviate from normal patterns, and by gradually coming to give acceptable accounts for
their behavior.[44]

Beyond illegitimacy and unreasonableness are special types of
situations in which accounts may not be acceptable. One such type
involves the incorrect invocation of "commitment" or "attachment"[45]
in account situations where one or the other, but only the correct one,
is permitted. By commitment we refer to that role orientation in which
one has through investiture become liable and responsible for certain
actions. By attachment we refer to the sense of vesting one's feelings
and identity in a role. Certain statuses, especially those dealing with
distasteful activities or acts that are condemned except when performed by licensed practitioners, are typically expected to invest their
incumbents with only commitment and not with attachment. Hang-
men who, when questioned about their occupation, profess to be emotionally attracted to killing, are not likely to have their account
honored. Indeed, distasteful tasks are often imputed to have a clandes-
tine but impermissible allure, and so those who regularly perform them

are often on their guard to assert their commitment, but not their attachment to the task.

Organizations systematically provide accounts for their members in a variety of situations. The rules of bureaucracy, for instance, make available accounts for actions taken toward clients—actions which, from the viewpoint of the client, are untoward.[46] Again, these accounts "work" because of a set of background expectations. Thus when people say they must perform a particular action because it is a rule of the organization, the account is regarded as at least reasonable, since "everyone knows" that people follow rules. Of course, the gravity of the event may discredit such accounts, as the trials of Nazi war criminals dramatically illustrate.[47]

Under certain situations behavior that would ordinarily require an account is normalized without interruption or any call for an account. Typically such situations are social conversations in which the values to be obtained by the total encounter supersede those which would otherwise require excuses or justifications. Two values that may override the requirement of accounts are *sociability* and *information*.

In the case of *sociability* the desire that the interactional circle be uninterrupted by any event that might break it calls for each interactant to weigh carefully whether or not the calling for an account might disrupt the entire engagement. When the gathering is a convivial one not dedicated to significant matters—that is, matters that have a proactive life beyond the engagement itself—the participants may overlook errors, inept statements, lies, or discrepancies in the statements of others. Parties often call for such behavior but are vulnerable to disruption by one who violates the unwritten rule of not questioning another too closely. In unserious situations in which strangers are privileged to interact as a primary group without future rights of similar interaction—such as in bars—the interactants may construct elaborate and self-contradictory biographies without fear of being called to account.[48]

In some engagements the interactants seek to obtain *information* from the speaker which is incidental to his main point but which might be withheld if any of the speaker's statements were called into account. Among the Japanese, for example, the significant item in a conversation may be circumscribed by a verbal wall of trivia and superfluous speech. To interrupt a speaker by calling for an account might halt the conversation altogether or detour the speaker away from disclosing the particularly valued pieces of information.[49] Among adolescent boys in American society engaged in a "bull session" it is usually inappropriate to challenge a speaker describing his sexual exploits since, no matter how embellished and exaggerated the account might be, it permits the hearers to glean knowledge about sex—ordinarily withheld from them in the regular channels of education—with impunity. Calling for an account in the midst of such disclosures, especially when the account would require a discussion of the speaker's morality, might cut off the hearers from obtaining precisely that kind of information which is in no other way available to them.[50]

So far we have discussed accounts in terms of their content, but it should be pointed out that accounts also differ in form or style. Indeed, as we will now suggest, the style of an account will have bearing on its honoring or dishonoring.

LINGUISTIC STYLES AND ACCOUNTS

We may distinguish five linguistic styles that frame the manner in which an account will be given and often indicate the social circle in which it will be most appropriately employed. These five styles, which in practice often shade into one another and are not unambiguously separated in ordinary life, are the *intimate, casual, consultative, formal,* and *frozen* styles.[51] These styles, as we shall see, are ordered on a scale of decreasing social intimacy.[52]

The *intimate* style is the socially sanctioned linguistic form employed among persons who share a deep, intense and personal relationship. The group within which it is employed is usually a dyad—lovers, a married pair, or very close friends. The group can be larger but not much larger, and when it reaches four or five it is strained to its limits. The verbal style employs single sounds or words, and jargon, to communicate whole ideas. An account given in this form may be illustrated by the situation in which a husband, lying beside his wife in bed, caresses her but receives no endearing response. His wife utters the single word, "pooped." By this term the husband understands that the account given in response to his unverbalized question, "Why don't you make love to me? After all I am your husband. You have wifely duties!" is "I realize that under ordinary circumstances I should and indeed would respond to your love making, but tonight I am too exhausted for that kind of activity. Do not take it to mean that I have lost affection for you, or that I take my wifely duties lightly."

The *casual* style is used among peers, in-group members and insiders. It is a style employed by those for whom the social distance is greater than that among intimates but is still within the boundaries of a primary relationship. Typically it employs ellipses, i.e., omissions, and slang. In casual style certain background information is taken for granted among the interactants and may be merely alluded to in order to give an account. Thus among those who are regular users of hallucinogenic drugs, the question "Why were you running about naked in the park?" might be answered, "I was 'on.' " The hearer will then know that the speaker was under the influence of a familiar drug and was engaged in an activity that is common in response to taking that drug.

While each style differs from that to which it is juxtaposed by degree, the difference between any two styles—skipping an interval on the aforementioned social intimacy scale—is one of kind. Thus intimate and casual styles differ only in degree from one another and suggest a slight but significant difference in social distance among the interactants, but the *consultative* style differs in kind from the intimate. Consultative style is that verbal form ordinarily employed when the amount of knowledge available to one of the interactants is unknown or problematic to the others. Typically in such an interaction the speaker supplies background information which he is unsure the hearer possesses, and the hearer continuously participates by means of linguistic signs and gestures which indicate that he understands what is said or that he requires more background information. In offering accounts in this form there is a definite element of "objectivity," i.e., of non-subjective and technical terms. The individual giving an account relies on reference to things and ideas outside the intimate and personal realm. In response to the question, "Why are you smoking marijuana? Don't you know that it's dangerous?", the individual might reply, "I smoke marijuana because everybody who's read the LaGuardia Report knows that it's not habit forming." But a casual response might be simply, "Don't be square."

Formal style is employed when the group is too large for informal co-participation to be a continuous part of the interaction. Typically it is suited to occasions when an actor addresses an audience greater than six. Listeners must then wait their turn to respond, or, if they interject comments, know that this will be an untoward event, requiring some kind of re-structuring of the situation. Speaker and audience are in an active and a passive role, respectively, and, if the group is large enough, may be obligated to speak or remain silent according to pre-established codes of procedure. Formal style may also be employed when speaker and auditor are in rigidly defined statuses. Such situations occur in bureaucratic organizations between persons in hierarchically differentiated statuses, or in the courtroom, in the interaction between judge and defendant.

Frozen style is an extreme form of formal style employed among those who are simultaneously required to interact and yet remain social strangers. Typically interaction in the frozen style occurs among those between whom an irremovable barrier exists. The barrier may be of a material or a social nature, or both. Thus pilots communicate to air scanners in a control tower in the same lingual style as prisoners of war to their captors or telephone operators to angered clients. Often the frozen accounts offered are tutored, memorized, or written down in advance, and they may be applicable to a variety of situations. Thus the prisoner of war reiterates his name, rank, and serial number to all questions and refers his interrogators to the Geneva Convention. The pilot replies to questions about his aberrant flight pattern, coming from the anonymous control tower, with a smooth flow of technical jargon quoted from his handbook on flying. The telephone operator refuses to become flustered or angered by the outraged demands and accusations of the caller unable to reach his party, and quotes from memory the rules of telephone conduct required of the situation.

In summary, then, accounts are presented in a variety of idioms. The idiomatic form of an account is expected to be socially suited to the circle into which it is introduced, according to norms of culture, subculture, and situation. The acceptance or refusal of an offered account in part depends on the appropriateness of the idiom employed. Failure to employ the proper linguistic style often results in a dishonoring of the account or calls for further accounts. Sometimes the situation results in requirements of compound accounting wherein an individual, having failed to employ idiomatic propriety in his first account, is required not only to reaccount for his original untoward act but also to present an account for the unacceptable language of his first account. Note that idiomatic errors on the part of a person giving an account provide an unusual opportunity for the hearer to dishonor or punish the speaker if he so wishes. Thus even if the content of the tendered account is such as to excuse or justify the act, a hearer who wishes to discredit the speaker may "trip him up" by shifting the subject away from the matter originally at hand and onto the form of the account given. Typical situations of this kind arise when persons of inferior status provide substantially acceptable accounts for their allegedly untoward behavior, to their inquiring superiors but employ idiomatically unacceptable or condemnable form. Thus school children who excuse their fighting with others by not only reporting that they were acting in self-defense, but also, and in the process, by using profanity, may still be punished for linguistic impropriety, even if they are let off for their original defalcation.[53]

STRATEGIES FOR AVOIDING ACCOUNTS

The vulnerability of actors to questions concerning their conduct varies with the situation and the status of the actors. Where hierarchies of authority govern the social situation, the institutionalized office may eliminate the necessity of an account, or even prevent the question from arising. Military officers are thus shielded from accountability to their subordinates. Where cultural distance and hierarchy are combined—as in the case of slaveholders vis-à-vis their new imported slaves—those enjoying the superior status are privileged to leave their subordinates in a perplexed and frightened state.[54]

Besides the invulnerability to giving accounts arising from the status and position of the actors are the strategies that can prevent their announcement. We may refer to these strategies as meta-accounts. Three such strategies are prominent: *mystification, referral, and identity switching.*[55]

When the strategy of *mystification* is employed an actor admits that he is not meeting the expectations of another, but follows this by pointing out that, although there are reasons for his unexpected actions, he cannot tell the inquirer what they are. In its simplest sense the actor says "It's a long story," and leaves it at that. Such accounts are most likely to be honored under circumstances which would normally hinder an elaborate account, as when students have a chance meeting while rushing off to scheduled classes.

More complicated versions of mystification are those that suggest that *alter* is not aware of certain facts—facts that are secret—which, if known, would explain the untoward action. Typically this is the response of the charismatic leader to his followers or the expert to his naive assistant. Thus does Jesus sometimes mystify his disciples and Sherlock Holmes his Dr. Watson. Finally, as already mentioned, certain statuses suggest mystification: in addition to charismatic leaders and experts at occult or little-understood arts are all those statuses characterized by specialized information including (but not limited to) doctors, lawyers, and spies.

Using the strategy of *referral,* the individual says, "I know I'm not meeting your expectations but if you wish to know why, please see. . . ." Typically referral is a strategy available to the sick and the subordinate. Illness, especially mental illness, allows the sick person to refer inquiries about his behavior to his doctor or psychiatrist. Subordinates may avoid giving accounts by designating superiors as the appropriate persons to be questioned. A special example of group referral is that which arises when accounts for the behavior of a whole people are avoided by sending the interrogator to the experts. Thus juvenile delinquents can refer inquiries to social workers, Hopi Indians to anthropologists, and unwed Negro mothers to the Moynihan report.

In *identity switching, ego* indicates to *alter* that he is not playing the role that *alter* believes he is playing. This is a way of saying to *alter,* "You do not know who I am." This technique is readily available since all individuals possess a multiplicity of identities. Consider the following example.[56] A working-class Mexican husband comes home from an evening of philandering. His wife suspects this and says, "Where were you?" He responds with: "None of your business, you're a wife." Here the husband is assuming that it is not the wife's job to pry into the affairs of her husband. She replies, "What kind of a father are you?" What the woman does here is to suggest that she is not a wife, but a mother—who is looking out for the welfare of the children. To this the husband replies: "I'm a man—and you're a woman." In other words, he is suggesting that, in this status of man, there are things that a woman just doesn't understand. We note in this example that the status of persons not only affects the honoring and non-honoring of accounts, but also determines who can call for an account and who can avoid it. Again it should be pointed out that the normal features of such interaction depend upon the actors sharing a common set of background expectancies.

NEGOTIATING IDENTITIES, AND ACCOUNTS

As our discussion of identity-switching emphasizes, accounts always occur between persons in roles—between husband and wife, doctor and patient, teacher and student, and so on. A normative| structure governs the nature and types of communication between the interactants, including whether and in what manner accounts may be required and given, honored or discredited.

Accounts, as suggested, presuppose an identifiable speaker and audience. The particular identities of the interactants must often be established as part of the encounter in which the account is presented.[57] In other words, people generate role identities for one another in social situations. In an account-giving situation, to cast *alter* in a particular role is to confer upon him the privilege of honoring a particular kind of account, the kind suitable to the role identity conferred and assumed for at least the period of the account. To assume an identity is to don the mantle appropriate to the account to be offered. Identity assumption and "alter-casting"[58] are prerequisites to the presentation of accounts, since the identities thus established interactionally "set" the social stage on which the drama of the account is to be played out.

The identities of speaker and audience will be negotiated as part of the encounter. Each of the interactants has a stake in the negotiations since the outcomes of the engagement will often depend on these preestablished identities. In competitive or bargaining situations[59] the interactants will each seek to maximize gains or minimize losses, and part of the strategy involved will be to assume and accept advantageous identities, refusing those roles that are disadvantageous to the situation. *Every account is a manifestation of the underlying negotiation of identities.*[60]

The most elementary form of identification is that of human and fellow human negotiated by the immediate perceptions of strangers who engage in abrupt and involuntary engagements. Thus once two objects on a street collide with one another and mutually perceive one another to be humans, an apology in the form of an excuse, or mutually paired excuses, will suffice. Those persons not privileged with full or accurate perception—the blind, myopic, or blindfolded—are not in a position to ascertain immediately whether the object with which they have collided is eligible to call for an account and to deserve an apology. In overcompensating for their inability to negotiate immediately such elementary identities, the persons so handicapped may indiscriminately offer apologies to everyone and everything with which they collide—doormen and doors, streetwalkers and street signs. On the other hand, their identification errors are forgiven as soon as their handicap is recognized.

Some objects are ambiguously defined with respect to their deserving of accounts. Animals are an example. House pets, especially dogs and cats are sometimes imputed to possess human attributes and are thus eligible for apologies and excuses when they are trodden upon by their masters. But insects and large beasts—ants and elephants, for example—do not appear to be normally eligible for accounts even when they are trodden upon by unwary (Occidental) humans.

However, there are instances wherein the anthropomorphosis of the human self is more difficult to negotiate than that of a dog. Racial minorities in caste societies often insist to no avail on the priority of their identity as "human beings" over their identification as members of a racial group.[61] Indeed the "Negro human-being" role choice dilemma is but one instance of a particular form of strategy in the negotiation of identities. The strategy involves the competition between ego and alter over particularistic versus universalistic role identities. In any encounter in which a disagreement is potential or has already occurred, or in any situation in which an account is to be offered, the particularistic or universalistic identity of the interactants might dictate the manner and outcome of the account situation. Each participant will strive for the advantageous identity. A Negro psychoanalyst with considerable experience in Europe and North Africa has shown how the form of address—either consultative or deprecatingly casual —and the tone used, are opening moves in the doctor's designation of his patient as European or Negro:

> Twenty European patients, one after another, came in: "Please sit down . . . Why do you wish to consult me?" Then comes a Negro or an Arab: "Sit there, boy. . . ."[62]

And, as the psychoanalyst points out, the identity imputed to the patient might be accepted or rejected. To reject the particularistic identity in favor of a universalistic one, the Negro patient might reply, "I am in no sense your boy, Monsieur"[63] and the negotiations for identities begin again or get detoured in an argument.

In an account situation there is a further complication. Once identities have been established and an account offered, the individual has committed himself to an identity and thus seemingly assumed the assets and liabilities of that role for the duration of the encounter. If he accepts the identity as permanent and unchangeable, however, he may have limited his range of subsequent accounts. And if he wishes to shift accounts to one appropriate to another identity he may also need to account for the switch in identities. Thus, in the face of a pejorative particularistic identity, a Negro might wish to establish his claim to a positive universalistic one devoid of the pejorative contents of the imputed one. However, once this new universalistic identity has been established, the Negro might wish to shift back to the particularistic one, if there are positive qualities to be gained thereby, qualities utterly lost by an unqualified acceptance of the universalistic identity.[64] But the switch might require an account itself.

Identity switching has retroactive dangers, since it casts doubt on the attachment the claimant had to his prior identity, and his attachment may have been a crucial element in the acceptability of his first account. On the other hand, the hearer of an account may have a vested interest in accepting the entire range of accounts and may thus accommodate or even facilitate the switch in identities. Thus the hearer may "rationalize" the prior commitment, or reinterpret its meaning so that the speaker may carry off subsequent accounts.[65] Another strategy available to a hearer is to engage in alter-casting for purposes of facilitating or frustrating an account. The fact that individuals have multiple identities makes them both capable of strategic identity change and vulnerable to involuntary identity imputations.

In ordinary life, accounts are usually phased.[66] One account generates the question which gives rise to another; the new account requires re-negotiation of identities; the identities necessitate excuses or justifications, improvisation and alter-casting; another account is given; another question arises, and so on. The following interview between a Soviet social worker and his client, a young woman, nicely illustrates this phenomenon.[67]

A girl of about nineteen years of age enters the social worker's office and sits down sighing audibly. The interview begins on a note of *mystification* which ends abruptly when the girl establishes her identity—abandoned wife.

> "What are you sighing so sadly for?" I asked. "Are you in trouble?" Lyuba raised her prim little head with a jerk, sighed pianissimo and smiled piteously.
> "No . . . it's nothing much. I *was* in trouble, but it's all over now. . . ."
> "All over, and you are still sighing about it?" I questioned further. Lyuba gave a little shiver and looked at me. A flame of interest had leaped into her earnest brown eyes.
> "Would you like me to tell you all about it?"
> "Yes, do."
> "It's a long story."
> "Never mind. . . ."
> "My husband has left me."

The interview carries on in what must be regarded as an unsuccessful approach by the social worker. He establishes that Lyuba still loves her wayward husband, has lost faith in men, and is unwilling to take his advice to forget her first husband and remarry. The abandoned wife turns out to be an identity with which the worker has difficulty coping. He, therefore, alter-casts with telling effect in the following manner.

> "Tell me, Lyuba, are your parents alive?"
> "Yes, they are. Daddy and Mummy! They keep on telling me off for having got married."
> "Quite right too."
> "No, it's not. What's right about it?"
> "Of course, they're right. You're still a child and already married and divorced."
> "Well . . . what about it! What's that got to do with them?"
> "Aren't you living with them?"
> "I have a room of my own. My husband left me and went to live with his . . . and the room is mine now. And I earn two hundred rubles. And I'm not a child! How can you call me a child?"

Note that little bits of information provide the cues for alter-casting, so that Lyuba's volunteering the fact of her parents' disapproval of her first marriage, provides the grounds for the social worker's recasting her in the child role. However, this new identity is rejected by Lyuba by further evidentiary assertions: she supports herself and maintains her own residence. The child role has been miscast. Even the social worker gives up his attempt at switching Lyuba out from her role as abandoned wife. He writes: "Lyuba looked at me in angry surprise and I saw that she was quite serious about this game she played in life." Thus negotiations for identities—as in financial transactions—usually end with both parties coming to an agreeable settlement.

CONCLUSION

The sociologist has been slow to take as a serious subject of investigation what is perhaps the most distinctive feature of humans—talk. Here we are suggesting a concern with one type of talk: the study of what constitutes "acceptable utterances"[68] for untoward action. The sociological study of communications has relegated linguistic utterances largely to linguists and has generally mapped out non-verbal behavior as its distinctive domain. We are suggesting that a greater effort is needed to formulate theory that will integrate both verbal and non-verbal behavior.[69]

Perhaps the most immediate task for research in this area is to specify the background expectations that determine the range of alternative accounts deemed culturally appropriate to a variety of recurrent situations. We want to know how the actors take bits and pieces of words and appearances and put them together to produce a perceivedly normal (or abnormal) state of affairs. This kind of inquiry crucially involves a study of background expectations.[70] On the basis of such investigations, the analyst should be able to provide a set of instructions on "how to give an account" that would be taken by other actors as "normal."[71] These instructions would specify how different categories of statuses affect the honoring of an account, and what categories of statuses can use what kinds of accounts.

Future research on accounts may fruitfully take as a unit of analysis the *speech community*.[72] This unit is composed of human aggregates in frequent and regular interaction. By dint of their association sharers of a distinct body of verbal signs are set off from other speech communities. By speech community we do not refer to language communities, distinguished by being composed of users of formally different languages. Nor do we refer simply to dialect communities, composed of persons who employ a common spoken language which is a verbal variant of a more widely used written language.

Speech communities define for their members the appropriate lingual forms to be used amongst themselves. Such communities are located in the social structure of any society. They mark off segments of society from one another, and also distinguish different kinds of activities. Thus, the everyday language of lower-class teenage gangs differs sharply from that of the social workers who interview them, and the language by which a science teacher demonstrates to his students how to combine hydrogen and oxygen in order to produce water differs from the language employed by the same teacher to tell his inquisitive six-year-old son how babies are created. The types of accounts appropriate to each speech community differ in form and in content. The usage of particular speech norms in giving an account has consequences for the speaker depending upon the relationship between the form used and the speech community into which it is introduced.

A single individual may belong to several speech communities at the same time, or in the course of a lifetime. Some linguistic devices (such as teenage argot) are appropriate only to certain age groups and are discarded as one passes into another age grouping; others, such as the linguistic forms used by lawyers in the presence of judges, are appropriate to certain status sets and are consecutively employed and discarded as the individual moves into and out of interactions with his various status partners. Some individuals are dwellers in but a single speech community; they move in circles in which all employ the same verbal forms. The aged and enfeebled members of class or ethnic ghettoes are an obvious example. Others are constant movers through differing speech communities, adeptly employing language forms suitable to the time and place they occupy. Social workers who face teenage delinquents, fellow workers, lawyers, judges, their own wives, and children, all in one day, are an example.

In concluding we may note that, since it is with respect to deviant behavior that we call for accounts, the study of deviance and the study of accounts are intrinsically related, and a clarification of accounts will constitute a clarification of deviant phenomena—to the extent that deviance is considered in an interactional framework.[73]

NOTES

[1]For a now classic statement and analysis of the Hobbesian question, see the discussion by Talcott Parsons, *The Structure of Social Action,* Glencoe, Ill.: Free Press, 1949, pp. 89–94.

[2]See, for instance, William Soskin and Vera John, "The Study of Spontaneous Talk," in *The Stream of Behavior,* Roger Barker, ed., N.Y.: Appleton-Century-Crofts, 1963, pp. 228–282. Much suggestive material and a complete bibliography can be found in Joyce O. Hertzler, *A Sociology of Language,* N.Y.: Random House, 1965.

[3]An account has a family resemblance to the verbal component of a "motive" in Weber's sense of the term. Weber defined a motive as "a complex of subjective meaning which seems to the actor himself or to the observer as an adequate ground for the conduct in question." Max Weber, *Theory of Social and Economic Organization,* Talcott Parsons and A. M. Henderson, trans., Glencoe, Ill.: Free Press, 1947, pp. 98–99. Following Weber's definition and building on G. H. Mead's social psychology and the work of Kenneth Burke, C. Wright Mills was among the first to employ the notion of accounts in his much neglected essay, "Situated Action and the Vocabulary of Motives," *American Sociological Review,* 6 (December, 1940), pp. 904–913. Contemporary British philosophy, following the leads of Ludwig Wittgenstein, has (apparently) independently advanced the idea of a "vocabulary of motives." An exemplary case is R. S. Peters' *The Concept of Motivation,* London: Routledge and Kegan Paul, 1958.

[4]The point is nicely illustrated by Jackson Toby, "Some Variables in Role Conflict Analysis," *Social Forces,* 30 (March, 1952), pp. 323–327.

[5]Thus by an account we include also those nonvocalized but linguistic explanations that arise in an actor's mind when he questions his own behavior. However, our concern is with vocalized accounts and especially those that are given in face-to-face relations.

[6]William J. Goode, *World Revolution and Family Patterns,* N.Y.: Free Press, 1963, pp. 254–256.

[7]Moreover, commonsense understandings that violate widespread cognitive knowledge, such as are asserted in statements like "The sun rises every morning and sets every night," or avowed in perceptions that a straight stick immersed in water appears bent, are expected to be maintained. Persons who always insist on the astronomically exact statement about the earth's relation to the sun might be considered officious or didactic, while those who see a straight stick in a pool might be credited with faulty eyesight. For a relevant discussion of social reactions to inquiries about taken-for-granted phenomena, see Harold Garfinkel, "Studies of the Routine Grounds of Everyday Activities," *Social Problems*, 11 (Winter, 1964), pp. 225–250, and "A Conception of and Experiments with 'Trust' as a Condition of Concerted Action," in *Motivation and Social Interaction*, O. J. Harvey, ed., N.Y.: Ronald Press, 1963, pp. 187–238.

[8]We have taken this formulation from J. L. Austin. See his *Philosophical Papers*, London: Oxford University Press, 1961, pp. 123–152.

[9]Austin, *Philosophical Papers*, p. 124.

[10]These types of excuses are to be taken as illustrative rather than as an exhaustive listing.

[11]Only where nothing is left to chance—as among the Azande, where particular misfortunes are accounted for by a ubiquitous witchcraft—is the excuse by accident not likely to occur. Azande do not assert witchcraft to be the sole cause of phenomena; they have a practical and realistic approach to events which would enjoy consensual support from Occidental observers. However, Azande account for what Occidentals would call "chance" or "coincidence" by reference to witchcraft. E. E. Evans-Pritchard writes: "We have no explanation of why the two chains of causation [resulting in a catastrophe] intersected at a certain time and in a certain place, for there is no interdependence between them. Azande philosophy can supply the missing link. . . . It is due to witchcraft. . . . Witchcraft explains the coincidence of these two happenings." *Witchcraft, Oracles and Magic Among the Azande*, London: Oxford University Press, 1937, p. 70.

[12]Defeasibility, or the capacity of being voided, is a concept developed by H. L. A. Hart. This section leans heavily on Hart's essay, "The Ascription of Responsibility and Rights," in *Logic and Language, First Series*, Anthony Flew, ed., Oxford: Basil Blackwell, 1960, pp. 145–166.

[13]For a general discussion of cultures in terms of their fatalistic orientations or universalist-achievement orientations, see Talcott Parsons, "A Revised Analytical Approach to the Theory of Social Stratification," in *Essays in Sociological Theory*, Glencoe, Ill.: Free Press, 1954, pp. 386–439. See also Parsons, *The Social System*, Glencoe, Ill.: Free Press, 1951.

[14]Thus, in the most famous study of the psychodynamics of prejudice, one of the characteristics of the intolerant or "authoritarian" personality is "externalization," that is, the attribution of causality of events believed to be within the actor's power or rational comprehension to uncontrollable forces beyond his influence or understanding. See T. W. Adorno, *et al., The Authoritarian Personality*, N.Y.: Harper and Row, 1950, pp. 474–475. See also Gordon W. Allport, *The Nature of Prejudice*, Garden City, N.Y.: Anchor Doubleday, 1958, p. 379. In a recent study an intermittently employed cab driver's insistence that there would inevitably be a revolution after which the world would be taken over by Negroes and Jews is recalled as one of several early warning cues that he is mentally ill. Marion Radke Yarrow, *et al.*, "The Psy-

chological Meaning of Mental Illness in the Family," in Thomas J. Scheff, ed., *Mental Illness and Social Processes*, N.Y.: Harper and Row, 1967, p. 35

[15]See Horace R. Cayton, "The Psychology of the Negro Under Discrimination," in Arnold Rose, ed., *Race Prejudice and Discrimination*, N.Y.: Knopf, 1953, pp. 276–290; and Bertram P. Karon, *The Negro Personality*, N.Y.: Springer, 1958, pp. 8–53, 140–160.

[16]David Matza, *Delinquency and Drift*, N.Y.: Wiley, 1964, pp. 88–90, 188–91.

[17]Herbert J. Gans, *The Urban Villagers*, N.Y.: Free Press, 1962, p. 49. According to another student of Italian-American life, slum-dwelling members of this subculture believe that "a man's health requires sexual intercourse at certain intervals." William F. Whyte, "A Slum Sex Code," *American Journal of Sociology*, 49 (July, 1943), p. 26.

[18]Oscar Lewis, *The Children of Sanchez*, N.Y.: Random House, 1961, p. 475.

[19]Gordon Westwood, *A Minority*, London: Longmans, Green, 1960, p. 46.

[20]For an interesting study showing that criminals believe that a fellow criminal's physical attractiveness will vary with type of crime—robbers are the most attractive, murders the least; rapists are more attractive than pedophiles, etc.—see Raymond J. Corsini, "Appearance and Criminality," *American Journal of Sociology*, 65 (July, 1959), pp. 49–51.

[21]Adorno, *The Authoritarian Personality*, pp. 233, 485; Allport, *The Nature of Prejudice*, pp. 235–249, suggests the historicity and uniqueness of each instance of scapegoating.

[22]Arturo de Hoyos and Genevieve de Hoyos, "The Amigo System and Alienation of the Wife in the Conjugal Mexican Family," in Bernard Farber, ed., *Kinship and Family Organization*, N.Y.: Wiley, 1966, pp. 102–115, esp., pp. 103–107.

[23]Lewis, *Children of Sanchez*, p. 143.

[24]Lewis, *Children of Sanchez*, p. 202.

[25]Lewis, *Children of Sanchez*, p. 86.

[26]Gresham M. Sykes and David Matza, "Techniques of Neutralization," *American Sociological Review*, 22 (December, 1957), pp. 667–669.

[27]One other neutralization technique mentioned by Sykes and Matza, "denial of responsibility," is subsumed in our schema under "appeal to defeasibility."

[28]Note that appeal to loyalties could be an *excuse* if the argument runs that X did do A under the influence of Y's domination or love, or under the coercive influence of Y's injury to him were he not to act, e.g., loss of love, blackmail, etc. In other words, appeal to loyalties is an excuse if X admits it was bad to do A, but refuses to monopolize responsibility for A in himself.

[29]Erving Goffman, *Asylums*, Garden City, N.Y.: Doubleday Anchor, 1961, pp. 150–151. The sad tale involves the most dramatic instance of the general process of reconstructing personal biography whereby—for example— a husband may account for his present divorce by reconstructing the history of earlier events in an ascending scale leading up to the final dissolution. The idea of a reconstruction of biography is a continual theme in the writings of Alfred Schutz. See his *Collected Papers*, Vol. I, Maurice Natanson, ed., The Hague: Martinus Nijhoff, 1962. A short clear summary of Schutz's contribution on the reconstruction of biography is found in Peter L. Berger, *Invitation to Sociology: A Humanistic Perspective*, Garden City, N.Y.: Doubleday An-

chor, 1963, pp. 54–65. Drawing on Schutz, Garfinkel details the concept of reconstruction of biography in a series of experiments on the "retrospective reading" of social action. See his "Common Sense Knowledge of Social Structures," in *Theories of the Mind,* ed. by Jordon M. Scher, Glencoe, Ill.: Free Press, 1962, pp. 689–712. The empirical use of the concept of retrospective reading of action is nicely illustrated by John I. Kitsuse, "Societal Reaction to Deviant Behavior," in *The Other Side,* Howard S. Becker, ed., N.Y.: Free Press, 1964, pp. 87–102.

[30]Goffman, *Asylums,* p. 152.

[31]Westwood, *A Minority,* p. 32.

[32]Tape-recorded interview, May 1967.

[33]Tape-recorded interview, June 1967.

[34]Erving Goffman, *Encounters,* Indianapolis: Bobbs-Merrill, 1961, pp. 45–48.

[35]Goffman, *Encounters,* p. 51.

[36]John Selden, *Table Talk,* 1696, quoted in Harry Johnson, *Sociology,* N.Y.: Harcourt, Brace, 1960, p. 552n.

[37]The term is borrowed from Harold Garfinkel. Besides the footnote references to Garfinkel already cited, see his *Studies in Ethnomethodology,* Englewood Cliffs, N.J.: Prentice-Hall, 1968. For an original discussion on how the meaning of an account depends upon background expectancies and a methodology for its study, see Harvey Sacks, *The Search for Help,* unpublished doctoral dissertation, University of California, Berkeley, 1966.

[38]On how background expectations are used to determine whether a person is judged criminal or sick see the neglected essay by Vilhelm Aubert and Sheldon L. Messinger, "The Criminal and the Sick," *Inquiry,* 1 (Autumn, 1958), pp. 137–160.

[39]This formulation is persistently (and we believe rightly) argued in the various writings of Ernest Becker. See especially *The Revolution in Psychiatry,* N.Y.: Free Press, 1964; and his essay "Mills' Social Psychology and the Great Historical Convergence on the Problem of Alienation," in *The New Sociology,* Irving L. Horowitz, ed., N.Y.: Oxford University Press, 1964, pp. 108–133.

[40]In the case of schizophrenics, it has been noted that they are individuals who construct overly elaborate accounts, i.e., accounts that are perceived as being elaborately constructed. These accounts, it appears, take the form of "building up" the possibilities of a situation that others find improbable. Thus the paranoid husband accounts for his frenzied state by relating that his wife went shopping—and, to him, going shopping constitutes the most opportune occasion to rendezvous secretly with a lover. In response to the inquirer, the paranoid asks: "If you wanted to meet a lover, wouldn't you tell your spouse you're going shopping?" For a general discussion, see Becker, *The Revolution in Psychiatry.*

[41]Erving Goffman, *Presentation of Self in Everyday Life,* University of Edinburgh, 1956.

[42]Albert J. Reiss, Jr., "The Social Integration of Queers and Peers," in Howard S. Becker, ed., *The Other Side,* pp. 181–210.

[43]Marguerite Sechehaye, *Autobiography of a Schizophrenic Girl,* N.Y.: Grune and Stratton, 1951.

[44]See Thomas Scheff, *Being Mentally Ill,* Chicago: Aldine Press, 1966. See also Erving Goffman, *Asylums.*

[45]These terms are adapted from Erving Goffman, *Behavior in Public Places,* N.Y.: Free Press, 1963, p. 36n, and Goffman, *Encounters,* pp. 105 ff.

[46]The theme is widely explored in the literature on formal organizations. For an early and perhaps still the clearest statement of the theme, see Robert K. Merton's widely reprinted "Bureaucratic Structure and Personality," available in *Complex Organizations,* Amitai Etzioni, ed., N.Y.: Holt, Rinehart and Winston, 1962, pp. 48–60.

[47]For a literary illustration, see the play by Peter Weiss, *The Investigation,* N.Y.: Atheneum Books, 1967.

[48]See Sherri Cavan, *Liquor Licences,* Chicago: Aldine Press, 1966, pp. 79–87.

[49]Edward T. Hall, *The Hidden Dimension,* Garden City, N.Y.: Doubleday, 1966, pp. 139–144.

[50]When a boy is interrupted by a call for an account in the midst of his own recounting of sexual exploits he may simply relapse into uncommunicative silence, change the subject, or withdraw from the group. To prevent any of these, and to aid in the continuity of the original story, the other members of the audience may urge the speaker to continue as before, assure him of their interest and support, and sharply reprove or perhaps ostracize from the group the person who called for the account.

[51]We have adapted these styles from Martin Joos, *The Five Clocks,* N.Y.: Harbinger Books, 1961.

[52]Each of these linguistic styles is associated with distinctive physical distances between the interactants. For a discussion of this point see Hall, *Hidden Dimension,* pp. 116–122.

[53]Besides the five linguistic styles discussed, we may note that accounts may be usefully distinguished in the manner of their *delivery.* For a cogent typology see Robert E. Pittenger, *et al., The First Five Minutes,* Ithaca, N.Y.: Paul Martineau, 1960, p. 255.

[54]Another kind of invulnerability arises in those situations in which physical presence is tantamount to task performance. Students in a classroom, parishoners in a church, and soldiers at a drill may be counted as present—their very visibility being all that is required for routine performance—although they might be away in the sense of daydreaming, musing on other matters, or relaxing into a reverie.

[55]For these terms, in the context of strategies for avoiding accounts, we are indebted to Gregory Stone.

[56]For this illustration we are again indebted to Gregory Stone. The illustration itself is derived from Lewis, *Children of Sanchez.*

[57]For an excellent discussion of this point as well as an insightful analysis of the concept of identity, see Anselm L. Strauss, *Mirrors and Masks,* Glencoe, Ill.: Free Press, 1959.

[58]The concept of "alter-casting" is developed by Eugene A. Weinstein and Paul Deutschberger, "Tasks, Bargains, and Identities in Social Interaction," *Social Forces,* V. 42 (May, 1964), pp. 451–456.

[59]See the brilliant discussion by Thomas C. Schelling, *The Strategy of Conflict,* N.Y.: Galaxy Books, 1963, pp. 21–52.

[60]The terms "identities" and "roles" may be used as synonymous in that roles are identities mobilized in a specific situation; whereas role is always situationally specific, identities are trans-situational.

[61]"An unconscious desire to be white, coupled with feelings of revulsion toward the Negro masses, may produce an assimilationist pattern of behavior at the purely personal level. Assimilation is in this sense a means of escape, a form of flight from 'the problem.' It involves a denial of one's racial identity which may be disguised by such sentiments as 'I'm not a Negro but a human being'—as if the two were mutually exclusive. This denial is accompanied by a contrived absence of race consciousness and a belittling of caste barriers. By minimizing the color line, the assimilationist loses touch with the realities of Negro life." Robert A. Bone, *The Negro Novel in America,* New Haven, Conn.: Yale University Press, 1965, p. 4.

[62]Frantz Fanon, *Black Skin, White Masks,* N.Y.: Grove Press, 1967, p. 32.

[63]Fanon, *Black Skin, White Masks,* p. 33.

[64]Fanon, *Black Skin, White Masks,* provides one of the most graphic examples of this phenomenon. For a socio-literary treatment, see St. Clair Drake, "Hide My Face?"—On Pan-Africanisms and Negritude," in Herbert Hill, ed., *Soon One Morning,* N.Y.: Knopf, 1963, pp. 77–105.

[65]Schelling, *Strategy of Conflict,* p. 34.

[66]For a discussion on the "phasing" of encounters, see Strauss, *Mirrors and Masks,* p. 44.

[67]The following is from A.S. Mackarenko, *The Collective Family,* Garden City, N.Y.: Doubleday Anchor, 1967, pp. 230–232.

[68]The term is borrowed from Noam Chomsky, *Aspects of a Theory of Syntax,* Cambridge, Mass.: M.I.T. Press, 1965, p. 10.

[69]To our knowledge the most persuasive argument for this need is made by Kenneth L. Pike, *Language in Relation to a Unified Theory of the Structure of Human Behavior,* Glendale: Summer Institute of Linguistics, 1954. A short, clear programmatic statement is found in Dell Hymes, "The Ethnography of Speaking," in Thomas Gladwin and William C. Sturtevant, eds., *Anthropology and Human Behavior,* Washington, D.C.: Anthropological Society of Washington, 1962, pp. 72–85. For an argument that stresses the analytic separation of the content of talk from the forms of talk, see the brief but lucid statement by Erving Goffman, "The Neglected Situation," in *The Ethnography of Communications,* John Gumperz and Dell Hymes, eds., *American Anthropologist,* 66 (December, 1964), Part 2, pp. 133–136.

[70]For the methodology of such studies sociologists may well investigate the anthropological technique of componential analysis, i.e., the study of contrast sets. The clearest statement of the method of componential analysis is that of Charles O. Frake, "The Ethnographic Study of Cognitive Systems," in Gladwin and Sturtevant, eds., *Anthropology and Human Behavior,* pp. 72–85. A related methodology is developed by Sacks, *The Search for Help.*

[71]See Charles O. Frake, "How to Ask for a Drink in Subanun," in *The Ethnography of Communications,* pp. 127–132.

[72]The idea of a "speech community" is usefully developed by John J. Gumperz in "Speech Variation and the Study of Indian Civilization," in *Language in Culture and Society,* Dell Hymes, ed., N.Y.: Harper and Row, 1964, pp. 416–423; and "Linguistic and Social Interaction in Two Communities," in *Ethnography of Communications,* pp. 137–153.

[73]We refer to the approach to deviance clearly summarized by Howard S. Becker, *Outsiders,* N.Y.: Free Press, 1963, especially pp. 1–18.

Part II

SOCIAL TYPING:
THE PROCESS OF
ATTACHING MEANINGS

4

Conditions of Successful
Degradation Ceremonies

HAROLD GARFINKEL[1]

Any communicative work between persons, whereby the public identity of an actor is transformed into something looked on as lower in the local scheme of social types, will be called a *status degradation ceremony.* Some restrictions on this definition may increase its usefulness. The identities referred to must be total identities. That is, these identities must refer to persons as motivational types rather than as behavioral types,[2] not to what a person may be expected to have done or to do (in Parsons' term,[3] to his "performances") but to what the group holds to be the ultimate grounds or reasons for his performance.[4]

The grounds on which a participant achieves what for him is adequate understanding of why he or another acted as he did are not treated by him in a utilitarian manner. Rather, the correctness of an imputation is decided by the participant in accordance with socially valid and institutionally recommended standards of "preference." With reference to these standards, he makes the crucial distinctions between appearances and reality, truth and falsity, triviality and importance, accident and essence, coincidence and cause. Taken together, the grounds, as well as the behavior that the grounds make explicable as the other person's conduct, constitute a person's identity. Together, they constitute the other as a social object. Persons identified by means of the ultimate reasons for their socially categorized and socially understood behavior will be said to be totally identified. The degradation ceremonies here discussed are those that are concerned with the alteration of total identities.

Reprinted from *American Journal of Sociology,* 61 (1956), pp. 420–424. Copyright © University of Chicago Press. Reprinted by permission.

It is proposed that only in societies that are completely demoralized, will an observer be unable to find such ceremonies, since only in total anomie are the conditions of degradation ceremonies lacking. Max Scheler[5] argued that there is no society that does not provide in the very features of its organization the conditions sufficient for inducing shame. It will be treated here as axiomatic that there is no society whose social structure does not provide, in its routine features, the conditions of identity degradation. Just as the structural conditions of shame are universal to all societies by the very fact of their being organized, so the structural conditions of status degradation are universal to all societies. In this framework the critical question is not whether status degradation occurs or can occur within any given society. Instead, the question is: Starting from any state of a society's organization, what program of communicative tactics will get the work of status degradation done?

First of all, two questions will have to be decided, at least tentatively: *What are we referring to behaviorally when we propose the product of successful degradation work to be a changed total identity?* And *what are we to conceive the work of status degradation to have itself accomplished or to have assumed as the conditions of its success?*

I

Degradation ceremonies fall within the scope of the sociology of moral indignation. Moral indignation is a social affect. Roughly speaking, it is an instance of a class of feelings particular to the more or less organized ways that human beings develop as they live out their lives in one another's company. Shame, guilt, and boredom are further important instances of such affects.

Any affect has its behavioral paradigm. That of shame is found in the withdrawal and covering of the portion of the body that socially defines one's public appearance—prominently, in our society, the eyes and face. The paradigm of shame is found in the phrases that denote removal of the self from public view, i.e., removal from the regard of the publicly identified other: "I could have sunk through the floor; I wanted to run away and hide; I wanted the earth to open up and swallow me." The feeling of guilt finds its paradigm in the behavior of self-abnegation—disgust, the rejection of further contact with or withdrawal from, and the bodily and symbolic expulsion of the foreign body, as when we cough, blow, gag, vomit, spit, etc.

The paradigm of moral indignation is *public* denunciation. We publicly deliver the curse: "I call upon all men to bear witness that he is not as he appears but is otherwise and *in essence*[6] of a lower species."

The social affects serve various functions both for the person as well as for the collectivity. A prominent function of shame for the person is that of preserving the ego from further onslaughts by withdrawing entirely its contact with the outside. For the collectivity shame is an "individuator." One experiences shame in his own time.

Moral indignation serves to effect the ritual destruction of the person denounced. Unlike shame, which does not bind persons together, moral indignation may reinforce group solidarity. In the market and in politics, a degradation ceremony must be counted as a secular form of communion. Structurally, a degradation ceremony bears close resemblance to ceremonies of investiture and elevation. How such a ceremony may bind persons to the collectivity we shall see when we take up the conditions of a successful denunciation. Our immediate question concerns the meaning of ritual destruction.

In the statement that moral indignation brings about the ritual destruction of the person being denounced, destruction is intended literally. The transformation of identities is the destruction of one social object and the constitution of another. The transformation does not involve the substitution of one identity for another, with the terms of the old one loitering about like the overlooked parts of a fresh assembly, any more than the woman we see in the department-store window that turns out to be a dummy carries with it the possibilities of a woman. It is not that the old object has been overhauled; rather it is replaced by another. One decalres, *"Now, it was otherwise in the first place."*

The work of the denunciation effects the recasting of the objective character of the perceived other: The other person becomes in the eyes of his condemners literally a different and *new* person. It is not that the new attributes are added to the old "nucleus." He is not changed, he is reconstituted. The former identity, at best, receives the accent of mere appearance. In the social calculus of reality representations and test, the former identity stands as accidental; the new identity is the "basic reality." What he is now is what, "after all," he was all along.[7]

The public denunciation effects such a transformation of essence by substituting another socially validated motivational scheme for that previously used to name and order the performances of the denounced. It is with reference to this substituted, socially validated motivational scheme as the essential grounds, i.e., the *first principles,* that his performances, past, present, and prospective, according to the witnesses, are to be properly and necessarily understood.[8] Through the interpretive work that respects this rule the denounced person becomes in the eyes of the witnesses a different person.

II

How can one make a good denunciation?[9]

To be successful, the denunciation must redefine the situations of those that are witnesses to the denunciation work. The denouncer, the party to be denounced (let us call him the perpetrator), and the thing that is being blamed on the perpetrator (let us call it the event) must be transformed as follows.[10]

1. Both event and perpetrator must be removed from the realm of their everyday character and be made to stand as "out of the ordinary."

2. Both event and perpetrator must be placed within a scheme of preferences that shows the following properties:

A. The preferences must not be for event A over event B, but for event of *type* A over event of *type* B. The same typing must be accomplished for the perpetrator. Event and perpetrator must be defined as instances of a uniformity and must be treated as a uniformity throughout the work of the denunciation. The unique, never recurring character of the event or perpetrator should be lost. Similarly, any sense of accident, coincidence, indeterminism, change, or momentary occurrence must not merely be minimized. Ideally, such measures should be inconceivable; at least they should be made false.

B. The witnesses must appreciate the characteristics of the typed person and event by referring the type to a dialectical counterpart. Ideally, the witnesses should not be able to contemplate the features of the denounced person without reference to the counterconception, as the profanity of an occurrence or a desire or a character trait, for example, is clarified by the references it bears to its opposite, the sacred. The features of the mad-dog murderer reverse the features of the peaceful citizen. The confessions of the Red can be read to each the meanings of patriotism. There are many contrasts available, and any aggregate of witnesses this side of a complete war of each against all will have a plethora of such schemata for effecting a "familiar," "natural," "proper," ordering of motives, qualities, and other events.

From such contrasts, the following is to be learned. If the denunciation is to take effect, the scheme must not be one in which the witness is allowed to elect the preferred. Rather, the alternatives must be such that the preferred is morally required. Matters must be so arranged that the validity of his choice, its justification, is maintained by the fact that he makes it.[11] The scheme of alternatives must be such as to place constraints upon his making a selection "for a purpose." Nor will the denunciation succeed if the witness is free to look beyond the fact that he makes the selection for evidence that the correct alternative has been chosen, as, for example, by the test of empirical consequences of the choice. The alternatives must be such that, in "choosing," he takes it for granted and beyond any motive for doubt that not choosing can mean only preference for its opposite.

3. The denouncer must so identify himself to the witnesses that during the denunciation they regard him not as a private but as a publicly known person. He must not portray himself as acting according to his personal, unique experiences. He must rather be regarded

as acting in his capacity as a public figure, drawing upon communally entertained and verified experience. He must act as a bona fide participant in the tribal relationships to which the witnesses subscribe. What he says must not be regarded as true for him alone, not even in the sense that it can be regarded by denouncer and witnesses as matters upon which they can become agreed. In no case, except in a most ironical sense, can the convention of true-for-reasonable-men be invoked. What the denouncer says must be regarded by the witnesses as true on the grounds of a socially employed metaphysics whereby witnesses assume that witnesses and denouncer are alike in essence.[12]

4. The denouncer must make the dignity of the supra-personal values of the tribe salient and accessible to view, and his denunciation must be delivered in their name.

5. The denouncer must arrange to be invested with the right to speak in the name of these ultimate values. The success of the denunciation will be undermined if, for his authority to denounce, the denouncer invokes the personal interests that he may have acquired by virtue of the wrong done to him or someone else. He must rather use the wrong he has suffered as a tribal member to invoke the authority to speak in the name of these ultimate values.

6. The denouncer must get himself so defined by the witnesses that they locate him as a supporter of these values.

7. Not only must the denouncer fix his distance from the person being denounced, but the witnesses must be made to experience their distance from him also.

8. Finally, the denounced person must be ritually separated from a place in the legitimate order, i.e., he must be defined as standing at a place opposed to it. He must be placed "outside," he must be made "strange."

These are the conditions that must be fulfilled for a successful denunciation. If they are absent, the denunciation will fail. Regardless of the situation when the denouncer enters, if he is to succeed in degrading the other man, it is necessary to introduce these features.[13]

Not all degradation ceremonies are carried on in accordance with publicly prescribed and publicly validated measures. Quarrels which seek the humiliation of the opponent through personal invective may achieve degrading on a limited scale. Comparatively few persons at a time enter into this form of communion, few benefit from it, and the fact of participation does not give the witness a definition of the other that is standardized beyond the particular group or scene of its occurrence.

The devices for effecting degradation vary in the feature and effectiveness according to the organization and operation of the system of action in which they occur. In our society the arena of degradation whose product, the redefined person, enjoys the widest transferability between groups has been rationalized, at least as to the institutional measures for carrying it out. The court and its officers have something like a fair monopoly over such ceremonies, and there they have become an occupational routine. This is to be contrasted with degradation undertaken as an immediate kinship and tribal obligation and carried out by those who, unlike our professional degraders in the law courts, acquire both right and obligation to engage in it through being themselves the injured parties or kin to the injured parties.

Factors conditioning the effectiveness of degradation tactics are provided in the organization and operation of the system of action within which the degradation occurs. For example, timing rules that provide for serial or reciprocal "conversations" would have much to do with the kinds of tactics that one might be best advised to use. The tactics advisable for an accused who can answer the charge as soon as it is made are in contrast with those recommended for one who had to wait out the denunciation before replying. Face-to-face contact is a different situation from that wherein the denunciation and reply are conducted by radio and newspaper. Whether the denunciation must be accomplished on a single occasion or is to be carried out over a sequence of "tries," factors like the territorial arrangements and movements of persons at the scene of the denunciation, the numbers of persons involved as accused, degraders, and witnesses, status claims of the contenders, prestige and power allocations among participants, all should influence the outcome.

In short, the factors that condition the success of the work of degradation are those that we point to when we conceive the actions of a number of persons as group-governed. Only some of the more obvious structural variables that may be expected to serve as predicters of the characteristics of denunciatory communicative tactics have been mentioned. They tell us not only how to construct an effective denunciation but also how to render denunciation useless.

NOTES

[1] Acknowledgment is gratefully made to Erving Goffman, National Institute of Mental Health, Bethesda, Maryland, and to Sheldon Messinger, Social Science Research Council predoctoral fellow, University of California, Los Angeles, for criticisms and editorial suggestions.

[2] These terms are borrowed from Alfred Schutz, "Common Sense and Scientific Interpretation of Human Action," *Philosophy and Phenomenological Research*, Vol. XIV, No. 1 (September, 1953).

[3] Talcott Parsons and Edward Shils, "Values, Motives, and Systems of Action," in Parsons and Shils (eds.), *Toward a General Theory of Action* (Cambridge: Harvard University Press, 1951).

[4]Cf. the writings of Kenneth Burke, particularly *Permanence and Change* (Los Altos, Calif.: Hermes Publications, 1954), and *A Grammar of Motives* (New York: Prentice-Hall, Inc., 1945).

[5]Richard Hays Williams, "Scheler's Contributions to the Sociology of Affective Action, with Special Attention to the Problem of Shame," *Philosophy and Phenomenological Research,* Vol. II, No. 3 (March, 1942).

[6]The man at whose hands a neighbor suffered death becomes a "murderer." The person who passes on information to enemies is really "in essence," "in the first place," "all along," "in the final analysis," "originally," an informer.

[7]Two themes commonly stand out in the rhetoric of denunciation: (1) the irony between what the denounced appeared to be and what he is seen now really to be where the new motivational scheme is taken as the standard and (2) a re-examination and redefinition of origins of the denounced. For the sociological relevance of the relationship between concerns for essence and concerns for origins see particularly Kenneth Burke, *A Grammar of Motives.*

[8]While constructions like "substantially a something" or "essentially a something" have been banished from the domain of scientific discourse, such constructions have prominent and honored places in the theories of motives, persons, and conduct that are employed in handling the affairs of daily life. Reasons can be given to justify the hypothesis that such constructions may be lost to a group's "terminology of motives" only if the relevance of socially sanctioned theories to practical problems is suspended. This can occur where interpersonal relations are trivial (such as during play) or, more interestingly, under severe demoralization of a system of activities. In such organizational states the frequency of status degradation is low.

[9]Because the paper is short, the risk must be run that, as a result of excluding certain considerations, the treated topics may appear exaggerated. It would be desirable, for example, to take account of the multitude of hedges that will be found against false denunciation, of the rights to denounce, of the differential apportionment of these rights, as well as the ways in which a claim, once staked out, may become a vested interest and may tie into the contests for economic and political advantage. Further, there are questions centering around the appropriate areanas of denunciation. For example, in our society the tribal council has fallen into secondary importance; among lay persons the denunciation has given way to the complaint to the authorities.

[10]These are the effects that the communicative tactics of the denouncer must be designed to accomplish. Put otherwise, in so far as the denouncer's tactics accomplish the reordering of the definitions of the situation of the witnesses to the denunciatory performances, the denouncer will have succeeded in effecting the transformation of the public identity of his victim. The list of conditions of this degrading effect are the determinants of the effect. Viewed in the scheme of a project to be rationally pursued, they are the adequate means. One would have to choose one's tactics for their efficiency in accomplishing these effects.

[11]Cf. Gregory Bateson and Jurgen Ruesch, *Communication: The Social Matrix of Psychiatry* (New York: W. W. Norton & Co., 1951), pp. 212–27.

[12]For bona fide members it is not that these are the grounds upon which we are agreed but upon which we are *alike,* consubstantial, in origin the same.

[13]Neither of the problems of possible communicative or organizational conditions of their effectiveness have been treated here in systematic fashion.

However, the problem of communicative tactics in degradation ceremonies is set in the light of systematically related conceptions. These conceptions may be listed in the following statements:

1. The definition of the situation of the witnesses (for ease of discourse we shall use the letter S) always bears a time qualification.

2. The S at t_2 is a function of the S at t_1. This function is described as an operator that transforms the S at t_1.

3. The operator is conceived as communicative work.

4. For a successful denunciation, it is required that the S at t_2 show specific properties. These have been specified previously.

5. The task of the denouncer is to alter the S's of the witnesses so that these S's will show the specified properties.

6. The "rationality" of the denouncer's tactics, i.e., their adequacy as a means for effecting the set of transformations necessary for effecting the identity transformation, is decided by the rule that the organizational and operational properties of the communicative net (the social system) are determinative of the size of the discrepancy between an intended and an actual effect of the communicative work. Put otherwise, the question is not that of the temporal origin of the situation but always and only how it is altered over time. The view is recommended that the definition of the situation at time 2 is a function of the definition at time 1 where this function consists of the communicative work conceived as a set of operations whereby the altered situation at time 1 is the situation at time 2. In strategy terms the function consists of the program of procedures that a denouncer should follow to effect the change of state S_{t1} to S_{t2}. In this paper S_{t1} is treated as an unspecified state.

5

Moral Passage: The Symbolic Process in Public Designations of Deviance

JOSEPH R. GUSFIELD

Recent perspectives on deviant behavior have focused attention away from the actor and his acts and placed it on the analysis of public reactions in labelling deviants as "outsiders."[1] This perspective forms the background for the present paper. In it I will analyze the implications which defining behavior as deviant has for the public designators. Several forms of deviance will be distinguished, each of which has a different kind of significance for the designators. The symbolic import of each type, I argue, leads to different public responses toward the deviant and helps account for the historical changes often found in treatment of such delinquents as alcoholics, drug addicts, and other "criminals," changes which involve a passage from one moral status to another.

INSTRUMENTAL AND SYMBOLIC FUNCTIONS OF LAW[2]

Agents of government are the only persons in modern societies who can legitimately claim to represent the total society. In support of their acts, limited and specific group interests are denied while a public and societal interest is claimed.[3] Acts of government "commit the group to action or to perform coordinated acts for general welfare."[4] This representational character of governmental officials and their

Reprinted from *Social Problems*, 15 (1967), pp. 175–188, by permission of the Journal of Social Problems and the Institute for the Study of Social Problems.

acts makes it possible for them not only to influence the allocation of resources but also to define the public norms of morality and to designate which acts violate them. In a pluralistic society these defining and designating acts can become matters of political issue because they support or reject one or another of the competing and conflicting cultural groups in the society.

Let us begin with a distinction between *instrumental* and *symbolic* functions of legal and governmental acts. We readily perceive that acts of officials, legislative enactments, and court decisions often affect behavior in an instrumental manner through a direct influence on the actions of people. The Wagner Labor Relations Act and the Taft-Hartley Act have had considerable impact on the conditions of collective bargaining in the United States. Tariff legislation directly affects the prices of import commodities. The instrumental function of such laws lies in their enforcement; unenforced they have little effect.

Symbolic aspects of law and government do not depend on enforcement for their effect. They are symbolic in a sense close to that used in literary analysis. The symbolic act "invites consideration rather than overt reaction."[5] There is a dimension of meaning in symbolic behavior which is not given in its immediate and manifest significance but in what the action connotes for the audience that views it. The symbol "has acquired a meaning which is added to its immediate intrinsic significance."[6] The use of the wine and wafer in the Mass or the importance of the national flag cannot be appreciated without knowing their symbolic meaning for the users. In analyzing law as symbolic we are oriented less to behavioral consequences as a means to a fixed end; more to meaning as an act, a decision, a gesture important in itself.

An action of a governmental agent takes on symbolic import as it affects the designation of public norms. A courtroom decision or a legislative act is a gesture which often glorifies the values of one group and demeans those of another. In their representational character, governmental actions can be seen as ceremonial and ritual performances, designating the content of public morality. They are the statement of what is acceptable in the public interest. Law can thus be seen as symbolizing the public affirmation of social ideals and norms as well as a means of direct social control. This symbolic dimension is given in the statement, promulgation, or announcement of law unrelated to its function in influencing behavior through enforcement.

It has long been evident to students of government and law that these two functions, instrumental and symbolic, may often be separated in more than an analytical sense. Many laws are honored as much in the breach as in performance.[7] Robin Williams has labelled such institutionalized yet illegal and deviant behavior the "patterned evasion of norms." Such evasion occurs when law proscribes behavior which nevertheless occurs in a recurrent socially organized manner and is seldom punished.[8] The kinds of crimes we are concerned with here quite clearly fall into this category. Gambling, prostitution, abortion, and public drunkenness are all common modes of behavior although laws exist designating them as prohibited. It is possible to see such systematic evasion as functioning to minimize conflicts between cultures by utilizing law to proclaim one set of norms as public morality and to use another set of norms in actually controlling that behavior.

While patterned evasion may perform such harmonizing functions, the passage of legislation, the acts of officials, and decisions of judges nevertheless have a significance as gestures of public affirmation. First, the act of public affirmation of a norm often persuades listeners that behavior and norm are consistent. The existence of law quiets and comforts those whose interests and sentiments are embodied in it.[9] Second, public affirmation of a moral norm directs the major institutions of the society to its support. Despite patterned practices of abortion in the United States, obtaining abortion does require access to a subterranean social structure and is much more difficult than obtaining an appendectomy. There are instrumental functions to law even where there is patterned evasion.

A third impact of public affirmation is the one that most interests us here. The fact of affirmation through acts of law and government expresses the public worth of one set of norms, of one subculture vis-à-vis those of others. It demonstrates which cultures have legitimacy and public domination, and which do not. Accordingly it enhances the social status of groups carrying the affirmed culture and degrades groups carrying that which is condemned as deviant. We have argued elsewhere that the significance of Prohibition in the United States lay less in its enforcement than in the fact that it occurred.[10] Analysis of the enforcement of Prohibition law indicates that it was often limited by the unwillingness of Dry forces to utilize all their political strength for fear of stirring intensive opposition. Great satisfaction was gained from the passage and maintenance of the legislation itself.[11]

Irrespective of its instrumental effects, public designation of morality is itself an issue generative of deep conflict. The designating gestures are dramatistic events, "since it invites one to consider the matter of motives in a perspective that, being developed in the analysis of drama, treats language and thought primarily as modes of action."[12] For this reason the designation of a way of behavior as violating public norms confers status and honor on those groups whose cultures are followed as the standard of conventionality, and derogates those whose cultures are considered deviant. My analysis of the American Temperance Movement has shown how the issue of drinking and abstinence became a politically significant focus for the conflicts between Protestant and Catholic, rural and urban, native and immigrant, middle class and lower class in American society. The political conflict lay in the efforts of an abstinent Protestant middle class to control the public affirmation of morality in drinking. Victory or defeat were consequently symbolic of the status and power of the cultures opposing each other.[13] Legal affirmation or rejection is thus important in what it symbolizes as well or instead of what it controls. Even if the law was broken, it was clear whose law it was.

DEVIANT NONCONFORMITY AND DESIGNATOR REACTION

In Durkheim's analysis of the indignant and hostile response to norm-violation, all proscribed actions are threats to the existence of the norm.[14] Once we separate the instrumental from the symbolic functions of legal and governmental designation of deviants, however, we can question this assumption. We can look at norm-violation from the standpoint of its effects on the symbolic rather than the instrumental character of the norm. Our analysis of patterned evasion of norms has suggested that a law weak in its instrumental functions may nevertheless perform significant symbolic functions. Unlike human limbs, norms do not necessarily atrophy through disuse. Standards of charity, mercy, and justice may be dishonored every day yet remain important statements of what is publicly approved as virtue. The sexual behavior of the human male and the human female need not be a copy of the socially sanctioned rules. Those rules remain as important affirmations of an acceptable code, even though they are regularly breached. Their roles as ideals are not threatened by daily behavior. In analyzing the violation of norms we will look at the implications of different forms of deviance on the symbolic character of the norm itself. *The point here is that the designators of deviant behavior react differently to different norm-sustaining implications of an act.* We can classify deviant behavior from this standpoint.

The Repentant Deviant

The reckless motorist often admits the legitimacy of traffic laws, even though he has broken them. The chronic alcoholic may well agree that both he and his society would be better if he could stay sober. In both cases the norm they have violated is itself unquestioned. Their deviation is a moral lapse, a fall from a grace to which they aspire. The homosexual who seeks a psychiatrist to rid himself of his habit has defined his actions similarly to those who have designated him as a deviant. There is a consensus between the designator and the deviant; his repentance confirms the norm.

Repentance and redemption seem to go hand-in-hand in court and church. Sykes and Matza have described techniques of neutralization which juvenile delinquents often use with enforcement agencies.

The juvenile delinquent would appear to be at least partially committed to the dominant social order in that he frequently exhibits guilt or shame when he violates its proscriptions, accords approval to certain conforming figures and distinguishes between appropriate and inappropriate targets for his deviance.[15]

A show of repentance is also used, say Sykes and Matza, to soften the indignation of law enforcement agents. A recent study of police behavior lends support to this. Juveniles apprehended by the police received more lenient treatment, including dismissal, if they appeared contrite and remorseful about their violations than if they did not. This difference in the posture of the deviant accounted for much of the differential treatment favoring middle-class "youngsters" as against lower-class "delinquents."[16]

The Sick Deviant

Acts which represent an attack upon a norm are neutralized by repentance. The open admission of repentance confirms the sinner's belief in the sin. His threat to the norm is removed and his violation has left the norm intact. Acts which we can perceive as those of sick and diseased people are irrelevant to the norm; they neither attack nor defend it. The use of morphine by hospital patients in severe pain is not designated as deviant behavior. Sentiments of public hostility and the apparatus of enforcement agencies are not mobilized toward the morphine-user. His use is not perceived as a violation of the norm against drug use, but as an uncontrolled act, not likely to be recurrent.[17]

While designations of action resulting from sickness do not threaten the norm, significant consequences flow from such definitions. Talcott Parsons has pointed out that the designation of a person as ill changes the obligations which others have toward the person and his obligations toward them.[18] Parsons' description sensitizes us to the way in which the sick person is a different social object than the healthy one. He has now become an object of welfare, a person to be helped rather than punished. Hostile sentiments toward sick people are not legitimate. The sick person is not responsible for his acts. He is excused from the consequences which attend the healthy who act the same way.[19]

Deviance designations, as we shall show below, are not fixed. They may shift from one form to another over time. Defining a behavior pattern as one caused by illness makes a hostile response toward the actor illegitimate and inappropriate. "Illness" is a social designation, by no means given in the nature of medical fact. Even left-handedness is still seen as morally deviant in many countries.

Hence the effort to define a practice as a consequence of illness is itself a matter of conflict and a political issue.

The Enemy Deviant

Writing about a Boston slum in the 1930s, William F. Whyte remarks:

> The policeman is subject to sharply conflicting pressures. On one side are the "good people" of Eastern City, who have written their moral judgments into law and demand through their newspapers that the law be enforced. On the other side are the people of Cornerville, who have different standards and have built up an organization whose perpetuation depends upon the freedom to violate the law.[20]

Whyte's is one of several studies that have pointed out the discrepancies between middle-class moralities embodied in law and lower-class moralities which differ sharply from them.[21] In Cornerville, gambling was seen as a respectable crime, just as antitrust behavior may be in other levels of the social structure. In American society, conflicts between social classes are often also cultural conflicts reflecting moral differences. Coincidence of ethnic and religious distinctions with class differences accentuates such conflicts between group values.

In these cases, the validity of the public designation is itself at issue. The publicly-defined deviant is neither repentant nor sick, but is instead an upholder of an opposite norm. He accepts his behavior as proper and derogates the public norm as illegitimate. He refuses to internalize the public norm into his self-definition. This is especially likely to occur in instances of business crimes. The buyer sees his action as legitimate economic behavior and resists a definition of it as immoral and thus prohibitable. The issue of off-track betting illustrates one area in which clashes of culture have been salient.

The designation of culturally legitimate behavior as deviant depends upon the superior power and organization of the designators. The concept of convention in this area, as Thrasymachus defined Justice for Socrates, is the will of the stronger. If the deviant is the politically weaker group, then the designation is open to the changes and contingencies of political fortunes. It becomes an issue of political conflict, ranging group against group and culture against culture in the effort to determine whose morals are to be designated as deserving of public affirmation.

It is when the deviant is also an enemy and his deviance is an aspect of group culture that the conventional norm is most explicitly and energetically attacked. When those once designated as deviant have achieved enough political power they may shift from disobedience to an effort to change the designation itself. This has certainly happened in the civil rights movement. Behavior viewed as deviant in the segregationist society has in many instances been moved into the realm of the problematic, now subject to political processes of conflict and compromise.

When the deviant and the designator perceive each other as enemies, and the designator's power is superior to that of the deviant, we have domination without a corresponding legitimacy. Anything which increases the power of the deviant to organize and attack the norm is thus a threat to the social dominance symbolized in the affirmation of the norm. Under such conditions the need of the designators to strengthen and enforce the norms is great. The struggle over the symbol of social power and status is focused on the question of the maintenance or change of the legal norm. The threat to the middle class in the increased political power of Cornerville is not that the Cornerville resident will gamble more; he already does gamble with great frequency. The threat is that the law will come to accept the morality of gambling and treat it as a legitimate business. If this happens, Boston is no longer a city dominated by middle-class Yankees but becomes one dominated by lower-class immigrants, as many think has actually happened in Boston. The maintenance of a norm which defines gambling as deviant behavior thus symbolizes the maintenance of Yankee social and political superiority. Its disappearance as a public commitment would symbolize the loss of that superiority.

The Cynical Deviant

The professional criminal commits acts whose designation as deviant is supported by wide social consensus. The burglar, the hired murderer, the arsonist, the kidnapper all prey on victims. While they may use repentance or illness as strategies to manage the impressions of enforcers, their basic orientation is self-seeking, to get around the rules. It is for this reason that their behavior is not a great threat to the norms although it calls for social management and repression. It does not threaten the legitimacy of the normative order.

DRINKING AS A CHANGING FORM OF DEVIANCE

Analysis of efforts to define drinking as deviant in the United States will illustrate the process by which designations shift. The legal embodiment of attitudes toward drinking shows how cultural conflicts find their expression in the symbolic functions of law. In the 160 years since 1800, we see all our suggested types of non-conforming behavior and all the forms of reaction among the conventional segments of the society.

The movement to limit and control personal consumption of alcohol began in the early nineteenth century, although some scattered attempts were made earlier.[22] Colonial legislation was aimed mainly at controlling the inns through licensing systems. While drunkenness occurred, and drinking was frequent, the rigid nature of the Colonial society, in both North and South, kept drinking from becoming an important social issue.[23]

The Repentant Drinker

The definition of the drinker as an object of social shame begins in the early nineteenth century and reaches full development in the late 1820s and early 1830s. A wave of growth in Temperance organizations in this period was sparked by the conversion of drinking men to abstinence under the stimulus of evangelical revivalism.[24] Through drinking men joining together to take the pledge, a norm of abstinence and sobriety emerged as a definition of conventional respectability. They sought to control themselves and their neighbors.

The norm of abstinence and sobriety replaced the accepted patterns of heavy drinking countenanced in the late eighteenth and early nineteenth centuries. By the 1870s rural and small-town America had defined middle-class morals to include the dry attitude. This definition had little need for legal embodiment. It could be enunciated in attacks on the drunkard which assumed that he shared the normative pattern of those who exhorted him to be better and to do better. He was a repentant deviant, someone to be brought back into the fold by moral persuasion and the techniques of religious revivalism.[25] His error was the sin of lapse from a shared standard of virtue. "The Holy Spirit will not visit, much less will He dwell within he who is under the polluting, debasing effects of intoxicating drink. The state of heart and mind which this occasions to him is loathsome and an abomination."[26]

Moral persuasion thus rests on the conviction of a consensus between the deviant and the designators. As long as the object of attack and conversion is isolated in individual terms, rather than perceived as a group, there is no sense of his deviant act as part of a shared culture. What is shared is the norm of conventionality; the appeal to the drinker and the chronic alcoholic is to repent. When the Woman's Anti-Whiskey Crusade of 1873–1874 broke out in Ohio, church women placed their attention on the taverns. In many Ohio towns these respectable ladies set up vigils in front of the tavern and attempted to prevent men from entering just by the fear that they would be observed.[27] In keeping with the evangelical motif in the Temperance movement, the Washingtonians, founded in 1848, appealed to drinkers and chronic alcoholics with the emotional trappings and oratory of religious meetings, even though devoid of pastors.[28]

Moral persuasion, rather than legislation, has been one persistent theme in the designation of the drinker as deviant and the alcoholic as depraved. Even in the depictions of the miseries and poverty of the chronic alcoholic, there is a decided moral condemnation which has been the hallmark of the American Temperance movement. Moral persuasion was ineffective as a device to wipe out drinking and drunkenness. Heavy drinking persisted through the nineteenth century and the organized attempts to convert the drunkard experienced much backsliding.[29] Nevertheless, defections from the standard did not threaten the standard. The public definition of respectability matched the ideals of the sober and abstaining people who dominated those parts of the society where moral suasion was effective. In the late nineteenth century those areas in which temperance sentiment was strongest were also those in which legislation was most easily enforceable.[30]

The Enemy Drinker

The demand for laws to limit alcoholic consumption appears to arise from situations in which the drinkers possess power as a definitive social and political group and, in their customary habits and beliefs, deny the validity of abstinence norms. The persistence of areas in which Temperance norms were least controlling led to the emergence of attempts to embody control in legal measures. The drinker as enemy seems to be the greatest stimulus to efforts to designate his act as publicly defined deviance.

In its early phase the American Temperance movement was committed chiefly to moral persuasion. Efforts to achieve legislation governing the sale and use of alcohol do not appear until the 1840s. This legislative movement had a close relationship to the immigration of Irish Catholics and German Lutherans into the United States in this period. These nonevangelical and/or non-Protestant peoples made up a large proportion of the urban poor in the 1840s and 1850s. They brought with them a far more accepting evaluation of drinking than had yet existed in the United States. The tavern and the beer parlor had a distinct place in the leisure of the Germans and the Irish. The prominence of this place was intensified by the stark character of the developing American slum.[31] These immigrant cultures did not contain a strong tradition of Temperance norms which might have made an effective appeal to a sense of sin. To be sure, excessive drunkenness was scorned, but neither abstinence nor constant sobriety were supported by the cultural codes.

Between these two groups—the native American, middle-class evangelical Protestant and the immigrant European Catholic or Lutheran occupying the urban lower class—there was little room for repentance. By the 1850s the issue of drinking reflected a general clash over cultural values. The Temperance movement found allies in its political efforts among the nativist movements.[32] The force and power of the anti-alcohol movements, however, were limited greatly by the political composition of the urban electorate, with its high proportion of immigrants. Thus the movement to develop legislation emerged in reaction to the appearance of cultural groups least responsive to the norms of abstinence and sobriety. The very effort to turn such informal norms into legal standards polarized the opposing forces and accentuated the symbolic import of the movement. Now that the issue had been joined, defeat or victory was a clear-cut statement of public dominance.

It is a paradox that the most successful move to eradicate alcohol emerged in a period when America was shifting from a heavy-drinking society, in which whiskey was the leading form of alcohol, to a moderate one, in which beer was replacing whiskey. Prohibition came as the culmination of the movement to reform the immigrant cultures and at the height of the immigrant influx into the United States.

Following the Civil War, moral persuasion and legislative goals were both parts of the movement against alcohol. By the 1880's an appeal was made to the urban, immigrant lower classes to repent and to imitate the habits of the American middle class as a route to economic and social mobility. Norms of abstinence were presented to the non-abstainer both as virtue and as expedience.[33] This effort failed. The new, and larger, immigration of 1890–1915 increased still further the threat of the urban lower class to the native American.

The symbolic effect of Prohibition legislation must be kept analytically separate from its instrumental, enforcement side. While the urban middle class did provide much of the organizational leadership to the Temperance and Prohibition movements, the political strength of the movement in its legislative drives was in the rural areas of the United States. Here, where the problems of drinking were most under control, where the norm was relatively intact, the appeal to a struggle against foreign invasion was the most potent. In these areas, passage of legislation was likely to make small difference in behavior. The continuing polarization of political forces into those of cultural opposition and cultural acceptance during the Prohibition campaigns (1906–1919), and during the drive for Repeal (1926–1933), greatly intensified the symbolic significance of victory and defeat.[34] Even if the Prohibition measures were limited in their enforceability in the metropolis there was no doubt about whose law was public and what way of life was being labelled as opprobrious.

After Repeal, as Dry power in American politics subsided, the designation of the drinker as deviant also receded. Public affirmation of the Temperance norm had changed and with it the definition of the deviant had changed. Abstinence was itself less acceptable. In the 1950s the Temperance movement, faced with this change in public norms, even introduced a series of placards with the slogan, "It's Smart *Not* to Drink."

Despite this normative change in the public designation of drinking deviance, there has not been much change in American drinking patterns. Following the Prohibition period the consumption of alcohol has not returned to its pre-1915 high. Beer has continued to occupy a more important place as a source of alcohol consumption. "Hard drinkers" are not as common in America today as they were in the nineteenth century. While there has been some increase in moderate drinking, the percentage of adults who are abstainers has remained approximately the same (one-third) for the past thirty years. Similarly, Dry sentiment has remained stable, as measured by local opinion results.[35] In short, the argument over deviance designation has been largely one of normative dominance, not of instrumental social control. The process of deviance designation in drinking needs to be understood in terms of symbols of cultural dominance rather than in the activities of social control.

The Sick Drinker

For most of the nineteenth century, the chronic alcoholic as well as the less compulsive drinker was viewed as a sinner. It was not until after Repeal (1933) that chronic alcoholism became defined as illness in the United States. Earlier actions taken toward promotion of the welfare of drinkers and alcoholics through Temperance measures rested on the moral supremacy of abstinence and the demand for repentance. The user of alcohol could be an object of sympathy, but his social salvation depended on a willingness to embrace the norm of his exhorters. The designation of alcoholism as sickness has a different bearing on the question of normative superiority. It renders the behavior of the deviant indifferent to the status of norms enforcing abstinence.

This realization appears to have made supporters of Temperance and Prohibition hostile to efforts to redefine the deviant character of alcoholism. They deeply opposed the reports of the Committee of Fifty in the late nineteenth century.[36] These volumes of reports by scholars and prominent men took a less moralistic and a more sociological and functional view of the saloon and drinking than did the Temperance Movement.

The soundness of these fears is shown by what did happen to the Temperance movement with the rise of the view that alcoholism is illness. It led to new agencies concerned with drinking problems. These excluded Temperance people from the circle of those who now define what is deviant in drinking habits. The National Commission on Alcoholism was formed in 1941 and the Yale School of Alcoholic Studies formed in 1940. They were manned by medical personnel, social workers, and social scientists, people now alien to the spirit of the abstainer. Problems of drinking were removed from the church and placed in the hands of the universities and the medical clinics. The tendency to handle drinkers through protective and welfare agencies rather than through police or clergy has become more frequent.

"The bare statement that 'alcoholism is a disease' is most misleading since . . . it conceals what is essential—that a step in public policy is being recommended, not a scientific discovery announced."[37] John Seeley's remark is an apt one. Replacement of the norm of sin and repentance by that of illness and therapy removes the onus of guilt and immorality from the act of drinking and the state of chronic alcoholism. It replaces the image of the sinner with that of a patient, a person to be helped rather than to be exhorted. No wonder that the Temperance movement has found the work of the Yale School, and often even the work of Alcoholics Anonymous, a threat to its own movement. It has been most limited in its cooperation with these organizations and has attempted to set up other organizations which might provide the face of Science in league with the tone of the movement.[38]

The redefinition of the alcoholic as sick thus brought into power both ideas and organizations antithetical to the Temperance movement. The norm protected by law and government was no longer the one held by the people who had supported Temperance and Prohibition. The hostility of Temperance people is readily understandable; their relative political unimportance is crucial to their present inability to make that hostility effective.

MOVEMENTS OF MORAL PASSAGE

In this paper we have called attention to the fact that deviance designations have histories; the public definition of behavior as deviant is itself changeable. It is open to reversals of political power, twists of public opinion, and the development of social movements and moral crusades. What is attacked as criminal today may be seen as sick next year and fought over as possibly legitimate by the next generation.

Movements to redefine behavior may eventuate in a moral passage, a transition of the behavior from one moral status to another. In analyzing movements toward the redefinition of alcohol use, we have dealt with moral crusades which were restrictive and others which were permissive toward drinking and toward drunkards. (We might have also used the word "alcoholics," suggesting a less disapproving and more medical perspective.) In both cases, however, the movements sought to change the public designation. While we are familiar with the restrictive or enforcing movements, the permissive or legitimizing movement must also be seen as a prevalent way in which deviants throw off the onus of their actions and avoid the sanctions associated with immoral activities.

Even where the deviants are a small and politically powerless group they may nevertheless attempt to protect themselves by influence over the process of designation. The effort to define themselves as ill is one plausible means to this end. Drug addiction as well as drunkenness is partially undergoing a change toward such redefinition.[39] This occurs in league with powerful groups in society, such as social workers, medical professionals, or university professors. The moral passage achieved here reduces the sanctions imposed by criminal law and the public acceptance of the deviant designation.

The "lifting" of a deviant activity to the level of a political, public issue is thus a sign that its moral status is at stake, that legitimacy is a possibility. Today the moral acceptance of drinking, marijuana and LSD use, homosexuality, abortion, and other "vices" is being publicly discussed, and movements championing them have emerged. Such movements draw into them far more than the deviants themselves. Because they become symbols of general cultural attitudes they call out partisans for both repression and permission. The present debate over drug addiction laws in the United States, for example, is carried out between defenders and opposers of the norm rather than between users and nonusers of the drugs involved.

As the movement for redefinition of the addict as sick has grown, the movement to strengthen the definition of addiction as criminal has responded with increased legal severity. To classify drug users as sick and the victims or clients as suffering from "disease" would mean a change in the agencies responsible for reaction from police enforcement to medical authorities. Further, it might diminish the moral disapproval with which drug use, and the reputed euphoric effects connected with it, are viewed by supporters of present legislation. Commenting on the clinic plan to permit medical dispensing of narcotics to licensed addicts, U.S. Commissioner of Narcotics Anslinger wrote:

> This plan would elevate a most despicable trade to the avowed status of an honorable business, nay, to the status of practice of a time-honored profession; and drug addicts would multiply unrestrained, to the irrevocable impairment of the moral fiber and physical welfare of the American people.[40]

In this paper we have seen that redefining moral crusades tends to generate strong counter-movements. The deviant as a cultural opponent is a more potent threat to the norm than is the repentant, or even the sick deviant. The threat to the legitimacy of the norm is a spur to the need for symbolic restatement in legal terms. In these instances of "crimes without victims" the legal norm is *not* the enunciator of a consensus within the community. On the contrary, it is when consensus is least attainable that the pressure to establish legal norms appears to be greatest.

NOTES

[1]Howard S. Becker, *Outsiders: Studies in the Sociology of Deviance,* Glencoe: Free Press, 1963, Chap. 1. A similar view is presented in John Kitsuse, "Societal Reaction to Deviant Behavior," *Social Problems,* 9 (Winter, 1962), pp. 247–56; Kai Erikson, "Sociology of Deviance," in E. McDonagh and J. Simpson, eds., *Social Problems,* New York: Holt, Rinehart and Winston, Inc., 1965, pp. 457–464, p. 458.

[2]The material of this section is more fully discussed in my book *Symbolic Crusade: Status Politics and the American Temperance Movement,* Urbana: University of Illinois Press, 1963, esp. Chap. 7.

[3]See the analysis of power as infused with collective goals in Parsons' criticism of C. Wright Mills, *The Power Elite:* Talcott Parsons, "The Distribution of Power in American Society," *World Politics,* 10 (October, 1957), p. 123, 144. [See his book, *Structure and Process,* Glencoe, Ill.: Free Press, 1960.]

[4]Francis X. Sutton, "Representation and the Nature of Political Systems," *Comparative Studies in Society and History,* 2 (October, 1959), pp. 1–10. In this paper Sutton shows that in some primitive societies, political officials function chiefly as representatives to other tribes rather than as law enforcers or policy-makers.

[5]Phillip Wheelwright, *The Burning Fountain,* Bloomington: Indiana University Press, 1964, p. 23.

[6]Talcott Parsons, *The Social System,* Glencoe, Ill.: Free Press, 1954, p. 286.

[7]Murray Edelman has shown this in his analysis of the discrepancy between legislative action and administrative agency operation. Murray Edelman, *The Symbolic Uses of Politics,* Urbana: University of Illinois Press, 1964.

[8]Robin Williams, *American Society,* New York: A. A. Knopf, 1960, pp. 372–96. Hyman Rodman's analysis of "lower-class value stretch" suggests yet another ambiguity in the concept of norm. He found that in Trinidad among lower-class respondents that *both* marriage and nonlegal marital union are normatively accepted, although marriage is preferred. Hyman Rodman, "Illegitimacy in the Caribbean Social Structure," *American Sociological Review,* 31 (October, 1966), pp. 673–683.

[9]Edelman, *Symbolic Uses of Politics,* Chap. 2. The author refers to this as a process of political quiescence. While Edelman's symbolic analysis is close to mine, his emphasis is on the reassurance function of symbols in relation to presumed instrumental affects. My analysis stresses the conflict over symbols as a process of importance apart from instrumental effects.

[10]Gusfield, *Symbolic Crusade,* pp. 117–126.

[11]Joseph Gusfield, "Prohibition: The Impact of Political Utopianism," in John Braeman, ed., *The 1920's Revisited,* Columbus: Ohio State University Press, forthcoming; Andrew Sinclair, *The Era of Excess,* New York: Harper Colophon Books, 1964, Chap. 10, pp. 13–14.

[12]Kenneth Burke, *A Grammar of Motives,* New York: Prentice-Hall, 1945, p. 393. Burke's writings have been the strongest influence on the mode of analysis presented here. Two other writers, whose works have been influential, themselves influenced by Burke, are Erving Goffman and Hugh D. Duncan.

[13]Gusfield, *Symbolic Crusade,* Chap. 5.

[14]Emile Durkheim, *The Division of Labor in Society*, trans. George Simpson, Glencoe, Ill.: The Free Press, 1947, especially at pp. 96–103. For a similar view see Lewis Coser, "Some Functions of Deviant Behavior and Normative Flexibility," *American Journal of Sociology*, 68 (September, 1962), pp. 172–182.

[15]Gresham Sykes and David Matza, "Techniques of Neutralization: A Theory of Delinquency," *American Sociological Review*, 22 (December, 1957), pp. 664–670, p. 666.

[16]Irving Piliavin and Scott Briar, "Police Encounters with Juveniles," *American Journal of Sociology*, 70 (September, 1964), pp. 206–214.

[17]This of course does not mean that the patient using morphine may not become an addict.

[18]Talcott Parsons and Renée Fox, "Illness, Therapy and the Modern Urban Family," *Journal of Social Issues*, 8 (1952), pp. 31–44.

[19]A somewhat similar distinction as that presented here can be found in Vilhelm Aubert and Sheldon Messinger, "The Criminal and the Sick," in V. Aubert, *The Hidden Society*, New York: The Bedminister Press, 1965, pp. 25–54.

[20]William F. Whyte, *Street-Corner Society*, Chicago: University of Chicago Press, 2nd edition, 1955, p. 138.

[21]See William Westley's analysis of the differences between the morality shared by the lower class and the police in contrast to that of the courts over such matters as gambling, prostitution, and sexual perversion. The courts take a sterner view of gamblers and prostitutes than do the police, who take a sterner view of the sexual offender. William Westley, "Violence and the Police," *American Journal of Sociology*, 59 (July, 1953), pp. 34–42.

[22]The best single account of Temperance activities before the Civil War is that of John Krout, *The Origins of Prohibition*, New York: A. A. Knopf, 1925.

[23]Krout, *Origins of Prohibition*, Chapters 1 and 2; also see Alice Earle, *Home Life in Colonial Days*, New York: Macmillan and Co., 1937, pp. 148–149; 156–165.

[24]Gusfield, *Symbolic Crusade*, pp. 44–51.

[25]Gusfield, *Symbolic Crusade*, pp. 69–86.

[26]*Temperance Manual* (no publisher listed, 1836), p. 46.

[27]See the typical account by Mother Stewart, one of the leaders in the 1873–74 Woman's War on Whiskey, in Eliza D. Steward, *Memories of the Crusade*, Columbus, Ohio: W. G. Hibbard, 2nd edition, 1889, pp. 139–143; also see *Standard Encyclopedia of the Alcohol Problem*, 6 (Westerville, Ohio: American Issue Publishing Co., 1930), pp. 2902–2905.

[28]Krout, *Origins of Prohibition*, Chap. 9.

[29]See the table of consumption of alcoholic beverages, 1850–1957, in Mark Keller and Vera Efron, "Selected Statistics on Alcoholic Beverage," reprinted in Raymond McCarthy, ed., *Drinking and Intoxication*, Glencoe, Ill.: The Free Press, 1959, p. 180.

[30]Joseph Rowntree and Arthur Sherwell, *State Prohibition and Local Option*, London: Hodden and Stoughton, 1900, using both systematic observation and analysis of federal tax payments, concluded (p. 253) that ". . . local veto in America has only been found operative outside the larger towns and cities."

[31]See the accounts of drinking habits among Irish and German immigrants in Oscar Handlin, *Boston's Immigrants,* Cambridge, Mass.: Harvard University Press, 1941, pp. 191–192, 201–209; Marcus Hansen, *The Immigrant in American History,* Cambridge, Mass.: Harvard University Press, 1940.

[32]Ray Billington, *The Protestant Crusade, 1800–1860,* New York: Macmillan and Co., 1938, Chap. 15; Gusfield, *Symbolic Crusade,* pp. 55–57.

[33]William F. Whyte, *Street-Corner Society,* p. 99. Whyte has shown this as a major attitude of social work and the settlement house toward slum-dwellers he studied in the 1930's. "The community was expected to adapt itself to the standards of the settlement house." The rationale for adaptation lay in its effects in promoting social mobility.

[34]Although a well-organized Temperance movement existed among Catholics, it was weakened by the Protestant drive for Prohibition. See Joan Bland, *Hibernian Crusade,* Washington, D.C.: Catholic University Press, 1951.

[35]See my analysis of American drinking in the post-Repeal era. Gusfield, "Prohibition: The Impact of Political Utopianism," *Symbolic Crusade.*

[36]The Committee of Fifty, a group of prominent educators, scientists, and clergymen, sponsored and directed several studies of drinking and the saloon. Their position as men unaffiliated to temperance organizations was intended to introduce unbiased investigation, often critical of Temperance doctrine. For two of the leading volumes see John Shaw Billing's, *The Physiological Aspects of the Liquor Problem,* Boston and New York: Houghton, Mifflin and Co., 1903; Raymond Calkins, *Substitutes for the Saloon,* Boston and New York: Houghton, Mifflin and Co., 1903.

[37]John Seeley, "Alcoholism Is a Disease: Implications for Social Policy," in D. Pittman and C. Snyder, eds., *Society, Culture and Drinking Patterns,* New York: John Wiley and Sons, 1962, pp. 586–593, at p. 593. For a description of the variety of definitions of alcoholism and drunkenness, as deviant and nondeviant, see the papers by Edwin Lemert, "Alcohol, Values and Social Control" and by Archer Tongue, "What the State Does About Alcohol and Alcoholism," both in the same volume.

[38]The WCTU during the 1950s persistently avoided support to Alcoholics Anonymous. The Yale School of Alcohol Studies was attacked and derogated in Temperance literature. A counterorganization, with several prominent pro-Dry scientists, developed, held seminars, and issued statements in opposition to Yale School publications.

[39]Many of the writings of sociologists interested in drug addiction have contained explicit demands for such redefinitions. See Becker, *Outsiders;* Alfred Lindesmith, *The Addict and the Law,* Bloomington: Indiana University Press, 1965, and David Ausubel, *Drug Addiction,* New York: Random House, 1958. The recent movement to redefine marijuana and LSD as legitimate is partially supported by such writings but is more saliently a movement of enemy deviants. The activities of Timothy Leary, Allen Ginsberg, and the "hipsters" is the most vocal expression of this movement.

[40]Harry Anslinger and William Tompkins, *The Traffic in Narcotics,* New York: Funk and Wagnalls Co., Inc., 1953, p. 186.

Part III

SOCIALIZATION INTO DEVIANCE

6

The Moral Career
of the Mental Patient

ERVING GOFFMAN

Traditionally the term *career* has been reserved for those who expect to enjoy the rises laid out within a respectable profession. The term is coming to be used, however, in a broadened sense to refer to any social strand of any person's course through life. The perspective of natural history is taken: unique outcomes are neglected in favor of such changes over time as are basic and common to the members of a social category, although occurring independently to each of them. Such a career is not a thing that can be brilliant or disappointing; it can no more be a success than a failure. In this light, I want to consider the mental patient, drawing mainly upon data collected during a year's participant observation of patient social life in a public mental hospital,[1] wherein an attempt was made to take the patient's point of view.

One value of the concept of career is its two-sidedness. One side is linked to internal matters held dearly and closely, such as image of self and felt identity; the other side concerns official position, jural relations, and style of life, and is part of a publicly accessible institutional complex. The concept of career, then, allows one to move back and forth between the personal and the public, between the self and its significant society, without having overly to rely for data upon what the person says he thinks he imagines himself to be.

This paper, then, is an exercise in the institutional approach to the study of self. The main concern will be with the *moral* aspects of career—that is, the regular sequence of changes that career entails in

Reprinted by special permission of The William Alanson White Psychiatric Foundation, Inc., from *Psychiatry*, 22 (1959), pp. 123–142. Copyright by the William Alanson White Foundation, Inc.

the person's self and in his framework of imagery for judging himself and others.[2]

The category mental patient itself will be understood in one strictly sociological sense. In this perspective, the psychiatric view of a person becomes significant only in so far as this view itself alters his social fate—an alteration which seems to become fundamental in our society when, and only when, the person is put through the process of hospitalization.[3] I therefore exclude certain neighboring categories: the undiscovered candidates who would be judged "sick" by psychiatric standards but who never come to be viewed as such by themselves or others, although they may cause everyone a great deal of trouble;[4] the office patient whom a psychiatrist feels he can handle with drugs or shock on the outside; the mental client who engages in psychotherapeutic relationships. And I include anyone, however robust in temperament, who somehow gets caught up in the heavy machinery of mental hospital servicing. In this way the effects of being treated as a mental patient can be kept quite distinct from the effects upon a person's life of traits a clinician would view as psychopathological.[5] Persons who become mental hospital patients vary widely in the kind and degree of illness that a psychiatrist would impute to them, and in the attributes by which laymen would describe them. But once started on the way, they are confronted by some importantly similar circumstances and respond to these in some importantly similar ways. Since these similarities do not come from mental illness, they would seem to occur in spite of it. It is thus a tribute to the power of social forces that the uniform status of mental patient can not only assure an aggregate of persons a common fate and eventually, because of this, a common character, but that this social reworking can be done upon what is perhaps the most obstinate diversity of human materials that can be brought together by society. Here there lacks only the frequent forming of a protective group life by ex-patients to illustrate in full the classic cycle of response by which deviant subgroupings are psychodynamically formed in society.

This general sociological perspective is heavily reinforced by one key finding of sociologically-oriented students in mental hospital research. As has been repeatedly shown in the study of nonliterate societies the awesomeness, distastefulness, and barbarity of a foreign culture can decrease in the degree that the student becomes familiar with the point of view to life that is taken by his subjects. Similarly, the student of mental hospitals can discover that the craziness or "sick behavior" claimed for the mental patient is by and large a product of the claimant's social distance from the situation that the patient is in, and is not primarily a product of mental illness. Whatever the refinements of the various patients' psychiatric diagnoses, and whatever the special ways in which social life on the "inside" is unique, the researcher can find that he is participating in a community not significantly different from any other he has studied.[6] Of course, while restricting himself to the off-ward grounds community of paroled patients, he may feel, as some patients do, that life in the locked wards is bizarre; and while on a locked admissions or convalescent ward, he may feel that chronic "back" wards are socially crazy places. But he need only move his sphere of sympathetic participation to the "worst" ward in the hospital, and this too can come into social focus as a place with a livable and continuously meaningful social world. This in no way denies that he will find a minority in any ward or patient group that continues to seem quite beyond the capacity to follow rules of social organization, or that the orderly fulfilment of normative expectations in patient society is partly made possible by strategic measures that have somehow come to be institutionalized in mental hospitals.

The career of the mental patient falls popularly and naturalistically into three main phases: the period prior to entering the hospital, which I shall call the *prepatient phase;* the period in the hospital, the *inpatient phase;* the period after discharge from the hospital, should this occur, namely, the *ex-patient phase.*[7] This paper will deal only with the first two phases.

THE PREPATIENT PHASE

A relatively small group of prepatients come into the mental hospital willingly, because of their own idea of what will be good for them, or because of wholehearted agreement with the relevant members of their family. Presumably these recruits have found themselves acting in a way which is evidence to them that they are losing their minds or losing control of themselves. This view of oneself would seem to be one of the most pervasively threatening things that can happen to the self in our society, especially since it is likely to occur at a time when the person is in any case sufficiently troubled to exhibit the kind of symptom which he himself can see. As Sullivan described it,

> What we discover in the self-system of a person undergoing schizophrenic changes or schizophrenic processes, is then, in its simplest form, an extremely fear-marked puzzlement, consisting of the use of rather generalized and anything but exquisitely refined referential processes in an attempt to cope with what is essentially a failure at being human—a failure at being anything that one could respect as worth being.[8]

Coupled with the person's disintegrative reevaluation of himself will be the new, almost equally pervasive circumstance of attempting to conceal from others what he takes to be the new fundamental facts about himself, and attempting to discover whether others too have discovered them.[9] Here I want to stress that perception of losing one's mind is based on culturally derived and socially engrained stereotypes as to the significance of symptoms such as hearing voices, losing temporal and spatial orientation, and sensing that one is being followed, and that many of the most spectacular and convincing of these symptoms in some instances psychiatrically signify merely a temporary emotional upset in a stressful situation, however terrifying to the person at the time. Similarly, the anxiety consequent upon this perception of oneself, and the strategies devised to reduce this anxiety, are not a product of abnormal psychology, but would be exhibited by any person socialized into our culture who came to conceive of himself as someone losing his mind. Interestingly, subcultures in American society apparently differ in the amount of ready imagery and encouragement they supply for such self-views, leading to differential rates of *self*-referral; the capacity to take this distintegrative view of oneself without psychiatric prompting seems to be one of the questionable cultural privileges of the upper classes.[10]

For the person who has come to see himself—with whatever justification—as mentally unbalanced, entrance to the mental hospital can sometimes being relief, perhaps in part because of the sudden transformation in the structure of his basic social situations. Instead of being to himself a questionable person trying to maintain a role as a full one, he can become an officially questioned person known to himself to be not so questionable as that. In other cases, hospitalization can make matters worse for the willing patient, confirming by the objective situation what has theretofore been a matter of the private experience of self.

Once the willing prepatient enters the hospital, he may go through the same routine of experiences as do those who enter unwillingly. In any case, it is the latter that I mainly want to consider, since in America at present these are by far the more numerous kind.[11] Their approach to the institution takes one of three classic forms: they come because they have been implored by their family or threatened with the abrogation of family ties unless they go "willingly"; they come by force under police escort; they come under misapprehension purposely induced by others, this last restricted mainly to youthful prepatients.

The prepatient's career may be seen in terms of an extrusory model; he starts out with relationships and rights, and ends up, at the beginning of his hospital stay, with hardly any of either. The moral aspects of this career, then, typically begin with the experience of abandonment, disloyalty, and embitterment. This is the case even though to others it may be obvious that he was in need of treatment, and even though in the hospital he may soon come to agree.

The case histories of most mental patients document offense against some arrangement for face-to-face living—a domestic establishment, a work place, a semipublic organization such as a church or store, a public region such as a street or park. Often there is also a record of some *complainant,* some figure who takes that action against the offender which eventually leads to his hospitalization. This may not be the person who makes the first move, but it is the person who makes what turns out to be the first effective move. Here is the *social* beginning of the patient's career, regardless of where one might locate the psychological beginning of his mental illness.

The kinds of offenses which lead to hospitalization are felt to differ in nature from those which lead to other extrusory consequences— to imprisonment, divorce, loss of job, disownment, regional exile, noninstitutional psychiatric treatment, and so forth. But little seems known about these differentiating factors; and when one studies actual commitments, alternate outcomes frequently appear to have been possible. It seems true, moreover, that for every offense that leads to an effective complaint, there are many psychiatrically similar ones that never do. No action is taken; or action is taken which leads to other extrusory outcomes; or ineffective action is taken, leading to the mere pacifying or putting off of the person who complains. Thus, as Clausen and Yarrow have nicely shown, even offenders who are eventually hospitalized are likely to have had a long series of ineffective actions taken against them.[12]

Separating those offenses which could have been used as grounds for hospitalizing the offender from those that are so used, one finds a vast number of what students of occupation call career contingencies.[13] Some of these contingencies in the mental patient's career have been suggested, if not explored, such as socioeconomic status, visibility of the offense, proximity to a mental hospital, amount of treatment facilities available, community regard for the type of treatment given in available hospitals, and so on.[14] For information about other contingencies one must rely on atrocity tales: a psychotic man is tolerated by his wife until she finds herself a boyfriend, or by his adult children until they move from a house to an apartment; an alcoholic is sent to a mental hospital because the jail is full, and a drug addict because he declines to avail himself of psychiatric treatment on the outside; a rebellious adolescent daughter can no longer be managed at home because she now threatens to have an open affair with an unsuitable companion; and so on. Correspondingly there is an equally important set of contingencies causing the person to bypass this fate. And should the person enter the hospital, still another set of contingencies will help determine when he is to obtain a discharge—such as the desire of his family for his return, the availability of a "manageable" job, and so on. The society's official view is that inmates of mental hospitals are there primarily because they are suffering from mental illness. However, in the degree that the "mentally ill" outside hospitals numerically approach or surpass those inside hospitals, one could say that mental patients *distinctively* suffer not from mental illness, but from contingencies.

Career contingencies occur in conjunction with a second feature of the prepatient's career—the *circuit of agents*—and agencies—that participate fatefully in his passage from civilian to patient status.[15] Here is an instance of that increasingly important class of social system whose elements are agents and agencies which are brought into systemic connection through having to take up and send on the same persons. Some of these agent roles will be cited now, with the understanding that in any concrete circuit a role may be filled more than once, and a single person may fill more than one of them.

First is the *next-of-relation*—the person whom the prepatient sees as the most available of those upon whom he should be able to most depend in times of trouble; in this instance the last to doubt his sanity and the first to have done everything to save him from the fate which, it transpires, he has been approaching. The patient's next-of-relation is usually his next of kin; the special term is introduced because he need not be. Second is the *complainant,* the person who retrospectively appears to have started the person on his way to the hospital. Third are the *mediators*—the sequence of agents and agencies to which the prepatient is referred and through which he is relayed and processed on his way to the hospital. Here are included police, clergy, general medical practitioners, office psychiatrists, personnel in public clinics, lawyers, social service workers, school teachers, and so on. One of these agents will have the legal mandate to sanction commitment and will exercise it, and so those agents who precede him in the process will be involved in something whose outcome is not yet settled. When the mediators retire from the scene, the prepatient has become an inpatient, and the significant agent has become the hospital administrator.

While the complainant usually takes action in a lay capacity as a citizen, an employer, a neighbor, or a kinsman, mediators tend to be specialists and differ from those they serve in significant ways. They have experience in handling trouble, and some professional distance from what they handle. Except in the case of policemen, and perhaps some clergy, they tend to be more psychiatrically oriented than the lay public, and will see the need for treatment at times when the public does not.[16]

An interesting feature of these roles is the functional effects of their interdigitation. For example, the feelings of the patient will be influenced by whether or not the person who fills the role of complainant also has the role of next-of-relation— an embarrassing combination more prevalent, apparently, in the higher classes than in the lower.[17] Some of these emergent effects will be considered now.[18]

In the prepatient's progress from home to the hospital he may participate as a third person in what he may come to experience as a kind of *alienative coalition*. His next-of-relation presses him into coming to "talk things over" with a medical practitioner, an office psychiatrist, or some other counselor. Disinclination on his part may be met by threatening him with desertion, disownment, or other legal action, or by stressing the joint and explorative nature of the interview. But typically the next-of-relation will have set the interview up, in the sense of selecting the professional, arranging for time, telling the professional something about the case, and so on. This move effectively tends to establish the next-of-relation as the responsible person to whom pertinent findings can be divulged, while effectively establishing the other as the patient. The prepatient often goes to the interview with the understanding that he is going as an equal of someone who is so bound together with him that a third person could not come between them in fundamental matters; this, after all, is one way in which close relationships are defined in our society. Upon arrival at the office the prepatient suddenly finds that he and his next-of-relation have not been accorded the same roles, and apparently that a prior understanding between the professional and the next-of-relation has been put in operation against him. In the extreme but common case the professional first sees the prepatient alone, in the role of examiner and diagnostician, and then sees the next-of-relation alone, in the role of advisor, while carefully avoiding talking things over seriously with them both together.[19] And even in those nonconsultative cases where public officials must forcibly extract a person from a family that wants to tolerate him, the next-of- relation is likely to be induced to "go along" with the official action, so that even here the prepatient may feel that an alienative coalition has been formed against him.

The moral experience of being third man in such a coalition is likely to embitter the prepatient, especially since his troubles have probably already led to some estrangement from his next-of-relation. After he enters the hospital, continued visits by his next-of-relation can give the patient the "insight" that his own best interests were being served. But the initial visits may temporarily strengthen his feeling of abandonment; he is likely to beg his visitor to get him out or at least to get him more privileges and to sympathize with the monstrousness of his plight—to which the visitor ordinarily can respond only by trying to maintain a hopeful note, by not "hearing" the requests, or by assuring the patient that the medical authorities know about these things and are doing what is medically best. The visitor then nonchalantly goes back into a world that the patient has learned is incredibly thick with freedom and privileges, causing the patient to feel that his next-of-relation is merely adding a pious gloss to a clear case of traitorous desertion.

The depth to which the patient may feel betrayed by his next-of-relation seems to be increased by the fact that another witnesses his betrayal—a factor which is apparently significant in many three-party situations. An offended person may well act forbearantly and accommodatively toward an offender when the two are alone, choosing peace ahead of justice. The presence of a witness, however, seems to add something to the implications of the offense. For then it is beyond the power of the offended and offender to forget about, erase, or suppress what has happened; the offense has become a public social fact.[20] When the witness is a mental health commission, as is sometimes the case, the witnessed betrayal can verge on a "degradation ceremony."[21] In such circumstances, the offended patient may feel that some kind of extensive reparative action is required before witnesses, if his honor and social weight are to be restored.

Two other aspects of sensed betrayal should be mentioned. First, those who suggest the possibility of another's entering a mental hospital are not likely to provide a realistic picture of how in fact it may strike him when he arrives. Often he is told that he will get required medical treatment and a rest, and may well be out in a few months or so. In some cases they may thus be concealing what they know, but I think, in general, they will be telling what they see as the truth. For here there is a quite relevant difference between patients and mediating professionals; mediators, more so than the public at large, may conceive of mental hospitals as short-term medical establishments where required rest and attention can be voluntarily obtained, and not as places of coerced exile. When the prepatient finally arrives he is likely to learn quite quickly, quite differently. He then finds that the information given him about life in the hospital has had the effect of his having put up less resistance to entering than he now sees he would have put up had he known the facts. Whatever the intentions of those who participated in his transition from person to patient, he may sense they have in effect "conned" him into his present predicament.

I am suggesting that the prepatient starts out with at least a portion of the rights, liberties, and satisfactions of the civilian and ends up on a psychiatric ward stripped of almost everything. The question here is how this stripping is managed. This is the second aspect of betrayal I want to consider.

As the prepatient may see it, the circuit of significant figures can function as a kind of betrayal funnel. Passage from person to patient may be effected through a series of linked stages, each managed by a different agent. While each stage tends to bring a sharp decrease in adult free status, each agent may try to maintain the fiction that no further decrease will occur. He may even manage to turn the prepatient over to the next agent while sustaining this note. Further, through words, cues, and gestures, the prepatient is implicitly asked by the current agent to join with him in sustaining a running line of polite small talk that tactfully avoids the administrative facts of the situation, becoming, with each stage, progressively more at odds with these facts. The spouse would rather not have to cry to get the prepatient to visit a psychiatrist; psychiatrists would rather not have a scene when the prepatient learns that he and his spouse are being seen separately and in different ways; the police infrequently bring a prepatient to the hospital in a strait jacket, finding it much easier all around to give him a cigarette, some kindly words, and freedom to relax in the back seat of the patrol car; and finally, the admitting psychiatrist finds he can do his work better in the relative quiet and luxury of the "admission suite" where, as an incidental consequence, the notion can survive that a mental hospital is indeed a comforting place. If the prepatient heeds all of these implied requests and is reasonably decent about the whole thing, he can travel the whole circuit from home to hospital without forcing anyone to look directly at what is happening or to deal with the raw emotion that his situation might well cause him to express. His showing consideration for those who are moving him toward the hospital allows them to show consideration for him, with the joint result that these interactions can be sustained with some of the protective harmony characteristic of ordinary face-to-face dealings. But should the new patient cast his mind back over the sequence of steps leading to hospitalization, he may feel that everyone's *current* comfort was being busily sustained while his long-range welfare was being undermined. This realization may constitute a moral experience that further separates him for the time from the people on the outside.[22]

   I would now like to look at the circuit of career agents from the point of view of the agents themselves. Mediators in the person's transition from civil to patient status—as well as his keepers, once he is in the hospital—have an interest in establishing a responsible next-of-relation as the patient's deputy or *guardian;* should there be no obvious candidate for the role, someone may be sought out and pressed into it. Thus while a person is gradually being transformed into a patient, a next-of-relation is gradually being transformed into a guardian. With a guardian on the scene, the whole transition process can be kept tidy. He is likely to be familiar with the prepatient's civil involvements and business, and can tie up loose ends that might otherwise be left to entangle the hospital. Some of the prepatient's abrogated civil rights can be transferred to him, thus helping to sustain the legal fiction that while the prepatient does not actually have his rights he somehow actually has not lost them.

   Inpatients commonly sense, at least for a time, that hospitalization is a massive unjust deprivation, and sometimes succeed in convincing a few persons on the outside that this is the case. It often turns out to be useful, then, for those identified with inflicting these deprivations, however justifiably, to be able to point to the cooperation and agreement of someone whose relationship to the patient places him above suspicion, firmly defining him as the person most likely to have the patient's personal interest at heart. If the guardian is satisfied with what is happening to the new inpatient, the world ought to be.[23]

Now it would seem that the greater the legitimate personal stake one part has in another, the better he can take the role of guardian to the other. But the structural arrangements in society which lead to the acknowledged merging of two persons' interests lead to additional consequences. For the person to whom the patient turns for help —for protection against such threats as involuntary commitment—is just the person to whom the mediators and hospital administrators logically turn for authorization. It is understandable, then, that some patients will come to sense, at least for a time, that the closeness of a relationship tells nothing of its trustworthiness.

There are still other functional effects emerging from this complement of roles. If and when the next-of-relation appeals to mediators for help in the trouble he is having with the prepatient, hospitalization may not, in fact, be in his mind. He may not even perceive the prepatient as mentally sick, or, if he does, he may not consistently hold to this view.[24] It is the circuit of mediators, with their greater psychiatric sophistication and their belief in the medical character of mental hospitals, that will often define the situation for the next-of-relation, assuring him that hospitalization is a possible solution and a good one, that it involves no betrayal, but is rather a medical action taken in the best interests of the prepatient. Here the next-of-relation may learn that doing his duty to the prepatient may cause the prepatient to distrust and even hate him for the time. But the fact that this course of action may have had to be pointed out and prescribed by professionals, and be defined by them as a moral duty, relieves the next-of-relation of some of the guilt he may feel.[25] It is a poignant fact that an adult son or daughter may be pressed into the role of mediator, so that the hostility that might otherwise be directed against the spouse is passed on to the child.[26]

Once the prepatient is in the hospital, the same guilt-carrying function may become a significant part of the staff's job in regard to the next-of-relation.[27] These reasons for feeling that he himself has not betrayed the patient, even though the patient may then think so, can later provide the next-of-relation with a defensible line to take when visiting the patient in the hospital and a basis for hoping that the relationship can be reestablished after its hospital moratorium. And of course this position, when sensed by the patient, can provide him with excuses for the next-of-relation, when and if he comes to look for them.[28]

Thus while the next-of-relation can perform important functions for the mediators and hospital administrators, they in turn can perform important functions for him. One finds, then, an emergent unintended exchange or reciprocation of functions, these functions themselves being often unintended.

The final point I want to consider about the prepatient's moral career is its peculiarly *retroactive* character. Until a person actually arrives at the hospital there usually seems no way of knowing for sure that he is destined to do so, given the determinative role of career contingencies. And until the point of hospitalization is reached, he or others may not conceive of him as a person who is becoming a mental patient. However, since he will be held against his will in the hospital, his next-of-relation and the hospital staff will be in great need of a rationale for the hardships they are sponsoring. The medical elements of the staff will also need evidence that they are still in the trade they were trained for. These problems are eased, no doubt unintentionally, by the case-history construction that is placed on the patient's past life, this having the effect of demonstrating that all along he had been becoming sick, that he finally became very sick, and that if he had not been hospitalized much worse things would have happened to him—all of which, of course, may be true. Incidentally, if the patient wants to make sense out of his stay in the hospital, and, as already suggested, keep alive the possibility of once again conceiving of his next-of-relation as a decent, well-meaning person, then he too will have reason to believe some of this psychiatric work-up of his past.

Here is a very ticklish point for the sociology of careers. An important aspect of every career is the view the person constructs when he looks backward over his progress; in a sense, however, the whole of the prepatient career derives from this reconstruction. The fact of having had a prepatient career, starting with an effective complaint, becomes an important part of the mental patient's orientation, but this part can begin to be played only after hospitalization proves that what he had been having, but no longer has, is a career as a prepatient.

THE INPATIENT PHASE

The last step in the prepatient's career can involve his realization— justified or not—that he has been deserted by society and turned out of relationships by those closest to him. Interestingly enough, the patient, especially a first admission, may manage to keep himself from coming to the end of this trail, even though in fact he is now in a locked mental hospital ward. On entering the hospital, he may very strongly feel the desire not to be known to anyone as a person who could possibly be reduced to these present circumstances, or as a person who conducted himself in the way he did prior to commitment. Consequently, he may avoid talking to anyone, may stay by himself when possible, and may even be "out of contact" or "manic" so as to avoid ratifying any interaction that presses a politely reciprocal role upon him and opens him up to what he has become in the eyes of others. When the next-of-relation makes an effort to visit, he may be rejected by mutism, or by the patient's refusal to enter the visiting room, these strategies sometimes suggesting that the patient still clings to a remnant of relatedness to those who made up his past, and is protecting this remnant from the final destructiveness of dealing with the new people that they have become.[29]

Usually the patient comes to give up this taxing effort at anonymity, at not-hereness, and begins to present himself for conventional social interaction to the hospital community. Thereafter he withdraws only in special ways—by always using his nickname, by signing his contribution to the patient weekly with his initial only, or by using the innocuous "cover" address tactfully provided by some hospitals; or he withdraws only at special times, when, say, a flock of nursing students makes a passing tour of the ward, or when, paroled to the hospital grounds, he suddenly sees he is about to cross the path of a civilian he happens to know from home. Sometimes this making of oneself available is called "settling down" by the attendants. It marks a new stand openly taken and supported by the patient, and resembles the "coming out" process that occurs in other groupings.[30]

Once the prepatient begins to settle down, the main outlines of his fate tend to follow those of a whole class of segregated establishments—jails, concentration camps, monasteries, work camps, and so on—in which the inmate spends the whole round of life on the grounds, and marches through his regimented day in the immediate company of a group of persons of his own institutional status.[31]

Like the neophyte in many of these "total institutions," the new inpatient finds himself cleanly stripped of many of his accustomed affirmations, satisfactions, and defenses, and is subjected to a rather full set of mortifying experiences: restriction of free movement; communal living; diffuse authority of a whole echelon of people; and so on. Here one begins to learn about the limited extent to which a conception of oneself can be sustained when the usual setting of supports for it are suddenly removed.

While undergoing these humbling moral experiences, the inpatient learns to orient himself in terms of the "ward system."[32] In public mental hospitals this usually consists of a series of graded living arrangements built around wards, administrative units called services, and parole statuses. The "worst" level involves often nothing but wooden benches to sit on, some quite indifferent food, and a small piece of room to sleep in. The "best" level may involve a room of one's own, ground and town privileges, contacts with staff that are relatively undamaging, and what is seen as good food and ample recreational facilities. For disobeying the pervasive house rules, the inmate will receive stringent punishments expressed in terms of loss of privileges; for obedience he will eventually be allowed to reacquire some of the minor satisfactions he took for granted on the outside.

The institutionalization of these radically different levels of living throws light on the implications for self of social settings. And this in turn affirms that the self arises not merely out of its possessor's interactions with significant others, but also out of the arrangements that are evolved in an organization for its members.

There are some settings which the person easily discounts as an expression or extension of him. When a tourist goes slumming, he may take pleasure in the situation not because it is a reflection of him but because it so assuredly is not. There are other settings, such as living rooms, which the person manages on his own and employs to influence in a favorable direction other persons' views of him. And there are still other settings, such as a work place, which express the employee's occupational status, but over which he has no final control, this being exerted, however tactfully, by his employer. Mental hospitals provide an extreme instance of this latter possibility. And this is due not merely to their uniquely degraded living levels, but also to the unique way in which significance for self is made explicit to the patient, piercingly, persistently, and thoroughly. Once lodged on a given ward, the patient is firmly instructed that the restrictions and deprivations he encounters are not due to such things as tradition or economy—and hence dissociable from self—but are intentional parts of his treatment, part of his need at the time, and therefore an expression of the state that his self has fallen to. Having every reason to initiate requests for better conditions, he is told that when the staff feels he is "able to manage" or will be "comfortable with" a higher ward level, then appropriate action will be taken. In short, assignment to a given ward is presented not as a reward or punishment, but as an expression of his general level of social functioning, his status as a person. Given the fact that the worst ward levels provide a round of life that inpatients with organic brain damage can easily manage, and that these quite limited human beings are present to prove it, one can appreciate some of the mirroring effects of the hospital.[33]

The ward system, then, is an extreme instance of how the physical facts of an establishment can be explicitly employed to frame the conception a person takes of himself. In addition, the official psychiatric mandate of mental hospitals gives rise to even more direct, even more blatant, attacks upon the inmate's view of himself. The more "medical" and the more progressive a mental hospital is—the more it attempts to be therapeutic and not merely custodial—the more he may be confronted by high-ranking staff arguing that his past has been a failure, that the cause of this has been within himself, that his attitude to life is wrong, and that if he wants to be a person he will have to change his way of dealing with people and his conceptions of himself. Often the moral value of these verbal assaults will be brought home to him by requiring him to practice taking this psychiatric view of himself in arranged confessional periods, whether in private sessions or group psychotherapy.

Now a general point may be made about the moral career of inpatients which has bearing on many moral careers. Given the stage that any person has reached in a career, one typically finds that he constructs an image of his life course—past, present, and future— which selects, abstracts, and distorts in such a way as to provide him with a view of himself that he can usefully expound in current situations. Quite generally, the person's line concerning self defensively brings him into appropriate alignment with the basic values of his society, and so may be called an *apologia*. If the person can manage to present a view of his current situation which shows the operation of favorable personal qualities in the past and a favorable destiny awaiting him, it may be called a *success story*. If the facts of a person's past and present are extremely dismal, then about the best he can do is to show that he is not responsible for what has become of him, and the term *sad tale* is appropriate. Interestingly enough, the more the person's past forces him out of apparent alignment with central moral values, the more often he seems compelled to tell his sad tale in any company in which he finds himself. Perhaps he partly responds to the need he feels in others of not having their sense of proper life courses affronted. In any case, it is among convicts, 'wino's,' and prostitutes that one seems to obtain sad tales the most readily.[34] It is the vicissitudes of the mental patient's sad tale that I want to consider now.

In the mental hospital, the setting and the house rules press home to the patient that he is, after all, a mental case who has suffered some kind of social collapse on the outside, having failed in some overall way, and that here he is of little social weight, being hardly capable of acting like a full-fledged person at all. These humiliations are likely to be most keenly felt by middle-class patients since their previous condition of life little immunizes them against such affronts; but all patients feel some downgrading. Just as any normal member of his outside subculture would do, the patient often responds to this situation by attempting to assert a sad tale proving that he is not "sick," that the "little trouble" he did get into was really somebody else's fault, that his past life course had some honor and rectitude, and that the hospital is therefore unjust in forcing the status of mental patient upon him. This self-respecting tendency is heavily institutionalized within the patient society where opening social contacts typically involve the participants' volunteering information about their current ward location and length of stay so far, but not the reasons for their stay—such interaction being conducted in the manner of small talk on the outside.[35] With greater familiarity, each patient usually volunteers relatively acceptable reasons for his hospitalization, at the same time accepting without open immediate question the lines offered by other patients. Such stories as the following are given and overtly accepted.

> I was going to night school to get a M.A. degree, and holding down a job in addition, and the load got too much for me.

> The others here are sick mentally but I'm suffering from a bad nervous system and that is what is giving me these phobias.

> I got here by mistake because of a diabetes diagnosis, and I'll leave in a couple of days. [The patient had been in seven weeks.]

> I failed as a child, and later with my wife I reached out for dependency.

> My trouble is that I can't work. That's what I'm in for. I had two jobs with a good home and all the money I wanted.[36]

The patient sometimes reinforces these stories by an optimistic definition of his occupational status: A man who managed to obtain an audition as a radio announcer styles himself a radio announcer; another who worked for some months as a copy boy and was then given a job as a reporter on a large trade journal, but was fired after three weeks, defines himself as a reporter.

A whole social role in the patient community may be constructed on the basis of these reciprocally sustained fictions. For these face-to-face niceties tend to be qualified by behind-the-back gossip that comes only a degree closer to the 'objective' facts. Here, of course, one can see a classic social function of informal networks of equals: they serve as one another's audience for self-supporting tales—tales that are somewhat more solid than pure fantasy and somewhat thinner than the facts.

But the patient's *apologia* is called forth in a unique setting, for few settings could be so destructive of self-stories except, of course, those stories already constructed along psychiatric lines. And this destructiveness rests on more than the official sheet of paper which attests that the patient is of unsound mind, a danger to himself and others—an attestation, incidentally, which seems to cut deeply into the patient's pride, and into the possibility of his having any.

Certainly the degrading conditions of the hospital setting belie many of the self-stories that are presented by patients; and the very fact of being in the mental hospital is evidence against these tales.

And of course, there is not always sufficient patient solidarity to prevent patient discrediting patient, just as there is not always a sufficient number of 'professionalized' attendants to prevent attendant discrediting patient. As one patient informant repeatedly suggested to a fellow patient:

If you're so smart, how come you got your ass in here?

The mental hospital setting, however, is more treacherous still. Staff has much to gain through discreditings of the patient's story—whatever the felt reason for such discreditings. If the custodial faction in the hospital is to succeed in managing his daily round without complaint or trouble from him, then it will prove useful to be able to point out to him that the claims about himself upon which he rationalizes his demands are false, that he is not what he is claiming to be, and that in fact he is a failure as a person. If the psychiatric faction is to impress upon him its views about his personal make-up, then they must be able to show in detail how their version of his past and their version of his character hold up much better than his own.[37] If both the custodial and psychiatric factions are to get him to cooperate in the various psychiatric treatments, then it will prove useful to disabuse him of *his* view of their purposes, and cause him to appreciate that they know what they are doing and are doing what is best for him. In brief, the difficulties caused by a patient are closely tied to his version of what has been happening to him, and if cooperation is to be secured, it helps if this version is discredited. The patient must "insightfully" come to take, or affect to take, the hospital's view of himself.

The staff also has ideal means—in addition to the mirroring effect of the setting—for denying the inmate's rationalizations. Current psychiatric doctrine defines mental disorder as something that can have its roots in the patient's earliest years, show its signs throughout the course of his life, and invade almost every sector of his current activity. No segment of his past or present need be defined, then, as beyond the jurisdiction and mandate of psychiatric assessment. Mental hospitals bureaucratically institutionalize this extremely wide mandate by formally basing their treatment on the patient upon his diagnosis and hence upon the psychiatric view of his past.

The case record is an important expression of this mandate. This dossier is apparently not regularly used, however, to record occasions when the patient showed capacity to cope honorably and effectively with difficult life situations. Nor is the case record typically used to provide a rough average or sampling of his past conduct. One of its purposes is to show the ways in which the patient is "sick" and the reasons why it was right to commit him and is right currently to keep him committed; and this is done by extracting from his whole life course a list of those incidents that have or might have had "symptomatic" significance.[38] The misadventures of his parents or siblings that might suggest a "taint" may be cited. Early acts in which the patient appeared to have shown bad judgment or emotional disturbance will be recorded. Occasions when he acted in a way which the layman would consider immoral, sexually perverted, weak-willed, childish, ill-considered, impulsive, and crazy may be described. Misbehaviors which someone saw as the last straw, as cause for immediate action, are likely to be reported in detail. In addition, the record will describe his state on arrival at the hospital—and this is not likely to be a time of tranquility and ease for him. The record may also report the false line taken by the patient in answering embarrassing questions, showing him as someone who makes claims that are obviously contrary to the facts:

> Claims she lives with oldest daughter or with sisters only when sick and in need of care; otherwise with husband, he himself says not for 12 years.

> Contrary to the reports from the personnel, he says he no longer bangs on the floor or cries in the morning.

> . . . conceals fact that she had her organs removed, claims she is still menstruating.

> At first she denied having had premarital sexual experience, but when asked about Jim she said she had forgotten about it 'cause it had been unpleasant.[39]

Where contrary facts are not known by the recorder, their presence is often left scrupulously an open question:

> The patient denied any heterosexual experiences nor could one trick her into admitting that she had ever been pregnant or into any kind of sexual indulgence, denying masturbation as well.

> Even with considerable pressure she was unwilling to engage in any projection of paranoid mechanisms.

> No psychotic content could be elicited at this time.[40]

And if in no more factual way, discrediting statements often appear in descriptions given of the patient's general social manner in the hospital:

> When interviewed, he was bland, apparently self-assured, and sprinkles high-sounding generalizations freely throughout his verbal productions.

Armed with a rather neat appearance and natty little Hit-
lerian mustache this 45-year-old man who has spent the last
five or more years of his life in the hospital, is making a very
successful hospital adjustment living within the role of a
rather gay liver and jim-dandy type of fellow who is not
only quite superior to his fellow patients in intellectual
respects but who is also quite a man with women. His speech
is sprayed with many multi-syllabled words which he generally uses in good context, but if he talks long enough on any
subject it soon becomes apparent that he is so completely
lost in this verbal diarrhea as to make what he says almost
completely worthless.[41]

The events recorded in the case history are, then, just the sort
that a layman would consider scandalous, defamatory, and discrediting. I think it is fair to say that all levels of mental hospital staff
fail, in general, to deal with this material with the moral neutrality
claimed for medical statements and psychiatric diagnosis, but instead
participate, by intonation and gesture if by no other means, in the lay
reaction to these acts. This will occur in staff-patient encounters as
well as in staff encounters at which no patient is present.

In some mental hospitals, access to the case record is technically
restricted to medical and higher nursing levels, but even here informal
access or relayed information is often available to lower staff levels.[42]
In addition, ward personnel are felt to have a right to know those
aspects of the patient's past conduct which, embedded in the reputation he develops, purportedly make it possible to manage him with
greater benefit to himself and less risk to others. Further, all staff
levels typically have access to the nursing notes kept on the ward,
which chart the daily course of each patient's disease, and hence his
conduct, providing for the near-present the sort of information the
case record supplies for his past.

I think that most of the information gathered in case records is
quite true, although it might seem also to be true that almost anyone's
life course could yield up enough denigrating facts to provide grounds
for the record's justification of commitment. In any case, I am not
concerned here with questioning the desirability of maintaining case
records, or the motives of staff in keeping them. The point is that these
facts about him being true, the patient is certainly not relieved from
the normal cultural pressure to conceal them, and is perhaps all the
more threatened by knowing that they are neatly available, and that
he has no control over who gets to learn them.[43] A manly looking
youth who responds to military induction by running away from the
barracks and hiding himself in a hotel room clothes closet, to be found
there, crying, by his mother; a woman who travels from Utah to
Washington to warn the President of impending doom; a man who dis-
robes before three young girls; a boy who locks his sister out of the

house, striking out two of her teeth when she tries to come back in through the window—each of these persons has done something he will have very obvious reason to conceal from others, and very good reason to tell lies about.

The formal and informal patterns of communication linking staff members tend to amplify the disclosive work done by the case record. A discreditable act that the patient performs during one part of the day's routine in one part of the hospital community is likely to be reported back to those who supervise other areas of his life, where he implicitly takes the stand that he is not the sort of person who could act that way.

Of significance here, as in some other social establishments, is the increasingly common practice of all-level staff conferences, where staff air their views of patients and develop collective agreement concerning the line that the patient is trying to take and the line that should be taken to him. A patient who develops a "personal" relation with an attendant, or manages to make an attendant anxious by eloquent and persistent accusations of malpractice can be put back into his place by means of the staff meeting, where the attendant is given warning or assurance that the patient is "sick." Since the differential image of himself that a person usually meets from those of various levels around him comes here to be unified behind the scenes into a common approach, the patient may find himself faced with a kind of collusion against him—albeit one sincerely thought to be for his own ultimate welfare.

In addition, the formal transfer of the patient from one ward or service to another is likely to be accompanied by an informal description of his characteristics, this being felt to facilitate the work of the employee who is newly responsible for him.

Finally, at the most informal of levels, the lunchtime and coffee break small talk of staff often turns upon the latest doings of the patient, the gossip level of any social establishment being here intensified by the assumption that everything about him is in some way the proper business of the hospital employee. Theoretically there seems to be no reason why such gossip should not build up the subject instead of tear him down, unless one claims that talk about those not present will always tend to be critical in order to maintain the integrity and prestige of the circle in which the talking occurs. And so, even when the impulse of the speakers seems kindly and generous, the implication of their talk is typically that the patient is not a complete person. For example, a conscientious group therapist, sympathetic with patients, once admitted to his coffee companions:

> I've had about three group disrupters, one man in particular—a lawyer [sotto voce] James Wilson—very bright—who just made things miserable for me, but I would always tell

him to get on the stage and do something. Well, I was getting desperate and then I bumped into his therapist, who
said that right now behind the man's bluff and front he
needed the group very much and that it probably meant
more to him than anything else he was getting out of the
hospital—he just needed the support. Well, that made me
feel altogether different about him. He's out now.

In general, then, mental hospitals systematically provide for circulation about each patient the kind of information that the patient is
likely to try to hide. And in various degrees of detail this information
is used daily to puncture his claims. At the admission and diagnostic
conferences, he will be asked questions to which he must give wrong
answers in order to maintain his self-respect, and then the true answer
may be shot back at him. An attendant whom he tells a version of his
past and his reason for being in the hospital may smile disbelievingly,
or say, "That's not the way I heard it," in line with the practical psychiatry of bringing the patient down to reality. When he accosts a
physician or nurse on the ward and presents his claims for more privileges or for discharge, this may be countered by a question which he
cannot answer truthfully without calling up a time in his past when
he acted disgracefully. When he gives his view of his situation during
group psychotherapy, the therapist, taking the role of interrogator,
may attempt to disabuse him of his face-saving interpretations and
encourage an interpretation suggesting that it is he himself who is to
blame and who must change. When he claims to staff or fellow pa-
patients that he is well and has never been really sick, someone may
give him graphic details of how, only one month ago, he was prancing
around like a girl, or claiming that he was God, or declining to talk or
eat, or putting gum in his hair.

Each time the staff deflates the patient's claims, his sense of what
a person ought to be and the rules of peer-group social intercourse
press him to reconstruct his stories; and each time he does this, the
custodial and psychiatric interests of the staff may lead them to discredit these tales again.

Behind these verbally instigated ups and downs of the self, is an
institutional base that rocks just as precariously. Contrary to popular
opinion, the "ward system" insures a great amount of internal social
mobility in mental hospitals, especially during the inmate's first year.
During that time he is likely to have altered his service once, his ward
three or four times, and his parole status several times; and he is likely
to have experienced moves in bad as well as good directions. Each of
these moves involves a very drastic alteration in level of living and in
available materials out of which to build a self-confirming round of
activities, an alteration equivalent in scope, say, to a move up or down
a class in the wider class system. Moreover, fellow inmates with whom

he has partially identified himself will similarly be moving, but in different directions and at different rates, thus reflecting feelings of social change to the person even when he does not experience them directly. As previously implied, the doctrines of psychiatry can reinforce the social fluctuations of the ward system. Thus there is a current psychiatric view that the ward system is a kind of social hothouse in which patients start as social infants and end up, within the year, on convalescent wards as resocialized adults. This view adds considerably to the weight and pride that staff can attach to their work, and necessitates a certain amount of blindness, especially at higher staff levels, to other ways of viewing the ward system, such as a method for disciplining unruly persons through punishment and reward. In any case, this resocialization perspective tends to overstress the extent to which those on the worst wards are incapable of socialized conduct and the extent to which those on the best wards are ready and willing to play the social game. Because the ward system is something more than a resocialization chamber, inmates find many reasons for "messing up" or getting into trouble, and many occasions, then, for demotion to less privileged ward positions. These demotions may be officially interpreted as psychiatric relapses or moral backsliding, thus protecting the resocialization view of the hospital, and these interpretations, by implication, translate a mere infraction of rules and consequent demotion into a fundamental expression of the status of the culprit's self. Correspondingly, promotions, which may come about because of ward population pressure, the need for a "working patient," or for other psychiatrically irrelevant reasons, may be built up into something claimed to be profoundly expressive of the patient's whole self. The patient himself may be expected by staff to make a personal effort to "get well," in something less than a year, and hence may be constantly reminded to think in terms of the self's success and failure.[44]

In such contexts inmates can discover that deflations in moral status are not so bad as they had imagined. After all, infractions which lead to these demotions cannot be accompanied by legal sanctions or by reduction to the status of mental patient, since these conditions already prevail. Further, no past or current delict seems to be horrendous enough in itself to excommunicate a patient from the patient community, and hence failures at right living lose some of their stigmatizing meaning.[45] And finally, in accepting the hospital's version of his fall from grace, the patient can set himself up in the business of "straightening up," and make claims of sympathy, privileges, and indulgence from the staff in order to foster this.

Learning to live under conditions of imminent exposure and wide fluctuation in regard, with little control over the granting or withholding of this regard, is an important step in the socialization of the patient, a step that tells something important about what it is like to be an inmate in a mental hospital. Having one's past mistakes and present progress under constant moral review seems to make for a special adaptation consisting of a less than moral attitude to ego-ideals. One's shortcomings and successes become too central and fluctuating an issue in life to allow the usual commitment of concern for other persons' views of them. It is not very practicable to try to sustain solid claims about oneself. The inmate tends to learn that degradations and reconstructions of the self need not be given too much weight, at the same time learning that staff and inmates are ready to view an inflation or deflation of a self with some indifference. He learns that a defensible picture of self can be seen as something outside oneself that can be constructed, lost, and rebuilt, all with great speed and some equanimity. He learns about the viability of taking up a standpoint— and hence a self—that is outside the one which the hospital can give and take away from him.

The setting, then, seems to engender a kind of cosmopolitan sophistication, a kind of civic apathy. In this unserious yet oddly exaggerated moral context, building up a self or having it destroyed becomes something of a shameless game, and learning to view this process as a game seems to make for some demoralization, the game being such a fundamental one. In the hospital, then, the inmate can learn that the self is not a fortress, but rather a small open city; he can become weary of having to show pleasure when held by troops of his own, and weary of having to show displeasure when held by the enemy. Once he learns what it is like to be defined by society as not having a viable self, this threatening definition—the threat that helps attach people to the self society accords them—is weakened. The patient seems to gain a new plateau when he learns that he can survive while acting in a way that society sees as destructive of him.

A few illustrations of this moral looseness and moral fatigue might be given. In state mental hospitals currently a kind of "marriage moratorium" appears to be accepted by patients and more or less condoned by staff. Some informal peer-group pressure may be brought against a patient who "plays around" with more than one hospital partner at a time, but little negative sanction seems to be attached to taking up, in a temporarily steady way, with a member of the opposite sex, even though both partners are known to be married, to have children, and even to be regularly visited by these outsiders. In short, there is license in mental hospitals to begin courting all over again, with the understanding, however, that nothing very permanent or serious can come of this. Like shipboard or vacation romances, these entanglements attest to the way in which the hospital is cut off from the outside community, becoming a world of its own, operated for the benefit of its own citizens. And certainly this moratorium is an expression of the alienation and hostility that patients feel for those on the outside to whom they were closely related. But in addition, one has evidence of the loosening effects of living in a world within a world, under conditions which make it difficult to give full seriousness to either of them.

The second illustration concerns the ward system. On the worst ward level, discreditings seem to occur the most frequently, in part because of lack of facilities, in part through the mockery and sarcasm that seem to be the occupational norm of social control for the attendants and nurses who administer these places. At the same time, the paucity of equipment and rights means that not much self can be built up. The patient finds himself constantly toppled, therefore, but with very little distance to fall. A kind of jaunty gallows humor seems to develop in some of these wards, with considerable freedom to stand up to the staff and return insult for insult. While these patients can be punished, they cannot, for example, be easily slighted, for they are accorded as a matter of course few of the niceties that people must enjoy before they can suffer subtle abuse. Like prostitutes in connection with sex, inmates on these wards have very little reputation or rights to lose and can therefore take certain liberties. As the person moves up the ward system, he can manage more and more to avoid incidents which discredit his claim to be a human being, and acquire more and more of the varied ingredients of self-respect; yet when eventually he does get toppled—and he does—there is a much further distance to fall. For instance, the privileged patient lives in a world wider than the ward, made up of recreation workers who, on request, can dole out cake, cards, table-tennis balls, tickets to the movies, and writing materials. But in absence of the social control of payment which is typically exerted by a recipient on the outside, the patient runs the risk that even a warmhearted functionary may, on occasion, tell him to wait until she has finished an informal chat, or teasingly ask why he wants what he has asked for, or respond with a dead pause and a cold look of appraisal.

Moving up and down the ward system means, then, not only a shift in self-constructive equipment, a shift in reflected status, but also a change in the calculus of risks. Appreciation of risks to his self-conception is part of everyone's moral experience, but an appreciation that a given risk level is itself merely a social arrangement is a rarer kind of experience, and one that seems to help to disenchant the person who has it.

A third instance of moral loosening has to do with the conditions that are often associated with the release of the inpatient. Often he leaves under the supervision and jurisdiction of his next-of-relation or of a specially selected and specially watchful employer. If he misbehaves while under their auspices, they can quickly obtain his readmission. He therefore finds himself under the special power of persons who ordinarily would not have this kind of power over him, and about whom, moreover, he may have had prior cause to feel quite bitter. In order to get out of the hospital, however, he may conceal his displeasure in this arrangement, and, at least until safely off the hospital rolls, act out a willingness to accept this kind of custody. These discharge procedures, then, provide a built-in lesson in overtly taking a role without the usual covert commitments, and seem further to separate the person from the worlds that others take seriously.

The moral career of a person of a given social category involves a standard sequence of changes in his way of conceiving of selves, including, importantly, his own. These half-buried lines of development can be followed by studying his moral experiences—that is, happenings which mark a turning point in the way in which the person views the world—although the particularities of this view may be difficult to establish. And note can be taken of overt tacks or strategies—that is, stands that he effectively takes before specifiable others, whatever the hidden and variable nature of his inward attachment to these presentations. By taking note of moral experiences and overt personal stands, one can obtain a relatively objective tracing of relatively subjective matters.

Each moral career, and behind this, each self, occurs within the confines of an institutional system, whether a social establishment such as a mental hospital or a complex of personal and professional relationships. The self, then, can be seen as something that resides in the arrangements prevailing in a social system for its members. The self in this sense is not a property of the person to whom it is attributed, but dwells rather in the pattern of social control that is exerted in connection with the person by himself and those around him. This special kind of institutional arrangement does not so much support the self as constitute it.

In this paper, two of these institutional arrangements have been considered by pointing to what happens to the person when these rulings are weakened. The first concerns the felt loyalty of his next-of-relation. The prepatient's self is described as a function of the way in which three roles are related, arising and declining in the kinds of affiliation that occur between the next-of-relation and the mediators. The second concerns the protection required by the person for the version of himself which he presents to others, and the way in which the withdrawal of this protection can form a systematic, if unintended, aspect of the working of an establishment. I want to stress that these are only two kinds of institutional rulings from which a self emerges for the participant; others, not considered in this paper, are equally important.

In the usual cycle of adult socialization one expects to find alienation and mortification followed by a new set of beliefs about the world and a new way of conceiving of selves. In the case of the mental hospital patient, this rebirth does sometimes occur, taking the form of a strong belief in the psychiatric perspective, or, briefly at least, a devotion to the social cause of better treatment for mental patients.

The moral career of the mental patient has unique interest, however; it can illustrate the possibility that in casting off the raiments of the old self—or in having this cover torn away—the person need not seek a new robe and a new audience before which to cower. Instead he can learn, at least for a time, to practice before all groups the amoral arts of shamelessness.

NOTES

[1]The study was conducted during 1955–56 under the auspices of the Laboratory of Socio-environmental Studies of the National Institute of Mental Health. The author is grateful to the Laboratory Chief, John A. Clausen, and to Dr. Winfred Overholser, Superintendent, and the late Dr. Jay Hoffman, then First Assistant Physician of Saint Elizabeths Hospital, Washington, D.C., for the ideal cooperation they freely provided. A preliminary report is contained in Goffman, "Interpersonal Persuasion," pp. 117–193; in *Group Processes: Transactions of the Third Conference*, edited by Bertram Schaffner; New York, Josiah Macy, Jr. Foundation, 1957. A shorter version of this paper was presented at the Annual Meeting of the American Sociological Society, Washington, D.C., August, 1957.

[2]Material on moral career can be found in early social anthropological work on ceremonies of status transition, and in classic social psychological descriptions of those spectacular changes in one's view of self that can accompany participation in social movements and sects. Recently new kinds of relevant data have been suggested by psychiatric interest in the problem of "identity" and sociological studies of work careers and "adult socialization."

[3]This point has recently been made by Elaine and John Cumming, *Closed Ranks;* Cambridge, Commonwealth Fund, Harvard Univ. Press, 1957; pp. 101–102. "Clinical experience supports the impression that many people define mental illness as 'That condition for which a person is treated in a mental hosptial.' . . . Mental illness, it seems, is a condition which afflicts people who must go to a mental institution, but until they do almost anything they do is normal." Leila Deasy has pointed out to me the correspondence here with the situation in white collar crime. Of those who are detected in this activity, only the ones who do not manage to avoid going to prison find themselves accorded the social role of the criminal.

[4]Case records in mental hospitals are just now coming to be exploited to show the incredible amount of trouble a person may cause for himself and others before anyone begins to think about him psychiatrically, let alone take psychiatric action against him. See John A. Clausen and Marian Radke Yarrow, "Paths to the Mental Hospital," *J. Social Issues* (1955) 11:25–32; August B. Hollingshead and Fredrick C. Redlich, *Social Class and Mental Illness;* New York, Wiley, 1958; pp. 173–174.

[5]An illustration of how this perspective may be taken to all forms of deviancy may be found in Edwin Lemert, *Social Pathology;* New York,

McGraw-Hill, 1951; see especially pp. 74–76. A specific application to mental defectives may be found in Stewart E. Perry, "Some Theoretic Problems of Mental Deficiency and Their Action Implications," Psychiatry (1954) 17:45–73; see especially p. 68.

[6]Conscientious objectors who voluntarily went to jail sometimes arrived at the same conclusion regarding criminal inmates. See, for example, Alfred Hassler, Diary of a Self-made Convict; Chicago, Regnery, 1954; p. 74.

[7]This simple picture is complicated by the somewhat special experience of roughly a third of ex-patients—namely, readmission to the hospital, this being the recidivist or "repatient" phase.

[8]Harry Stack Sullivan, Clinical Studies in Psychiatry, Helen Swick Perry, Mary Ladd Gawel, and Martha Gibbon, eds., New York, Norton, 1956; pp. 184–185.

[9]This moral experience can be contrasted with that of a person learning to become a marihuana addict, whose discovery that he can be 'high' and still 'op' effectively without being detected apparently leads to a new level of use. See Howard S. Becker, "Marihuana Use and Social Control," Social Problems (1955) 3:35–44; see especially pp. 40–41.

[10]See footnote 2; Hollingshead and Redlich, Social Class and Mental Illness, p. 187. Table 6, where relative frequency is given of self-referral by social class grouping.

[11]The distinction employed here between willing and unwilling patients cuts across the legal one, of voluntary and committed, since some persons who are glad to come to the mental hospital may be legally committed, and of those who come only because of strong familial pressure, some may sign themselves in as voluntary patients.

[12]Clausen and Yarrow; see footnote 4.

[13]An explicit application of this notion to the field of mental health may be found in Edwin M. Lemert, "Legal Commitment and Social Control," Sociology and Social Research (1946) 30:370–378.

[14]For example, Jerome K. Meyers and Leslie Schaffer, "Social Stratification and Psychiatric Practice: A Study of an Outpatient Clinic," Amer. Sociological Rev. (1954) 19:307–310. Lemert, see footnote 5: pp. 402–403. Patients in Mental Institutions, 1941; Washington, D.C., Department of Commerce, Bureau of the Census, 1941; p. 2.

[15]For one circuit of agents and its bearing on career contingencies, see Oswald Hall, "The Stages of a Medical Career," Amer. J. Sociology (1948) 53:227–336.

[16]See Cumming, Closed Ranks, p. 92.

[17]Hollingshead and Redlich, Social Class and Mental Illness, p. 187.

[18]For an analysis of some of these circuit implications for the inpatient, see Leila C. Deasy and Olive W. Quinn, "The Wife of the Mental Patient and the Hospital Psychiatrist," J. Social Issues (1955) 11:49–60. An interesting illustration of this kind of analysis may also be found in Alan G. Gowman, "Blindness and the Role of Companion," Social Problems (1956) 4:68–75. A general statement may be found in Robert Merton, "The Role Set: Problems in Sociological Theory," British J. Sociology (1957) 8:106–120.

[19]I have one case record of a man who claims he thought he was taking his wife to see the psychiatrist, not realizing until too late that his wife had made the arrangements.

[20]A paraphrase from Kurt Riezler, "Comment on 'The Social Psychology of Shame,'" Amer. J. Sociology (1943) 48:458.

[21]See Harold Garfinkel, "Conditions of Successful Degradation Ceremonies," *Amer. J. Sociology* (1956) 61:420–424.

[22]Concentration camp practices provide a good example of the function of the betrayal funnel in inducing cooperation and reducing struggle and fuss, although here the mediators could not be said to be acting in the best interests of the inmates. Police picking up persons from their homes would sometimes joke good-naturedly and offer to wait while coffee was being served. Gas chambers were fitted out like delousing rooms, and victims taking off their clothes were told to note where they were leaving them. The sick, aged, weak, or insane who were selected for extermination were sometimes driven away in Red Cross ambulances to camps referred to by terms such as "observation hospital." See David Boder. *I Did Not Interview the Dead;* Urbana, Univ. of Illinois Press, 1949; p. 81; and Elie A. Cohen, *Human Behavior in the Concentration Camp;* London, Cape, 1954; pp. 32, 37, 107.

[23]Interviews collected by the Clausen group at the National Institute of Mental Health suggest that when a wife comes to be a guardian, the responsibility may disrupt previous distance from in-laws, leading either to a new supportive coalition with them or to a marked withdrawal from them.

[24]For an analysis of these nonpsychiatric kinds of perception, see Marian Radke Yarrow, Charlotte Green Schwartz, Harriet S. Murphy, and Leila Calhoun Deasy, "The Psychological Meaning of Mental Illness in the Family," *J. Social Issues* (1955) 11: 12–24; Charlotte Green Schwartz, "Perspectives on Deviance: Wives' Definitions of their Husbands' Mental Illness," *Psychiatry* (1957) 20:275–291.

[25]This guilt-carrying function is found, of course, in other role-complexes. Thus, when a middle-class couple engages in the process of legal separation or divorce, each of their lawyers usually takes the position that his job is to acquaint his client with all of the potential claims and rights, pressing his client into demanding these, in spite of any nicety of feelings about the rights and honorableness of the ex-partner. The client, in all good faith, can then say to self and to the ex-partner that the demands are being made only because the lawyer insists it is best to do so.

[26]Recorded in the Clausen data.

[27]This point is made by Cumming, *Closed Ranks,* p. 129.

[28]There is an interesting contrast here with the moral career of the tuberculosis patient. I am told by Julius Roth that tuberculous patients are likely to come to the hospital willingly, agreeing with their next-of-relation about treatment. Later in their hospital career, when they learn how long they yet have to stay and how depriving and irrational some of the hospital rulings are, they may seek to leave, be advised against this by the staff and by relatives, and only then begin to feel betrayed.

[29]The inmate's initial strategy of holding himself aloof from ratifying contact may partly account for the relative lack of group formation among inmates in public mental hospitals, a connection that has been suggested to me by William R. Smith. The desire to avoid personal bonds that would give license to the asking of biographical questions could also be a factor. In mental hospitals, of course, as in prisoner camps, the staff may consciously break up incipient group formation in order to avoid collective rebellious action and other ward disturbances.

[30]A comparable coming out occurs in the homosexual world, when a person finally comes frankly to present himself to a "gay" gathering not as a tourist but as someone who is "available." See Evelyn Hooker. "A Prelim-

inary Examination of Group Behavior of Homosexuals," *J. Psychology* (1956) 42:217–225; especially p. 221. A good fictionalized treatment may be found in James Baldwin's *Giovanni's Room;* New York, Dial, 1956; pp. 41–63. A familiar instance of the coming out process is no doubt to be found among prepubertal children at the moment one of these actors sidles *back* into a room that had been left in an angered huff and injured *amour-propre.* The phrase itself presumably derives from a *rite-de-passage* ceremony once arranged by upper-class mothers for their daughters. Interestingly enough, in large mental hospitals the patient sometimes symbolizes a complete coming out by his first active participation in the hospital-wide patient dance.

[31]See Goffmann, "Characteristics of Total Institutions," pp. 43–84; in *Proceedings of the Symposium of Preventive and Social Psychiatry:* Washington, D.C., Walter Reed Army Institute of Research, 19

[32]A good description of the ward system may be found in Ivan Belknap, *Human Problems of a State Mental Hospital;* New York, McGraw-Hill, 1956; see especially p. 164.

[33]Here is one way in which mental hospitals can be worse than concentration camps and prisons as places in which to "do" time; in the latter, self-insulation from the symbolic implications of the settings may be easier. In fact, self-insulation from hospital settings may be so difficult that patients have to employ devices for this which staff interpret as psychotic symptoms.

[34]In regard to convicts, see Anthony Heckstall-Smith, *Eighteen Months;* London, Wingate, 1954; pp. 52–53. For 'wino's' see the discussion in Howard G. Bain, "A Sociological Analysis of the Chicago Skid-Row Lifeway;" unpublished M.A. thesis, Deptartment of Sociology, University of Chicago, Sept., 1950; especially "The Rationale of the Skid-Row Drinking Group," pp. 141–146. Bain's neglected thesis is a useful source of material on moral careers.

Apparently one of the occupational hazards of prostitution is that clients and other professional contacts sometimes persist in expressing sympathy by asking for a defensible dramatic explanation for the fall from grace. In having to bother to have a sad tale ready, perhaps the prostitute is more to be pitied than damned. Good examples of prostitute sad tales may be found in Sir Henry Mayhew, "Those that Will Not Work," pp. 210–272; in his *London Labour and the London Poor,* Vol. 4; London, Griffin, Bohn, and Cox, 1862. For a contemporary source, see *Women of the Streets,* edited by C. H. Rolph; London, Zecker and Warburg, 1955; especially p. 6. "Almost always, however, after a few comments on the police, the girl would begin to explain how it was that she was in the life, usually in terms of self-justification." Lately, of course, the psychological expert has helped out the profession in the construction of wholly remarkable sad tales. See, for example, Harold Greenwald, *Call Girl;* New York, Ballantine, 1958.

[35]A similar self-protecting rule has been observed in prisons. Thus, Hassler, see footnote 6, in describing a conversation with a fellow-prisoner: "He didn't say much about why he was sentenced and I didn't ask him, that being the accepted behavior in prison" (p. 76). A novelistic version for the mental hospital may be found in J. Kerkhoff, *How Thin the Veil: A Newspaperman's Story of His Own Mental Crack-up and Recovery;* New York Greenberg, 1952; p. 27.

[36]From the writer's field notes of informal interaction with patients, transcribed as near verbatim as he was able.

[37]The process of examining a person psychiatrically and then altering or reducing his status in consequence is known in hospital and prison parlance as *bugging,* the assumption being that once you come to the attention of the testers you either will automatically be labeled crazy or the process of testing itself will make you crazy. Thus psychiatric staff are sometime seen not as *discovering* whether you are sick, but as *making* you sick; and "Don't bug me, man," can mean, "Don't pester me to the point where I'll get upset." Sheldon Messinger has suggested to me that this meaning of bugging is related to the other colloquial meaning, of wiring a room with a secret microphone to collect information usable for discrediting the speaker.

[38]While many kinds of organizations maintain records of their members, in almost all of these some socially significant attributes can only be included indirectly, being officially irrelevant. But since mental hospitals have a legitimate claim to deal with the "whole" person, they need *officially* recognize no limits to what they consider relevant, a sociologically interesting license. It is an odd historical fact that persons concerned with promoting civil liberties in other areas of life tend to favor giving the psychiatrist complete discretionary power over the patient. Apparently it is felt that the more power possessed by medically qualified administrators and therapists, the better the interests of the patients will be served. Patients, to my knowledge, have not been polled on this matter.

[39]Verbatim transcriptions of hospital case record material.

[40]Verbatim transcriptions of hospital case record material.

[41]Verbatim transcriptions of hospital case record material.

[42]However, some mental hospitals do have a "hot file" of selected records which can be taken out only by special permission. These may be records of patients who work as administration office messengers and might otherwise snatch glances at their own files; of inmates who had elite status in the environing community; and of inmates who may take legal action against the hospital and hence have a special reason to maneuver access to their records. Some hospitals even have a "hot-hot file," kept in the superintendent's office. In addition, the patient's professional title, especially if it is a medical one, is sometimes purposely omitted from his file card. All of these exceptions to the general rule for handling information show, of course, the institution's realization of some of the implications of keeping mental hospital records. For a further example, see Harold Taxel, "Authority Structure in a Mental Hospital Ward," unpublished M.A. thesis, Dept. of Sociology, Univ. of Chicago, 1953; pp. 11–12.

[43]This is the problem of "information control" that many groups suffer from to varying degrees. See Goffman, "Discrepant Roles," Ch. 4, pp. 86–106; in *Presentation of Self in Everyday Life;* Monograph No. 2, Univ. of Edinburgh, Social Science Research Centre, 1956. A suggestion of this problem in relation to case records in prisons is given by James Peck in his story, "The Ship that Never Hit Port," in *Prison Etiquette,* edited by Holley Cantine and Dachine Rainer; Bearsville, N.Y., The Retort Press, 1950.

"The hacks of course hold all the aces in dealing with any prisoner because they can always write him up for inevitable punishment. Every infraction of the rules is noted in the prisoner's jacket, a folder which records all the details of the man's life before and during imprisonment. There are general reports written by the work detail screw, the cell block screw, or some other screw who may have overheard a conversation. Tales pumped from stool pigeons are also included.

"Any letter which interests the authorities goes into the jacket. The mail censor may make a photostatic copy of a prisoner's entire letter, or merely copy a passage. Or he may pass the letter on to the warden. Often an inmate called out by the warden or parole officer is confronted with something he wrote so long ago he had forgotten all about it. It might be about his personal life or his political views—a fragment of thought that the prison authorities felt was dangerous and filed for later use" (p. 66).

[44]For this and other suggestions, I am indebted to Charlotte Green Schwartz.

[45]In the hospital I studied there did not seem to be a kangaroo court, and so, for example, an engaging alcoholic, who managed to get two very well-liked student nurses sent home for drinking with him, did not apparently suffer much for his betrayal of the desires of the peer group.

7

Definitions of Time and Recovery in Paralytic Polio Convalescence

FRED DAVIS

It is an oft-repeated, although seldom analyzed, truism that recovery from a disease is as much a psychological process as it is a physiochemical process. The rate and extent of the recovery are presumed to be influenced significantly by optimism, the will to get well, and self-confidence in the body's recuperative process. More often than not, these traits and motivations are assumed to be inherent in the patient; he brings them, pre-formed, to the sickbed, and they serve to his recuperative advantage. Seldom does the precise role played by the hospital and its personnel in this psychological process of recovery come under scrutiny.

In the course of a long-range, longitudinal study of the psychological and social impact of paralytic poliomyelitis on children and their families, the author and his associates have examined the ways in which the hospital and its personnel structure and define the recuperative motivations and orientations of the stricken child and his parents. More concretely, we have examined the ways in which therapeutic personnel attempt to gear the child and his family to an acceptance of institutional and somewhat special definitions of the patient's paralysis and progress in recovery—definitions which, is might be added, both draw upon broad cultural values and motivational patterns and, in a number of respects, conflict with them.

Reprinted from *American Journal of Sociology,* 61 (1956), pp. 582–587. Copyright © University of Chicago Press. Reprinted by permission. The author was aided by a grant from the National Foundation for Infantile Paralysis. Footnotes have been renumbered.

Let us consider the situation of the child who is stricken with paralytic poliomyelitis. In a very real sense he is thrown into an entirely new world from the one to which he is accustomed. The paralysis affects not only his ability to manipulate his own body but also severely alters his customary motor relations with significant persons and social objects. In a great many cases he cannot walk for several months following the acute attack. He is taken away from family and playmates and set down in strange surroundings where the routine is unfamiliar and where the faces of those who minister to his needs change with great frequency. No longer is he the only child or one among several children. He is one among many. Generally, he has only the vaguest idea of what is being done to him and why it is being done. In short, the child and his parents are confronted by an unknown world which requires definition of its procedures and purposes as well as its relationship to the everyday world with which they are familiar.

This paper will consider the question of how the hospital and its personnel—especially the physiotherapist, who is most actively involved in the polio child's day-by-day treatment—go about effectuating what W. I. Thomas has called the "definition of the situation." Two aspects are singled out for discussion. These are the definition of time and the definition of progress in recovery.

Let us begin with the definition of time. When the stricken child is first admitted to the hospital in the acute stage of poliomyelitis, doctors, nurses, and other attending personnel are inevitably, and understandably, bombarded by the family with such questions as: How long will it be? When can I have my child back? etc. The children themselves, although often in a high fever and suffering from muscle spasms, at first ask incessantly when their parents will come for them and when they will be sent home. A few weeks later, upon admission to the convalescent hospital—the scene of the long-term pull toward recovery—the same questions are raised by parent and child, albeit with somewhat less persistence and a certain sense of resignation learned from what has already transpired.

Invariably, what happens to the children and families we have studied is that an initial perspective of short-time hospital confinement with associated thoughts of rapid recovery is, within a few weeks after the acute onset, replaced by a long-term perspective wherein the extent of ultimate recovery from the paralysis is viewed in a more qualified and ambiguous fashion. As a physiotherapist at one of the Baltimore convalescent hospitals has put it: "When they come in here, the children think in terms of days. Very soon they're thinking in terms of weeks and not long after that in terms of months."

How is this change in time perspective brought about? Of course, to begin with, a large part of this, obviously, is accomplished by the doctor in communicating to the parent specific facts about the nature and course of the disease, knowledge with which even a well-informed parent is only slightly familiar. But it is important to examine the situational and institutional contexts of communication between expert and layman to understand the lengthening of the time perspective.

Very significant is, of course, the discrepancy in power in the doctor-patient relationship. Little need be said on this oft-noted point, except to repeat the observation made by Parsons in his discussion of medical practice, namely, that, when the patient is placed in the hands of the doctor, he and his family relinquish, in effect, all *technical* responsibility for the patient's treatment and somatic recovery.[1] Said a father whose nine-year-old daughter was paralyzed in the lower extremities: "I've never felt so helpless in all my life. There's nothing you can do except put your trust in the doctors and hope for the best."

This in itself constitutes an important point of leverage for the doctor as he begins to redefine the time perspective of parent and child. However, although a good deal of factual knowledge regarding the course of the disease is imparted to the parent, in polio, as in so many pathological conditions, much is unknown, and the practitioner is confronted by significant areas of therapeutic uncertainty. This uncertainty is for the most part on the socially crucial questions of the rate of recovery and the ultimate extent of disability with which the patient will be left. It is thus necessary for the doctor somehow to communicate to the parents that the uncertainty stems from the nature of the disease itself and not from therapeutic incompetence or an unwillingness to speak the truth. His status as an expert generally insures that the child and his parents will believe him. That it is not always so, however, is attested to by the "shopping around" inside and outside the hospital which numerous parents in our study engage in.

"Shopping around" inside the hospital usually means that the parents direct inquiries at physiotherapists and nurses and sometimes at other parents whom they meet on visiting days and who, they feel, may be more knowledgeable than themselves. As can be expected, this rarely provides the answers they are seeking. Other parents, they soon learn, are as much in the dark as they. As subordinates of the doctor, the nurses are most averse, as a rule, to making prognosticatory statements of any kind. Beyond "handling" the parents with the customary retort that the patient "is doing fine" or "as well as can be expected," they invariably refer them to the doctor.

The physiotherapist, however, does generally possess an intimate knowledge of the child's condition; sometimes she knows more than the doctor. Early in the convalescent period she is likely to have reached certain well-founded conclusions concerning the type and degree of residual muscle damage. But, partly because the communication of prognoses is the professional responsibility of the doctor and partly because the probable in polio convalescence is by no means certain, she is careful not to speak her mind in full or go into too great detail. When pressed by the parents for definitive statements concerning the child's future, she, too, refers them to the doctor.

"Shopping around" outside the hospital typically involves consultations by the parents with other doctors and talks with suddenly discovered, near or distant, neighbors whose children have had polio. The former is seldom satisfactory in that the private practitioner, on the basis of what the parents can tell him, is in less of a position to prognosticate or offer reassurance than is the doctor who is resident in the hospital. And visits with neighbors who have faced polio in their own families generally result in an exchange of experiences and beliefs which, at best, pertain to but a few cases. The cases they hear about display so much variability in onset and outcome that the parents soon come to feel that few, if any, generalizations are possible. All these frustrating encounters serve only to reinforce the doctor's initial injunction that "much is unknown and only time will tell." "Time" in this context connotes, of course, a long time.

Another important factor in the lengthening of the time perspective is the gradient approach to recovery which the hospital institutes: treatment procedures are so progressively arranged and serve so clearly to delineate the sequence of benchmarks on the road to recovery that time begins to be conceived as measured intervals in the striving toward a goal. The significance of this for the child will be discussed later. Here let us briefly consider some implications for the parent.

Parents are permitted to visit their children in the hospital only once or twice a week at regularly scheduled times. This in itself frequently imparts to their time perspective a certain attenuated periodicity. Further, in the course of these visits they soon become aware that they are able to observe only slight changes from week to week and are led to believe anew that recovery is a long, slow process. This belief is reinforced by doctor and physiotherapist, who caution the parent "not to expect too much too quickly." Optimism is not completely discouraged, however, for it is an attitude of "restrained hopefulness" which hospital personnel typically regard as most conducive to establishing a proper therapeutic environment. Thus, the physiotherapist at a polio convalescent hospital told a parent who phoned almost daily to inquire about her child's condition: "Mrs. Smith, if you call me every day, there's not much progress I can report in Harry's condition. But, if you would call me every other week, I think I'll be able to give you a good report." Such periodic reports, along with the ordered sequence of physiotherapeutic exercises and formal muscle checks taken at six-week intervals, also have the effect of directing the parents' expectations to points in the future.

Thus far we have been considering the hospital's management of time perspective chiefly with reference to the family of the paralyzed child. How does the institution manage to lengthen the child's own time perspective? Of predominant importance in this connection is the loosening of the child's affective ties with home and his immersion in the subculture of sickness. As long as the child senses his separation from parents and home acutely and unremittingly, the incorporation of hospital routine and values in his motivational system is mechanical at best. The passage of each day is keenly felt as but further forced separation from the familiar and loved. In the phraseology of the hospital personnel, this child is not "a co-operative patient."

The rapid immersion of the child in the subculture of sickness proceeds on many well-charted fronts. In general, this is accomplished by restricting parents' visits to once or twice a week; by the hospital personnel's assuming in surrogate fashion many of the functions of parents; by duplicating in the hospital many of the activities and diversions of the home (e.g., television, games, picture and comic books, group play, etc.); by a reward and punishment system, both formal and informal, which sanctions good behavior and cooperative attitudes as these are defined by the treatment personnel; and—most important of all, perhaps— by the fact of living in a milieu in which sickness is the norm rather than the deviation and which permits the child to relate in a more thorough and structured fashion to a common universe of special meanings, goals, and evaluative rankings.

This raises, in passing, the interesting problem of certain dysfunctional consequences in the very thorough assimilation of hospital definitions and values which many of the children experience during their convalescent stay. For the values of the hospital are not precisely those of the society to which the child will have to return one day. The severely paralyzed child who after long treatment is able to get out of bed and move about on crutches has, in the eyes of the physiotherapist, for example, made marked and important progress. Naturally, he and others in the hospital encourage and support him in this conviction. To outsiders—and possibly to his parents—he may just be a poor crippled kid. Hence, a number of the children in our study, particularly those approaching adolescence, voice reluctance and strong foreboding when discharge time draws near. Growing increasingly aware of the trauma frequently attending the shift from hospital to home, some polio convalescent centers have begun to institute a policy whereby the children are allowed home for several weekend visits a month or so prior to discharge. There remains, however, the broader problem of the extent to which the values of the two worlds can be effectively reconciled without detriment to either.

Before taking up the question of how the hospital defines progress in recovery, let us consider some of the latent functions of the lengthening of the time perspective. First, it encourages the paralyzed child to shift his attention from the ultimate hope of walking, running, playing ball, etc., to such short-range goals as sitting up in bed, moving a specific muscle, and locomotion in a wheel chair. Second, for the treatment personnel—especially the doctor—it serves the purpose of blocking repetitive and incessant questioning by the family. Because recovery is defined as slow and full of uncertainty, many parents soon begin to feel that there is not much point in "pestering" the busy doctor, particularly if they will be told very little, as is generally the case. Hence the doctor can either rightly or wrongly shed some of the onerous burden of continually answering questions and devote himself more fully to what he regards as his significant duties, namely, diagnosis, prescription, and treatment. Third, from the parents' standpoint, the lengthening of the time perspective provides them sufficient time to assimilate the crisis and thereupon gradually to reorganize their attitudes in accordance with the changed circumstances of their child's life. Particularly significant is the psychological time required for the parents to accept the fact that their child, as is so often the case, will be left with a residual disability.

Customarily we think of recovery from a disease or ailment as a more or less spontaneous process. True, there are the usual medical interventions and medications, but we assume for the most part that the feeling of getting well is a subjective state which hardly requires definition. Yet closer examination reveals a whole class of pathological conditions in which this would not seem to be the case. Questions can be raised as to whether the experience of recovery from any disease or ailment is ever as subjectively spontaneous as we think, but, in particular, we refer to those conditions in which the precise course and extent of recovery are obscured by uncertainty factors and where, as a rule, the patient's state upon recovery is significantly different from what it was originally. Certain mental diseases, diabetes, numerous cardiac conditions, and paralytic poliomyelitis seem to fall in this class.

What distinguishes this class of pathology is that without the explanations provided by the therapeutic personnel as well as the implicit cues in the treatment procedures, the patient would have little way of sensing progress and knowing that he is getting better. It has been pointed out, for example, that in mental disease an important first step around which ward-treatment procedures are structured is for the patient to recognize verbally that he is sick and to express an intention to get better. This is institutionally labeled as "achieving insight." When this occurs, the patient's course of treatment is changed accordingly.[2] In recovery from paralytic polio, signs and movement tendencies, similar in form although different in content, are also structured into the everyday treatment procedures and interaction between physiotherapist and patient. These treatment procedures, in general, involve a graduated, step-by-step approach by the patient toward what the doctor and physiotherapist calculate to be optimal muscle functioning within the limits imposed by the initial muscle damage. Very frequently, of course, this means something less than total recovery of muscle use.

Consider the example of a child with extensive muscle damage in

one leg which permits him neither to stand nor to walk. Treatment
may begin on a stretcher bed on which the physiotherapist bends and
manipulates the paralyzed leg to the point of pain. Besides familiariz-
ing the physiotherapist with the exact site and extent of muscle damage, this procedure serves to indicate to the child that the leg is
potentially of use, something which a passive regime of bed rest would
not make evident so early. Several days later the child may be suspended for the first time in the hydrotherapy pool, where the buoy-
ancy of the water permits him to move the damaged leg about more
easily than he could on dry land. This in itself is a rewarding and plea-
surable experience and serves to reinforce the sense of muscle potential. In the course of several months the child may progress from moving the leg to and fro while lying prone upon a mat on the floor of the
physiotherapy room, to standing up while being held by the physiotherapist, to ambulating up and down a ramp while he supports himself on arm rails, to taking his first tentative steps with the aid of
braces or crutches, or both.

As each phase of the treatment is being mastered, the child is prepared by the physiotherapist for the next phase. The progression not
only defines his recovery for him but also functions as something of a
reward for the efforts he has made. New movements and sensations he
experiences in his leg are referred by him to the physiotherapist for
definitions as to whether they are "good" or "mean anything." In
short, even though his disability when viewed by the layman might
turn out to be marked, in his physiotherapeutic experiences he learns
by word and deed that he is "getting well." In addition, particular
physiotherapeutic routines become so intimately associated with particular stages of motion and ambulation that the former frequently
comes to be thought of by the children as an indispensable condition
for the latter. This led one perceptive twelve-year-old at a polio convalescent center to remark somewhat sarcastically: "Nobody around
here walks until after they've had their second muscle check." Physiotherapists are concerned lest the polio convalescents "sneak in too
many walks" prior to the appointed time. This concern certainly stems
in large degree from the possible harmful effects on gait and body-
muscle balance which premature ambulation can cause. At the same
time, though, the "scheduling" of so critical a physical advance as
ambulation suggests that factors like patient morale[3] and maintaining
routinized treatment procedures are also at play.

The treatment procedures in a very real sense tap the deep and
implicit faith of parents and children concerning the efficacy of "will
power" in overcoming adverse circumstances. The gradient structur-
ing of the recovery process not only gives a public demonstration of
the concept of will power but, as their child moves from state to stage,
gives fresh assurances that he has successfully demonstrated this quality. Therefore, the paralytic polio treatment procedure is of the quin-

tessence of the Protestant ideology of achievement in America—namely, slow, patient, and regularly applied effort in pursuit of a long-range goal. Moreover, the great amount of activity and application called for in the physiotherapeutic regime, as well as the elaborate technological apparatus surrounding it, leave little room for doubt that something is being done, thereby further reassuring the child and his parents. This accords in significant respects with what Parsons has termed the "activity bias" of American medical practice,[4] especially as it relates to the problem of coping with uncertainty. In this connection it is interesting to report that, while many orthopedic surgeons privately doubt that physiotherapy per se contributes anything beyond that which natural recuperative processes themselves accomplish, most realize, if only unconsciously, that it fulfils important psychological functions like those touched on here.

What has been written here refers chiefly to the effect of patterned institutional schema on the stricken child and his family. This is not to say that all cases proceed alike or that significant deviations from the pattern cannot be found. Indeed, they can, and they constitute an ongoing source of strain in the functioning of the treatment system. An examination of these aspects of the treatment system must, however, await another occasion.

NOTES

[1]Talcott Parsons, *The Social System* (Glencoe, Ill.: Free Press, 1951), chap. 10.

[2]Private communication with Erving Goffman.

[3]In the course of their work physiotherapists must frequently take into account how rapid progress by some children affects the morale of those who progress more slowly.

[4]Parsons, *The Social System*.

Part IV

THE PROCESS
OF ACCOMMODATION

8

The Adjustment of the Family
to the Crisis of Alcoholism

JOAN K. JACKSON

I. INTRODUCTION

Although the subjects *families under stress* and *alcoholism* have both received increased attention from sociologists in recent years, very little has appeared on the families of alcoholics. Standard textbooks on the family devote a few pages or a chapter to "the disgraced family" and, in passing, comment that one type of disgraced family is that of the alcoholic. In a few books dealing with alcoholism, the family's problems are recognized and advice is offered to its members on how to treat the alcoholic. But there is little information on the effect of alcoholism on the division of labor within the family, on the interaction patterns, on the family's integration, on the roles of family members, or on the ongoing functions of the family.

Mowrer (1), based on case studies of alcoholics and their wives, and of controls, stated that the status of the male alcoholic in marriage becomes inferior to that of his wife. Sexual relationships are unsatisfactory due to the inadequacies of both partners. In the conclusion, there is a suggestion that family attitudes towards alcoholics are direct resultants of the alcoholism.

Reprinted by permission from *Quarterly Journal of Studies in Alcohol,* 15 (1954), pp. 562–586. Copyright by Journal of Studies on Alcohol, Inc., New Brunswick, N.J. 08903.

This report, from the Department of Psychiatry, University of Washington School of Medicine, Seattle, Washington, is part of an alcoholism project which has been supported by the State of Washington Research Fund under Initiative 171.

Bacon (2) suggested that although on the whole "excessive drinking and factors in personality leading to excessive drinking tend to preclude or debar marriage," some of those alcoholics who do marry become excessively dependent on their wives. Baker (3) noted that treatment of the wife is often as important as treatment of the inebriate. She also mentioned the personality disturbances frequently found in children of alcoholics.

A few articles have dealt with the wives of alcoholics from a psychological viewpoint. Futterman (4) concluded that there is much clinical evidence to suggest that the wife "unconsciously, because of her own needs, seems to encourage her husband's alcoholism." He suggested that when the husband becomes sober the wife often decompensates and begins to show symptoms of neurotic disturbance. Whalen (5) and Price (6) substantially agree that the wife contributes to the alcoholism of the husband and shows personality difficulties. Whalen delineates four types of personalities common to wives of alcoholics. She goes further than Futterman, suggesting that certain types of women marry alcoholics in order to satisfy deep, unconscious needs. Price found wives of alcoholics to be nervous, hostile, basically dependent people, although on the surface they appeared to be adequate. They were unable to cope with the drinking by their husbands and accepted no responsibility for it. The wife at the time of her marriage was depicted as an insecure person who expected her husband to be a strong, dependable, responsible person.[1]

None of the studies deals with the way in which the family as a unit attempts to adjust to an alcoholic parent. None views these adjustments on a time continuum.

The studies of the wives of alcoholics impute psychological traits to the wife, as judged from her behavior after her husband has reached an advanced stage of alcoholism, and posit that these psychological traits would have been found prior to the onset of drinking. None of the articles conceptualizes the behavior of the wife, or the personality traits inferred from this behavior, as a reaction to a cumulative crisis in which the wife experiences progressively more stress.

These articles imply or state directly that the wife is responsible for some of her husband's drinking and, because of her own unconscious personality needs, encourages his excessive drinking. The reasoning seems to be somewhat as follows: The wife takes some kind of action; the husband soon thereafter resumes drinking. A causal connection is assumed to exist between the two events, and this assumption may receive further reinforcement when the husband states that this action was the reason why he drank. As the wife's behavior (from the viewpoint of an observer) was dysfunctional in achieving her consciously stated ends, and as she may persist in this behavior over a period of time, it is assumed that she is driven to act in this manner by an unconscious need to have her husband drink. These conceptions raise several problems. (*1*) There is no evidence that the husband drank because of this or any other form of action on the part of his wife. Nor is there any evidence that if the wife had not taken this action he would not have resumed his drinking. To make a causal connection between the behavior of the wife and the drinking of her husband requires that we know why alcoholics drink excessively, and can specify the type of behavior or other personal relationships which will precipitate or minimize drinking episodes. Our present verified knowledge of alcoholism does not include this information. (*2*) Before a conclusion can be reached that the wife has an unconscious need to have her husband continue to drink, we must be able to demonstrate that if she were given information on how to terminate the drinking, she would not or could not make use of this information. Again, knowledge of the appropriate behavior which would lead to the end of drinking is lacking, both to the wife who consciously wishes to have a sober husband, and to those who attempt to advise her. The question of unconscious needs will thus remain in the realm of theory until knowledge of alcoholism expands sufficiently to permit a test of this hypothesis. Alternate hypotheses might be: (*a*) that some of the wife's behavior has a more immediate motivation, that is, that it serves to release situationally induced tension, and that such behavior is followed only incidentally by more drinking by the husband; (*b*) that some of the wife's behavior is intended to stabilize the family and that, in so doing, it precipitates a situation which leads to further drinking by the husband. When viewed in the context of what is best for the husband, such behavior might be judged as dysfunctional; viewed in the context of the rest of the family, it might appear to be functional.

Sources of Data

Over a 3-year period, the present investigator has been an active participant in the Alcoholics Anonymous Auxiliary in Seattle. This group is composed partly of women whose husbands are or were members of Alcoholics Anonymous, and partly of women whose husbands are excessive drinkers but have never contacted Alcoholics Anonymous. At a typical meeting one-fifth would be the wives of Alcoholics Anonymous members who have been sober for some time; the husband of another fifth would have recently joined the fellowship; the remainder would be equally divided between those whose husbands were "on and off" the Alcoholics Anonymous program and those whose husbands had as yet not had any contact with Alcoholics Anonymous.

At least an hour and a half of each formal meeting of this group is taken up with a frank discussion of the current family problems of the members. As in other meetings of Alcoholics Anonymous the questions are posed by describing the situation which gives rise to the problem and the answers are a narration of the personal experiences of other wives who have had a similar problem, rather than direct advice. Verbatim shorthand notes have been taken of all discussions, at the request of the group, who also make use of the notes for the group's purposes. Informal contact has been maintained with past and present members. In the past 3 years 50 women have been members of this group.

The families represented by these women are at present in many different stages of adjustment and have passed through several stages during the past few years. The continuous contact over a prolonged period permits generalizations about processes and changes in family adjustments.

In addition, in connection with research on hospitalized alcoholics, many of their wives have been interviewed. The interviews with the hospitalized alcoholics, as well as with male members of Alcoholics Anonymous, have also provided information on family interactions. Further information has been derived from another group of wives, not connected with Alcoholics Anonymous, and from probation officers, social workers and court officials.

The following presentation is limited insofar as it deals only with families seeking help for the alcoholism of the husband. Other families are known to have solved the problem through divorce, often without having attempted to help the alcoholic member first. Others never seek help and never separate. There were no marked differences between the two groups seeking help, one through the hospital and one through the A.A. Auxiliary. The wives of hospitalized alcoholics gave a history of the family crisis similar to that given by women in the Auxiliary.

A second limitation is that only the families of male alcoholics are dealt with. It is recognized that the findings cannot be generalized to the families of alcoholic women without further research. Due to differences between men and women in their roles in the family as well as in the pattern of drinking, it would be expected that male and female alcoholics would in some ways have a different effect on family structure and function.

A third limitation is imposed for the sake of clarity and brevity: only the accounts of the wives of their attempts to stabilize their family adjustments will be dealt with. For any complete picture, the view of the alcoholic husband would also have to be included.

It must be emphasized that this paper deals with the definitions of the family situations by the wives, rather than with the actual situation. It has been noted that frequently wife and husband do not agree on what has occurred. The degree to which the definition of the situation by the wife or husband correlates with actual behavior is a question which must be left for further research.

The families represented in this study are from the middle and lower classes. The occupations of the husbands prior to excessive drinking include small business owners, salesmen, business executives, skilled and semiskilled workers. Prior to marriage the wives have been nurses, secretaries, teachers, saleswomen, cooks, or waitresses. The economic status of the childhood families of these husbands and wives ranged from very wealthy to very poor.

Method

From the records of discussions of the Alcoholics Anonymous Auxiliary, the statements of each wife were extracted and arranged in a time sequence. Notes on informal contacts were added at the point in the sequence where they occurred. The interviews with the wives of hospitalized alcoholics were similarly treated. These working records on individual families were then examined for uniformities of behavior and for regularities in changes over time.

The similarities in the process of adjustment to an alcoholic family member are presented here as stages of variable duration. It should be stressed that only the similarities are dealt with. Although the wives have shared the patterns dealt with here, there have been marked differences in the length of time between stages, in the number of stages passed through up to the present time, and in the relative importance to the family constellation of any one type of behavior. For example, all admitted nagging, but the amount of nagging was variable.

When the report of this analysis was completed it was read before a meeting of the Auxiliary with a request for correction of any errors in fact or interpretation. Corrections could be presented either anonymously or publicly from the floor. Only one correction was suggested and has been incorporated. The investigator is convinced that her relationship with the group is such that there would be no reticence about offering corrections. Throughout her contact with this group her role has been that of one who is being taught, very similar to the role of the new member. The overall response of the group to the presentation indicated that the members individually felt that they had been portrayed accurately.

The sense of having similar problems and similar experiences is indicated also in the reactions of new members to the Auxiliary's summarization of the notes of their discussions. Copies of these summaries are given to new members, who commonly state that they find it a relief to see that their problems are far from unique and that there are methods which successfully overcome them.

Statement of the Problem

For purposes of this presentation, the family is seen as involved in a cumulative crisis. All family members behave in a manner which they hope will resolve the crisis and permit a return to stability. Each member's action is influenced by his previous personality structure, by his previous role and status in the family group, and by the history of the crisis and its effects on his personality, roles and status up to that point. Action is also influenced by the past effectiveness of that particular action as a means of social control before and during the crisis. The behavior of family members in each phase of the crisis contributes to the form which the crisis takes in the following stages and sets limits on possible behavior in subsequent stages.

Family members are influenced, in addition, by the cultural definitions of alcoholism as evidence of weakness, inadequacy, or sinfulness; by the cultural prescriptions for the roles of family members; and by the cultural values of family solidarity, sanctity, and self-sufficiency. Alcoholism in the family poses a situation defined by the culture as shameful but for the handling of which there are no prescriptions which are effective or which permit direct action not in conflict with other cultural prescriptions. While in crises such as illness or death the family members can draw on cultural definitions of appropriate behavior for procedures which will terminate the crisis, this is not the case with alcoholism in the family. The cultural view has been that alcoholism is shameful and should not occur. Only recently has any information been offered to guide families in their behavior toward their alcoholic member and, as yet, this information resides more in technical journals than in the media of mass communication. Thus, in facing alcoholism, the family is in an unstructured situation and must find the techniques for handling it through trial and error.

II. STAGES IN FAMILY ADJUSTMENT TO AN ALCOHOLIC MEMBER

The Beginning of the Marriage

At the time marriage was considered, the drinking of most of the men was within socially acceptable limits. In a few cases the men were already alcoholics but managed to hide this from their fiancées. They drank only moderately or not at all when on dates and often avoided friends and relatives who might expose their excessive drinking. The relatives and friends who were introduced to the fiancée were those who had hopes that "marriage would straighten him out" and thus said nothing about the drinking. In a small number of cases the men spoke with their fiancées of their alcoholism. The women had no conception of what alcoholism meant, other than that it involved more than the usual frequency of drinking, and they entered the marriage with little more preparation than if they had known nothing about it.

Stage 1. Incidents of excessive drinking begin and, although they are sporadic, place strains on the husband-wife interaction. In attempts to minimize drinking, problems in marital adjustment not related to the drinking are avoided.

Stage 2. Social isolation of the family begins as incidents of excessive drinking multiply. The increasing isolation magnifies the importance of family interactions and events. Behavior and thought become drinking-centered. Husband-wife adjustment deteriorates and tension rises. The wife begins to feel self-pity and to lose her self-confidence as her behavior fails to stabilize her husband's drinking. There is an attempt still to maintain the original family structure, which is disrupted anew with each episode of drinking, and as a result the children begin to show emotional disturbance.

Stage 3. The family gives up attempts to control the drinking and begins to behave in a manner geared to relieve tension rather than achieve long-term ends. The disturbance of the children becomes more marked. There is no longer an attempt to support the alcoholic in his roles as husband and father. The wife begins to worry about her own sanity and about her inability to make decisions or act to change the situation.

Stage 4. The wife takes over control of the family and the husband is seen as a recalcitrant child. Pity and strong protective feelings largely replace the earlier resentment and hostility. The family becomes more stable and organized in a manner to minimize the disruptive behavior of the husband. The self-confidence of the wife begins to be rebuilt.

Stage 5: The wife separates from her husband if she can resolve the problems and conflicts surrounding this action.

Stage 6: The wife and children reorganize as a family without the husband.

Stage 7: The husband achieves sobriety and the family, which had become organized around an alcoholic husband, reorganizes to include a sober father and experiences problems in reinstating him in his former roles.

Stage 1. Attempts to Deny the Problem

Usually the first experience with drinking as a problem arises in a social situation. The husband drinks in a manner which is inappropriate to the social setting and the expectations of others present. The wife feels embarrassed on the first occasion and humiliated as it occurs more frequently. After several such incidents she and her husband talk over his behavior. The husband either formulates an explanation for the episode and assures her that such behavior will not occur again, or he refuses to discuss it at all. For a time afterward he drinks appropriately and drinking seems to be a problem no longer. The wife looks back on the incidents and feels that she has exaggerated them, feesl ashamed of herself for her disloyalty and for her behavior. The husband, in evaluating the incident, feels shame also and vows such episodes will not recur. As a result, both husband and wife attempt to make it up to the other and, for a time, try to play their conceptions of the ideal husband and wife roles, minimizing or avoiding other difficulties which arise in the marriage. They thus create the illusion of a "perfect" marriage.

Eventually another inappropriate drinking episode occurs and the pattern is repeated. The wife worries but takes action only in the situations in which inappropriate drinking occurs, as each long intervening period of acceptable drinking behavior convinces her that a recurrence is unlikely. As time goes on, in attempting to cope with individual episodes, she runs the gamut of possible trial and error behaviors, learning that none is permanently effective.

If she speaks to other people about her husband's drinking, she is usually assured that there is no need for concern, that her husband can control his drinking and that her fears are exaggerated. Some friends possibly admit that his drinking is too heavy and give advice on how they handled similar situations with their husbands. These friends convince her that her problem will be solved as soon as she hits upon the right formula for dealing with her husband's drinking.

During this stage the husband-wife interaction is in no way "abnormal." In a society in which a large proportion of the men drink, most wives have at some time had occasion to be concerned, even though only briefly, with an episode of drinking which they considered inappropriate (7). In a society in which the status of the family depends on that of the husband, the wife feels threatened by any behavior on his part which might lower it. Inappropriate drinking is regarded by her as a threat to the family's reputation and standing in the community. The wife attempts to exert control and often finds herself blocked by the sacredness of drinking behavior to men in America. Drinking is a private matter and not any business of the wife's. On the whole, a man reacts to his wife's suggestion that he has not adequately controlled his drinking with resentment, rebelliousness, and a display of emotion which makes rational discussion difficult. The type of husband-wife interaction outlined in this stage has occurred in many American families in which the husband never became an excessive drinker.

Stage 2. Attempts to Eliminate the Problems

Stage 2 begins when the family experiences social isolation because of the husband's drinking. Invitations to the homes of friends become less frequent. When the couple does visit friends, drinks are not served or are limited, thus emphasizing the reason for exclusion from other social activities of the friendship group. Discussions of drinking begin to be sidestepped awkwardly by friends, the wife, and the husband.

By this time the periods of socially acceptable drinking are becoming shorter. The wife, fearing that the full extent of her husband's drinking will become known, begins to withdraw from social participation, hoping to reduce the visibility of his behavior, and thus the threat to family status.

Isolation is further intensified because the family usually acts in accordance with the cultural dictate that it should be self-sufficient and manage to resolve its own problems without recourse to outside aid. Any experiences which they have had with well-meaning outsiders, usually relatives, have tended to strengthen this conviction. The husband has defined such relatives as interfering and the situation has deteriorated rather than improved.

With increasing isolation, the family members begin to lose perspective on their interaction and on their problems. Thrown into closer contact with one another as outside contacts diminish, the behavior of each member assumes exaggerated importance. The drinking behavior becomes the focus of anxiety. Gradually all family difficulties become attributed to it. (For example, the mother who is cross with her children will feel that, if her husband had not been drinking, she would not have been so tense and would not have been angry.) The fear that the full extent of drinking may be discovered mounts steadily; the conceptualization of the consequences of such a discovery becomes increasingly vague and, as a result, more anxiety-provoking. The family feels different from others and alone with its shameful secret.

Attempts to cover up increase. The employer who calls to inquire about the husband's absence from work is given excuses. The wife is afraid to face the consequences of loss of the husband's pay check in addition to her other concerns. Questions from the children are evaded or they are told that their father is ill. The wife lives in terror of the day when the children will be told by others of the nature of the "illness." She is also afraid that the children may describe their father's symptoms to teachers or neighbors. Still feeling that the family must solve its own problems, she keeps her troubles to herself and hesitates to seek outside help. If her husband beats her, she will bear it rather than call in the police. (Indeed, often she has no idea that this is even a possibility.) Her increased isolation has left her without the advice of others as to sources of help in the community. If she knows of them, an agency contact means to her an admission of the complete failure of her family as an independent unit. For the middle-class woman particularly, recourse to social agencies and law enforcement agencies means a terrifying admission of loss of status.

During this stage, husband and wife are drawing further apart.

Each feels resentful of the behavior of the other. When this resentment is expressed, further drinking occurs. When it is not, tension mounts and the next drinking episode is that much more destructive of family relationships. The reasons for drinking are explored frantically. Both husband and wife feel that if only they could discover the reason, all members of the family could gear their behavior to making drinking unnecessary. The discussions become increasingly unproductive, as it is the husband's growing conviction that his wife does not and cannot understand him.

On her part, the wife begins to feel that she is a failure, that she has been unable to fulfill the major cultural obligations of a wife to meet her husband's needs. With her increasing isolation, her sense of worth derives almost entirely from her roles as wife and mother. Each failure to help her husband gnaws away at her sense of adequacy as a person.

Periods of sobriety or socially acceptable drinking still occur. These periods keep the wife from making a permanent or stable adjustment. During them her husband, in his guilt, treats her like a queen. His behavior renews her hope and rekindles positive feelings toward him. Her sense of worth is bolstered temporarily and she grasps desperately at her husband's reassurance that she is really a fine person and not a failure and an unlovable shrew. The periods of sobriety also keep her family from facing the inability of the husband to control his drinking. The inaccuracies of the cultural stereotype of the alcoholic—particularly that he is in a constant state of inebriation—also contribute to the family's rejection of the idea of alcoholism, as the husband seems to demonstrate from time to time that he can control his drinking.

Family efforts to control the husband become desperate. There are no culturally prescribed behavior patterns for handling such a situation and the family is forced to evolve its own techniques. Many different types of behavior are tried but none brings consistent results; there seems to be no way of predicting the consequences of any action that may be taken. All attempts to stabilize or structure the situation to permit consistent behavior fail. Threats of leaving, hiding his liquor away, emptying the bottles down the drain, curtailing his money, are tried in rapid succession, but none is effective. Less punitive methods, as discussing the situation when he is sober, babying him during hangovers, and trying to drink with him to keep him in the home, are attempted and fail. All behavior becomes oriented around the drinking, and the thought of family members becomes obsessive on this subject. As no action seems to be successful in achieving its goal, the wife persists in trial-and-error behavior with mounting frustration. Long-term goals recede into the background and become secondary to just keeping the husband from drinking today.

There is still an attempt to maintain the illusion of husband-wife-children roles. When father is sober, the children are expected to give him respect and obedience. The wife also defers to him in his role as head of the household. Each drinking event thus disrupts family functioning anew. The children begin to show emotional disturbances as a result of the inconsistencies of parental behavior. During periods when the husband is drinking the wife tries to shield them from the knowledge and effects of his behavior, at the same time drawing them closer to herself and deriving emotional support from them. In sober periods, the father tries to regain their favor. Due to experiencing directly only pleasant interactions with their father, considerable affection is often felt for him by the children. This affection becomes increasingly difficult for the isolated wife to tolerate, and an additional source of conflict. She feels that she needs and deserves the love and support of her children and, at the same time, she feels it important to maintain the children's picture of their father. She counts on the husband's affection for the children to motivate a cessation of drinking as he comes to realize the effects of his behavior on them.

In this stage, self-pity begins to be felt by the wife, if it has not entered previously. It continues in various degrees throughout the succeeding stages. In an attempt to handle her deepening sense of inadequacy, the wife often tries to convince herself that she is right and her husband wrong, and this also continues through the following stages. At this point the wife often resembles what Whalen (5) describes as "The Sufferer."

Stage 3. Disorganization

The wife begins to adopt a "What's the use?" attitude and to accept her husband's drinking as a problem likely to be permanent. Attempts to understand one another become less frequent. Sober periods still engender hope, but hope qualified by skepticism; they bring about a lessening of anxiety and this is defined as happiness.

By this time some customary patterns of husband-wife-children interaction have evolved. Techniques which have had some effectiveness in controlling the husband in the past or in relieving pent-up frustration are used by the wife. She nags, berates or retreats into silence. Husband and wife are both on the alert, the wife watching for increasing irritability and restlessness which mean a recurrence of drinking, and the husband for veiled aspersions on his behavior or character.

The children are increasingly torn in their loyalties as they become tools in the struggle between mother and father. If the children are at an age of comprehension, they have usually learned the true nature of their family situation, either from outsiders or from their mother, who has given up attempts to bolster her husband's position as father. The children are often bewildered but questioning their parents brings no satisfactory answers as the parents themselves do not understand what is happening. Some children become terrified; some have increasing behavior problems within and outside the home; others seem on the surface to accept the situation calmly.[2]

During periods of the husband's drinking, the hostility, resentment and frustrations felt by the couple is allowed expression. Both may resort to violence—the wife in self-defense or because she can find no other outlet for her feelings. In those cases in which the wife retaliates to violence in kind, she feels a mixture of relief and intense shame at having deviated so far from what she conceives to be "the behavior of a normal woman."

When the wife looks at her present behavior, she worries about her "normality." In comparing the person she was in the early years of her marriage with the person she has become, she is frightened. She finds herself nagging and unable to control herself. She resolves to stand up to her husband when he is belligerent but instead finds herself cringing in terror and then despises herself for her lack of courage. If she retaliates with violence, she is filled with self-loathing at behaving in an "unwomanly" manner. She finds herself compulsively searching for bottles, knowing full well that finding them will change nothing, and is worried because she engages in such senseless behavior. She worries about her inability to take constructive action of any kind. She is confused about where her loyalty lies, whether with her husband or her children. She feels she is a failure as a wife, mother and person. She believes she should be strong in the face of adversity and instead feels herself weak.

The wife begins to find herself avoiding sexual contact with her husband when he has been drinking. Sex under these circumstances, she feels, is sex for its own sake rather than an indication of affection for her. Her husband's lack of consideration of her needs to be satisfied leaves her feeling frustrated. The lack of sexual responsiveness reflects her emotional withdrawal from him in other areas of family life. Her husband, on his part, feels frustrated and rejected; he accuses her of frigidity and this adds to her concern about her adequacy as a woman.[3]

By this time the opening wedge has been inserted into the self-sufficiency of the family. The husband has often been in difficulty with the police and the wife has learned that police protection is available. An emergency has occurred in which the seeking of outside help was the only possible action to take; subsequent calls for aid from outsiders do not require the same degree of urgency before they can be undertaken. However, guilt and a lessening of self-respect and self-confidence accompany this method of resolving emergencies. The husband intensifies these feelings by speaking of the interference of outsiders, or of his night in jail.

In Stage 3 all is chaos. Few problems are met constructively. The husband and wife both feel trapped in an intolerable, unstructured situation which offers no way out. The wife's self-assurance is almost completely gone. She is afraid to take action and afraid to let things remain as they are. Fear is one of the major characteristics of this stage: fear of violence, fear of personality damage to the children, fear for her own sanity, fear that relatives will interfere, and fear that they will not help in an emergency. Added to this, the family feels alone in the world and helpless. The problems, and the behavior of family members in attempting to cope with them, seem so shameful that help from others is unthinkable. They feel that attempts to get help would meet only with rebuff, and that communication of the situation will engender disgust.

At this point the clinical picture which the wife presents is very similar to what Whalen (5) has described as "The Waverer."

Stage 4. Attempts to Reorganize in Spite of the Problems

Stage 4 begins when a crisis occurs which necessitates that action be taken. There may be no money or food in the house; the husband may have been violent to the children; or life on the level of Stage 3 may have become intolerable. At this point some wives leave, thus entering directly into Stage 5.

The wife who passes through Stage 4 usually begins to ease her husband out of his family roles. She assumes husband and father roles. This involves strengthening her role as mother and putting aside her role as wife. She becomes the manager of the home, the discipliner of the children, the decision-maker; she becomes somewhat like Whalen's (5) "Controller." She either ignores her husband as much as possible or treats him as her most recalcitrant child. Techniques are worked out for getting control of his pay check, if there still is one, and money is doled out to her husband on the condition of his good behavior. When he drinks, she threatens to leave him, locks him out of the house, refuses to pay his taxi bills, leaves him in jail overnight rather than pay his bail. Where her obligations to her husband conflict with those to her children, she decides in favor of the latter. As she views her husband increasingly as a child, pity and a sense of being desperately needed by him enter. Her inconsistent behavior toward him, deriving from the lack of predictability inherent in the situation up to now, becomes reinforced by her mixed feelings toward him.

In this stage the husband often tries to set his will against hers in decisions about the children. If the children have been permitted to stay with a friend overnight, he may threaten to create a scene unless they return immediately. He may make almost desperate efforts to gain their affection and respect, his behavior ranging from getting them up in the middle of the night to fondle them to giving them stiff lectures on children's obligations to fathers. Sometimes he will attempt to align the males of the family with him against the females. He may openly express resentment of the children and become beligerent toward them physically or verbally.

Much of the husband's behavior can be conceptualized as resulting from an increasing awareness of his isolation from the other members of the family and their steady withdrawal of respect and affection. It seems to be a desperate effort to regain what he has lost, but without any clear idea of how this can be accomplished—an effort to change a situation in which everyone is seen as against him; and, in reality, this is becoming more and more true. As the wife has taken over control of the family with some degree of success, he feels, and becomes, less and less necessary to the ongoing activity of the family. There are fewer and fewer roles left for him to play. He becomes aware that members of the family enjoy each other's company without him. When he is home he tries to enter this circle of warmth or to smash it. Either way he isolates himself further. He finds that the children discuss with the mother how to manage him and he sees the children acting on the basis of their mother's idea of him. The children refuse to pay aggention to his demands: they talk back to him in the same way that they talk back to one another, adding pressure on him to assume the role of just another child. All this leaves him frustrated and, as a result, often aggressive or increasingly absent from home.

The children, on the whole, become more settled in their behavior as the wife takes over the family responsibilities. Decisions are made by her and upheld in the face of their father's attempts to interfere. Participation in activities outside the home is encouraged. Their patterns of interaction with their father are supported by the mother. Whereas in earlier stages the children often felt that there were causal connections between their actions and their father's drinking, they now accept his unpredictability. "Well," says a 6-year old, "I'll just have to get used to it. I have a drunken father."

The family is more stabilized in one way but in other ways insecurities are multiplied. Pay checks are received less and less regularly. The violence or withdrawal of the father increases. When he is away the wife worries about automobile accidents or injury in fights, which become more and more probable as time passes. The husband may begin to be seriously ill from time to time; his behavior may become quite bizarre. Both of these signs of increasing illness arouse anxiety in the family.

During this stage hopes may rise high for father's "reform" when he begins to verbalize wishes to stop drinking, admits off and on his inability to stop, and sounds desperate for doing something about his drinking. Now may begin the trek to sanitariums for the middle-class alcoholic, to doctors, or to Alcoholics Anonymous. Where just the promise to stop drinking has failed to revive hope, sobriety through outside agencies has the ability to rekindle it brightly. There is the feeling that at last he is "taking really constructive action." In failure the discouragement is deeper. Here another wedge has been inserted into the self-sufficiency of the family.

By this time the wedges are many. The wife, finding she has managed to bring some semblance of order and stability to her family, while not exactly becoming a self-assured person, has regained some sense of worth which grows a little with each crisis she meets successfully. In addition, the very fact of taking action to stabilize the situation brings relief. On some occasion she may be able to approach social agencies for financial help, often during a period when the husband has temporarily deserted or is incarcerated. She may have gone to the family court; she may have consulted a lawyer about getting a restraining order when the husband was in a particularly belligerent state. She has begun to learn her way around among the many agencies which offer help.

Often she has had a talk with an Alcoholics Anonymous member and has begun to look into what is known about alcoholism. If she has attended a few Alcoholics Anonymous meetings, her sense of shame has been greatly alleviated as she finds so many others in the same boat. Her hopes rise as she meets alcoholics who have stopped drinking, and she feels relieved at being able to discuss her problems openly for the first time with an audience which understands fully. She begins to gain perspective on her problem and learns that she herself is involved in what happens to her husband, and that she must change. She exchanges techniques of management with other wifes and receives their support in her decisions.

She learns that her husband is ill rather than merely "ornery," and this often serves to quell for the time being thoughts about leaving him which have begun to germinate as she has gained more self-confidence. She learns that help is available but also that her efforts to push him into help are unavailing. She is not only supported in her recently evolved behavior of thinking first of her family, but now this course also emerges from the realm of the unconceptualized and is set in an accepted rationale. She feels more secure in having a reason and a certainty that the group accepts her as "doing the right thing." When she reports deviations from what the group thinks is the "right way," her reasons are understood; she receives solid support but there is also pressure on her to alter her behavior again toward the acceptable. Blaming and self-pity are actively discouraged. In group discussions she still admits to such feelings but learns to recognize them as they arise and to go beyond them to more productive thinking.

How much her altered behavior changes the family situation is uncertain, but it helps her and gives her security from which to venture forth to further actions of a consistent and constructive type, constructive at least from the point of view of keeping her family on as even a keel as possible in the face of the disruptive influence of the husband. With new friends whom she can use as a sounding board for plans, and with her growing acquaintance with the alternatives and possible patterns of behavior, her thinking ceases to be circular and unproductive. Her anxiety about her own sanity is alleviated as she is reassured by others that they have experienced the same concern and that the remedy is to get her own life and her family under better control. As she accomplishes this, the difference in her feelings about herself convinces her that this is so.

Whether or not she has had a contact with wives of Alcoholics Anonymous members or other wives who have been through a similar experience and have emerged successfully, the very fact of taking hold of her situation and gradually making it more manageable adds to her self-confidence. As her husband is less and less able to care for himself or his family, she begins to feel that he needs her and that without her he would be destroyed. Such a feeling makes it difficult for her to think of leaving him. His almost complete social isolation at this point and his cries for help reinforce this conviction of being needed.

The drinking behavior is no longer hidden. Others obviously know about it, and this becomes accepted by the wife and children. Already isolated and insulated against possible rejection, the wife is often surprised to find that she has exaggerated her fears of what would happen were the situation known. However, the unpredictability of her husband's behavior makes her reluctant to form social relationships which could be violently disrupted or to involve others in the possible consequences of his behavior.

Stage 5. Efforts to Escape the Problems

Stage 5 may be the terminal one for the marriage. In this stage the wife separates from her husband. Sometimes the marriage is reestablished after a period of sobriety, when it appears certain that the husband will not drink again. If he does revert to drinking, the marriage is sometimes finally terminated but with less emotional stress than the first time. If the husband deserts, being no longer able to tolerate his lack of status in his family, Stage 6 may be entered abruptly.

The events precipitating the decision to terminate the marriage may be near-catastrophic, as when there is an attempt by the husband to kill the wife or children, or they may appear trivial to outsiders, being only the last straw to an accumulation of years.

The problems in coming to the decision to terminate the marriage cannot be underestimated. Some of these problems derive from emotional conflicts; some are related to very practical circumstances in the situation; some are precipitated by the conflicting advice of outsiders. With several children dependent on her, the wife must decide whether the present situation is more detrimental to them than future situations she can see arising if she should leave her husband. The question of where the money to live on will come from must be thought out. If she can get a job, will there be enough to provide for child care also while she is away from home? Should the children, who have already experienced such an unsettled life, be separated from her to be cared for by others? If the family still owns its own home, how can she retain control of it? If she leaves, where can she go? What can be done to tide the family over until her first earnings come in? How can she ensure her husband's continued absence from the home and thus be certain of the safety of individuals and property in her absence? These are only a small sample of the practical issues that must be dealt with in trying to think her way through to a decision to terminate the marriage.

Other pressures act on her to impede the decision-making process. "If he would only stay drunk till I carry out what I intend to do," is a frequent statement. When the husband realizes that his wife really means to leave, he frequently sobers up, watches his behavior in the home, plays on her latent and sometimes conscious feelings of her responsibility for the situation, stresses his need for her and that without her he is lost, tears away at any confidence she has that she will be able to manage by herself, and threatens her and the children with injury or with his own suicide if she carries out her intention.

The children, in the meantime, are pulling and pushing on her emotions. They think she is "spineless" to stay but unfair to father's chances for ultimate recovery if she leaves. Relatives, who were earlier alienated in her attempts to shield her family but now know of the situation, do not believe in its full ramifications. They often feel she is exaggerating and persuade her to stay with him. Especially is this true in the case of the "solitary drinker." His drinking has been so well concealed that the relatives have no way of knowing the true nature of the situation. Other relatives, afraid that they will be called on for support, exert pressure to keep the marriage intact and the husband thereby responsible for debts. Relatives who feel she should leave him overplay their hands by berating the husband in such a manner as to evoke her defense of him. This makes conscious the positive aspects of her relationship with him, causing her to waver in her decision. If she consults organized agencies, she often gets conflicting advice. The agencies concerned with the well-being of the family may counsel leaving; those concerned with rehabilitating the husband may press her to stay. In addition, help from public organizations almost always involves delay and is frequently not forthcoming at the point where she needs it most.

The wife must come to terms with her own mixed feelings about her husband, her marriage and herself before she can decide on such a step as breaking up the marriage. She must give up hope that she can be of any help to her husband. She must command enough self-confidence, after years of having it eroded, to be able to face an unknown future and leave the security of an unpalatable but familiar past and present. She must accept that she has failed in her marriage, not an easy thing to do after having devoted years to stopping up the cracks in the family structure as they appeared. Breaking up the marriage involves a complete alteration in the life goals toward which all her behavior has been oriented. It is hard for her to rid herself of the feeling that she married him and he is her responsibility. Having thought and planned for so long on a day-to-day basis, it is difficult to plan for a long-term future.

Her taking over the family raises her self-confidence but failure to carry through on decisions undermines the new gains that she has made. Vacillation in her decisions tends to exasperate the agencies trying to help her, and she begins to feel that help from them may not be forthcoming if she finally decides to leave.

Some events, however, help her to arrive at a decision. During the absences of her husband she has seen how manageable life can be and how smoothly her family can run. She finds that life goes on without him. The wife who is working comes to feel that "my husband is a luxury I can no longer afford." After a few short-term separations in which she tries out her wings successfully, leaving comes to look more possible. Another step on the path to leaving is the acceptance of the idea that, although she cannot help her husband, she can help her family. She often reaches a state of such emotional isolation from her husband that his behavior no longer disturbs her emotionally but is only something annoying which upsets daily routines and plans.

Stage 6. Reorganization of Part of the Family

The wife is without her husband and must reorganize her family on this basis. Substantially the process is similar to that in other divorced families, but with some additions. The divorce rarely cuts her relationships to her husband. Unless she and her family disappear, her husband may make attempts to come back. When drunk, he may endanger her job by calls at her place of work. He may attempt violence against members of the family, or he may contact the children and work to gain their loyalty so that pressure is put on the mother to accept him again. Looking back on her marriage, she forgets the full impact of the problem situation on her and on the children and feels more warmly toward her husband, and these feelings can still be manipulated by him. The wide circulation of information on alcoholism as an illness engenders guilt about having deserted a sick man. Gradually, however, the family becomes reorganized.

Stage 7. Recovery and Reorganization of the Whole Family

Stage 7 is entered if the husband achieves sobriety, whether or not separation has preceded. It was pointed out that in earlier stages most of the problems in the marriage were attributed to the alcoholism of the husband, and thus problems in adjustment not related directly to the drinking were unrecognized and unmet. Also, the "sober personality" of the husband was thought of as the "real" personality, with a resulting lack of recognition of other factors involved in his sober behavior, such as remorse and guilt over his actions, leading him to act to the best of his ability like "the ideal husband" when sober. Irritation or other signs of growing tension were viewed as indicators of further drinking, and hence the problems giving rise to them were walked around gingerly rather than faced and resolved. Lack of conflict and lack of drinking were defined as indicating a perfect adjustment. For the wife and husband facing a sober marriage after many years of an alcoholic marriage, the expectations of what marriage without alcoholism will be are unrealistically idealistic, and the reality of marriage almost inevitably brings disillusionments. The expectation that all would go well and that all problems be resolved with the cessation of the husband's drinking cannot be met and this threatens the marriage from time to time.

The beginning of sobriety for the husband does not bring too great hope to the family at first. They have been through this before but are willing to help him along and stand by him in the new attempt. As the length of sobriety increases, so do the hopes for its permanence and efforts to be of help. The wife at first finds it difficult to think more than in terms of today, waking each morning with fear of what the day will bring and sighing with relief at the end of each sober day.

With the continuation of sobriety, many problems begin to crop up. Mother has for years managed the family, and now father again wishes to be reinstated in his former roles. Usually the first role reestablished is that of breadwinner, and the economic problems of the family begin to be alleviated as debts are gradually paid and there is enough left over for current needs. With the resumption of this role, the husband feels that the family should also accept him at least as a partner in the management of the family. Even if the wife is willing to hand over some of the control of the children, for example, the children often are not able to accept this change easily. Their mother has been both parents for so long that it takes time to get used to the idea of consulting their father on problems and asking for his decisions. Often the father tries too hard to manage this change overnight, and the very pressure put on the children toward this end defeats him. In addition, he is unable to meet many of the demands the children make on him because he has never really become acquainted with them or learned to understand them and is lacking in much necessary background knowledge of their lives.

The wife, who finds it difficult to conceive of her husband as permanently sober, feels an unwillingness to let control slip from her hands. At the same time she realizes that reinstatement of her husband in his family roles is necessary to his sobriety. She also realizes that the closer his involvement in the family the greater the probability of his remaining sober. Yet she remembers events in the past in which his failure to handle his responsibilities was catastrophic to the family. Used to avoiding anything which might upset him, the wife often hesitates to discuss problems openly. At times, if she is successful in helping him to regain his roles as father, she feels resentful of his intrustion into territory she has come to regard as hers. If he makes errors in judgment which affect the family adversely, her former feelings of being his superior may come to the fore and affect her interaction with him. If the children begin to turn to him, she may feel a resurgence of self-pity at being left out and find herself attempting to swing the children back toward herself. Above all, however, she finds herself feeling resentful that some other agency achieved what she and the children could not.

Often the husband makes demands for obedience, for consideration and for pampering which members of the family feel unable to meet. He may become rather euphoric as his sobriety continues and feel superior for a time.

Gradually, however, the drinking problem sinks into the past and marital adjustment at some level is achieved. Even when this has occurred, the drinking problem crops up occasionally, as when the time comes for a decision about whether the children should be permitted to drink. The mother at such times becomes anxious, sees in the child traits which remind her of her husband, worries whether these are the traits which mean future alcoholism. At parties, at first, she is watchful and concerned about whether her husband will take a drink or not. Relatives and friends may, in a party mood, make the husband the center of attention by emphasizing his nondrinking. They may unwittingly cast aspersions on his character by trying to convince him that he can now "drink like a man." Some relatives and friends have gone so far as secretly to "spike" a nonalcoholic drink and then cry "bottoms up!" without realizing the risk of reactivating patterns from the past.

If sobriety has come through Alcoholics Anonymous, the husband frequently throws himself so wholeheartedly into A.A. activities that his wife sees little of him and feels neglected. As she worries less about his drinking, she may press him to cut down on these activities. That this is dangerous, since A.A. activity is correlated with success in Alcoholics Anonymous, has been shown by Lahey (9). Also, the wife discovers that, though she has a sober husband, she is by no means free of alcoholics. In his Twelfth Step work, he may keep the house filled with men he is helping. In the past her husband has avoided self-searching; and now he may become excessively introspective, and it may be difficult for her to deal with this.

If the husband becomes sober through Alcoholics Anonymous and the wife participates actively in groups open to her, the thoughts of what is happening to her, to her husband and to her family will be verbalized and interpreted within the framework of the Alcoholics Anonymous philosophy and the situation will probably be more tolerable and more easily worked out.

III. SUGGESTIONS FOR FURTHER RESEARCH

The above presentation has roughly delineated sequences and characteristics of family adjustment to an alcoholic husband. A more detailed delineation of the stages is required. The extent to which these findings, based on families seeking help, can be generalized to other families of alcoholics needs to be determined, and differences between these families and others specified. Consideration should be given to the question of correspondence between the wife's definition of the situation and that which actually occurs.

Further research is needed on the factors which determine the rate of transition through the stages, and on the factors which retard such a transition, sometimes to the extent that the family seems to remain in the same stage almost permanently. In the group studied, the majority passed from one stage to the next but took different lengths of time to make the transition. Those wives whose husbands have been sober a long time had all passed through all the stages. None of the long-term members remained in the same stage throughout the time that the group was under study.

Other problems which require clarification are: (a) What are the factors within families which facilitate a return to sobriety or hamper it? (b) What variations in family behavior are determined by social class? (c) What problems are specific to the different types of drinking patterns of the husband—for example, the periodic drinker, the steady drinker, the solitary drinker, the sociable drinker, the drinker who becomes belligerent, and the drinker who remains calm? There are indications in the data gathered in the present study that such specific problems arise.

IV. SUMMARY

The onset of alcoholism in a family member has been viewed as precipitating a cumulative crisis for the family. Seven critical stages have been delineated. Each stage affects the form which the following one will take. The family finds itself in an unstructured situation which is undefined by the culture. Thus it is forced to evolve techniques of adjustment by trial and error. The unpredictability of the situation, added to its lack of structure, engenders anxiety in family members which gives rise to personality difficulties. Factors in the culture, in the environment, and within the family situation prolong the crisis and deter the working out of permanent adjustment patterns. With the arrest of the alcoholism, the crisis enters its final stage. The family attempts to reorganize to include the ex-alcoholic and makes adjustments to the changes which have occurred in him.

It has been suggested that the clinical picture presented by the wife to helping agencies is not only indicative of a type of basic personality structure but also of the stage in family adjustment to an alcoholic. That the wives of alcoholics represent a rather limited number of personality types can be interpreted in two ways, which are not mutually exclusive.

(a) That women with certain personality attributes tend to select alcoholics or potential alcoholics as husbands in order to satisfy unconscious personality needs;

(b) That women undergoing similar experiences of stress, within similarly unstructured situations, defined by the culture and reacted to by members of the society in such a manner as to place limits on the range of possible behavior, will emerge from this experience showing many similar neurotic personality traits. As the situation evolves some of these personality traits will also change. Changes have been observed in the women studied which correlate with altered family interaction patterns. This hypothesis is supported also by observations on the behavior of individuals in other unstructured situations, in situations involving conflicting goals and loyalties, and in situations in which they were isolated from supporting group interaction. It is congruent also with the theory of reactions to increased and decreased stress.

NOTES

[1]It may be noted that this is the culturally prevalent expectation of a husband by women in American society. This may be evidence that most American women are dependent but, if so, dependency loses its relevance to the problem of selecting or adjusting to an alcoholic spouse.

[2]Some effects of alcoholism of the father on children have been discussed by Newell (8).

[3]It is of interest here that marriage counselors and students of marital adjustment are of the opinion that unhappy marriage results in poor sexual adjustment more often than poor sexual adjustment leads to unhappy marriage. If this proves to be true, it would be expected that most wives of alcoholics would find sex distasteful while their husbands are drinking. The wives of the inactive alcoholics report that their sexual adjustments with their husbands are currently satisfactory; many of those whose husbands are still

drinking state that they enjoyed sexual relationships before the alcoholism was established.

REFERENCES

1. Mowrer, H. R. A psychocultural analysis of the alcoholic. Amer. sociol. Rev. 5: 546–557, 1940.
2. Bacon, S. D. Excessive drinking and the institution of the family. In: Alcohol, Science and Society; Lecture 16. New Haven; Quarterly Journal of Studies on Alcohol; 1945.
3. Baker, S. M. Social case work with inebriates. In: Alcohol, Science and Society; Lecture 27. New Haven; Quarterly Journal of Studies on Alcohol; 1945.
4. Futterman, S. Personality trends in wives of alcoholics. J. psychiat. soc. Work 23: 37–41, 1953.
5. Whalen, T. Wives of alcoholics: four types observed in a family service agency. Quart. J. Stud. Alc. 14: 632–641, 1953.
6. Price, G. M. A study of the wives of 20 alcoholics. Quart. J. Stud. Alc. 5: 620–627, 1945.
7. Club and Educational Bureaus of Newsweek. Is alcoholism everyone's problem? Platform, N.Y., p. 3, Jan. 1950.
8. Newell, N. Alcoholism and the father-image. Quart. J. Stud. Alc. 11: 92–96, 1950.
9. Lahey, W. W. A Comparison of Social and Personal Factors Identified with Selected Members of Alcoholics Anonymous. Master's Thesis; University of Southern California; 1950.

9

Deviance Disavowal:
The Management of Strained
Interaction by
the Visibly Handicapped

FRED DAVIS

A recurring issue in social relations is the refusal of those who are viewed as deviant[1] to concur in the verdict. Or, if in some sense it can be said that they do concur, they usually place a very different interpretation on the fact or allegation than do their judges. In our society this is especially true of deviance which results from ascription (e.g., the Negro) as against that which partakes to some significant degree of election (e.g., the homosexual). And, while it may be conjectured that ultimately neither the Negro nor the homosexual would be cast in a deviant role were it not for society's devaluation of these attributes in the first place, barring such a hypothetical contingency it remains the more persuasive argument in a democracy to be able to claim that the social injury from which one suffers was in no way self-inflicted.

Reprinted from *Social Problems,* 9 (1961), pp. 120–132, by permission of the Journal of Social Problems and the Institute for the Study of Social Problems. The Study from which this paper derives was supported by a grant from the Association for the Aid of Crippled Children. The author acknowledges the help and advice of Stephen A. Richardson and David Klein and wishes to thank Frances E. MacGregor, Cornell Medical Center, New York, for case materials from her research files. See Frances C. MacGregor et al., *Facial Deformities and Plastic Surgery: A Psychosocial Study* (Springfield, Ill.: Charles C. Thomas, 1953).

142

In these pages I wish to discuss another kind of non-self-inflicted social injury, the visible physical handicap. My aim though is not to survey and describe the many hardships of the visibly handicapped,[2] but to analyze certain facets of their coping behavior as it relates to the generalized imputations of deviance they elicit from society, imputations which many of them feel it necessary to resist and reject.

There are, of course, many areas in which such imputations bear heavily upon them: employment, friendship, courtship, sex, travel, recreation, residence, education. But the area I treat here is enmeshed to some extent in all of these without being as categorically specific as any. I refer to situations of sociability, and more specifically to that genre of everyday intercourse which has the characteristics of being: 1. face-to-face; 2. prolonged enough to permit more than a fleeting glimpse or exchange, but not so prolonged that close familiarity immediately ensues; 3. intimate to the extent that the parties must pay more than perfunctory attention to one another, but not so intimate that the customary social graces can be dispensed with; and 4. ritualized to the extent that all know in general what to expect, but not so ritualized as to preclude spontaneity and the slightly novel turn of events. A party or other social affair, a business introduction, getting to know a person at work, meeting neighbors, dealing with a salesman, conversing with a fellow passenger, staying at a resort hotel—these are but a few of the everyday social situations which fall within this portion of the spectrum of sociability, a range of involvement which can also be thought of as the zone of first impressions.

In interviews I conducted with a small number of very articulate and socially skilled informants who were visibly handicapped[3] I inquired into their handling of the imputation that they were not "normal, like everyone else." This imputation usually expresses itself in a pronounced stickiness of interactional flow and in the embarrassment of the normal by which he conveys the all too obvious message that he is having difficulty in relating to the handicapped person[4] as he would to "just an ordinary man or woman." Frequently he will make *faux pas,* slips of the tongue, revealing gestures and inadvertent remarks which overtly betray this attitude and place the handicapped person in an even more delicate situation.[5] The triggering of such a chain of interpersonal incidents is more likely with new persons than with those with whom the handicapped have well-established and continuing relations. Hence, the focus here is on more or less sociable occasions, it being these in which interactional discomfort is felt most acutely and coping behavior is brought into relief most sharply.

Because the visibly handicapped do not comprise a distinct minority group or subculture, the imputations of generalized deviance that they elicit from many normals are more nearly genuine interactional emergents than conventionalized sequelae to intergroup stereotyping as, for example, might obtain between a Negro and white.

A sociable encounter between a visibly handicapped person and a normal is usually more subject to ambiguity and experimentation in role postures than would be the case were the parties perceived by each other primarily in terms of member group characteristics. The visibly handicapped person must with each new acquaintance explore the *possibilities* of a relationship. As a rule there is no ready-made symbolic shorthand (e.g., "a Southerner can't treat a Negro as a social equal," "the Irish are anti-Semantic," "working-class people think intellectuals are effeminate") for anticipating the quality and degree of acceptance to be accorded him. The exchange must be struck before its dangers and potentialities can be seen and before appropriate corrective maneuvers can be fed into the interaction.[6]

THE HANDICAP AS THREAT
TO SOCIABLE INTERACTION

Before discussing how the visibly handicapped cope with difficult interaction, it is appropriate to first consider the general nature of the threat posed to the interactional situation *per se* as a result of their being perceived routinely (if not necessarily according to some prevalent stereotype) as "different, odd, estranged from the common run of humanity," etc.; in short, other than normal. (Achieving ease and naturalness of interaction with normals serves naturally as an important index to the handicapped person of the extent to which his preferred definition of self—i.e., that of someone who is merely different physically but not socially deviant—has been accepted. Symbolically, as long as the interaction remains stiff, strained or otherwise mired in inhibition, he has good reason to believe that he is in effect being denied the status of social normalcy he aspires to or regards as his due.) The threat posed by the handicap to sociability is, at minimum, fourfold: its tendency to become an exclusive focal point of the interaction, its potential for inundating expressive boundaries, its discordance with other attributes of the person and, finally, its ambiguity as a predicator of joint activity. These are not discrete entities in themselves as much as varying contextual emergents which, depending on the particular situation, serve singly or in combination to strain the framework of normative rules and assumptions in which sociability develops. Let us briefly consider each in turn.

A Focal Point of Interaction

The rules of sociable interation stipulate a certain generality and diffuseness in the attentions that parties are expected to direct to each other. Even if only superficially, one is expected to remain oriented to the whole person and to avoid the expression of a precipitous or fixed concern with any single attribute of his, however noteworthy or laudable it may be.[7] When meeting someone with a visible handicap, a number of perceptual and interpretative responses occur which make adherence to this rule tenuous for many. First, there is the matter of visibility as such. By definition, the visibly handicapped person cannot control his appearance sufficiently so that its striking particularity will not call a certain amount of concentrated attention to itself.[8] Second, the normal, while having his attention so narrowly channeled, is immediately constrained by the requirements of sociability to act as if he were oriented to the totality of the other rather than to that which is uppermost in his awareness, i.e., the handicap. Although the art of sociability may be said to thrive on a certain playful discrepancy between felt and expressed interests, it is perhaps equally true that when these are too discrepant strain and tension begin to undermine the interaction. (Conversely, when not discrepant enough, flatness and boredom frequently ensue.)[9] Whether the handicap is overtly and tactlessly responded to as such or, as is more commonly the case, no explicit reference is made to it, the underlying condition of heightened, narrowed, awareness causes the interaction to be articulated too exclusively in terms of it. This, as my informants described it, is usually accompanied by one or more of the familiar signs of discomfort and stickiness: the guarded references, the common everyday words suddenly made taboo, the fixed stare elsewhere, the artificial levity, the compulsive loquaciousness, the awkward solemnity.[10]

Second-order interactional elaborations of the underlying impedance are also not uncommon. Thus, for example, the normal may take great pains to disguise his awareness, an exertion that is usually so effortful and transparent that the handicapped person is then enjoined to disguise his awareness of the normal's disguise. In turn, the normal sensing the disguise erected in response to his disguise . . . and so forth. But unlike the infinitely multiplying reflections of an object located between opposing mirrors, this process cannot sustain itself for long without the pretense of unawareness collapsing, as witness the following report by a young woman:

> I get suspicious when somebody says, "Let's go for a uh, ah [imitates confused and halting speech] push with me down the hall," or something like that. This to me is suspicious because it means that they're aware, really aware, that there's a wheelchair here, and that this is probably uppermost with them. . . . A lot of people in trying to show you that they don't care that you're in a chair will do crazy things. Oh, there's one person I know who constantly kicks my chair, as if to say "I don't care that you're in a wheelchair. I don't even know that it's there." But that is just an indication that he *really* knows it's there.

Inundating Potential

The expressive requirements of sociability are such that rather strict limits obtain with respect to the types and amount of emotional display that are deemed appropriate. Even such fitting expressions as gaiety and laughter can, we know, reach excess and lessen satisfaction with the occasion. For many normals, the problem of sustaining sociable relations with someone who is visibly handicapped is not wholly that of the discrepancy of the inner feeling evoked, e.g., pity, fear, repugnance, avoidance. As with much else in sociability, a mere discrepancy of the actor's inner state with the social expectation need not result in a disturbance of interaction. In this instance it is specifically the marked dissonance of such emotions with those outward expressions deemed *most* salient for the occasion (e.g., pleasure, identification, warm interest) that seems to result frequently in an inundation and enfeeblement of the expressive controls of the individual. With some persons, the felt intrusion of this kind of situationally inappropriate emotion is so swift and overwhelming as to approximate a state of shock, leaving them expressively naked, so to speak. A pointed incident is told by a young blind girl:

> One night when I was going to visit a friend two of the people from my office put me into a taxi. I could tell that at first the taxi driver didn't know I was blind because for a while there he was quite a conversationalist. Then he asked what these sticks were for [a collapsible cane]. I told him it was a cane, and then he got so different. . . . He didn't talk about the same things that he did at first. Before this happened he joked and said, "Oh, you're a very quiet person. I don't like quiet people, they think too much." And he probably wouldn't have said that to me had he known I was blind because he'd be afraid of hurting my feelings. He didn't say anything like that afterwards.

The visibly handicapped are of course aware of this potential for inundating the expressive boundaries of situations and many take precautions to minimize such occurrences as much as possible. Thus, an interior decorator with a facial deformity would, when admitted to a client's house by the maid, station himself whenever he could so that the client's entrance would find him in a distantly direct line of vision from her. This, he stated, gave the client an opportunity to compose herself, as she might not be able to were she to come upon him at short range.

Contradiction of Attributes

Even when the inundating potential is well contained by the parties and the normal proves fully capable of responding in a more differentiated fashion to the variety of attributes presented by the handicapped person (e.g., his occupational identity, clothes, speech, intelligence, interests, etc.), there is frequently felt to be an unsettling discordance between these and the handicap. Sociable interaction is made more difficult as a result because many normals can only resolve the seeming incongruence by assimilating or subsuming (often in a patronizing or condescending way) the other attributes to that of the handicap, a phenomenon which in analogous connections has been well described by Hughes.[11] Thus, one informant, a strikingly attractive girl, reports that she frequently elicits from new acquaintances the comment, "How strange that someone so pretty should be in a wheelchair." Another informant, a professional worker for a government agency, tells of the fashionable female client who after having inquired on how long the informant had been in her job remarked, "How nice that you have something to do." Because the art of sociability deigns this kind of reductionism of the person, expressions of this type, even when much less blatant, almost invariably cast a pall on the interaction and embarrass the recovery of smooth social posture. The general threat inherent in the perceived discordance of personal attributes is given pointed expression by still another informant, a paraplegic of upper middle class background who comments on the attitude of many persons in his class:

> Now, where this affects them, where this brace and a crutch would affect them, is if they are going someplace or if they are doing something, they feel that, first, you would call attention and, second—you wouldn't believe this but it's true; I'll use the cruelest words I can—no cripple could possibly be in their social stratum.

Ambiguous Predicator

Finally, to the extent to which sociability is furthered by the free and spontaneous initiation of joint activity (e.g., dancing, games, going out to eat; in short, "doing things") there is frequently considerable ambiguity as regard the ability of the handicapped person to so participate and as regards the propriety of efforts which seek to ascertain whether he wants to. For the normal who has had limited experience with the handicapped it is by no means always clear whether, for example, a blind person can be included in a theater party or a crippled person in a bowling game. Even if not able to engage in the projected activity as such, will he want to come along mainly for the sake of company? How may his preferences be gauged without, on the one hand, appearing to make a thing out of the proposal or, on the other, conveying the impression that his needs and limitations are not being sufficiently considered? Should he refuse, is it genuine or is he merely offering his hosts a polite, though half-hearted, out? And, for each enigma thus posed for the normal, a counter-enigma is posed for the handicapped person. Do they really want him? Are they merely being polite? In spite of the open invitation, will his acceptance and presence lessen somehow their enjoyment of the activity? It is easy to see how a profusion of anticipatory ambiguities of this kind can strain the operative assumptions underlying sociable relations.

PROCESS OF DEVIANCE DISAVOWAL
AND NORMALIZATION

The above features then, may be said to comprise the threat that a visible handicap poses to the framework of rules and assumptions that guide sociability. We may now ask how socially adept handicapped persons cope with it so as to either keep it at bay, dissipate it, or lessen its impact upon the interaction. In answering this question we will not consider those broad personality adjustments of the person (e.g., aggression, denial, compensation, dissociation, etc.) which at a level once removed, so to speak, can be thought of as adaptive or maladaptive for, among other things, sociability. Nor, at the other extreme, is it possible in the allotted space to review the tremendous variety of specific approaches, ploys, and stratagems that the visibly handicapped employ in social situations. Instead, the analysis will attempt to delineate in transactional terms the stages through which a sociable relationship with a normal typically passes, assuming, of course, that the confrontation takes place and that both parties possess sufficient social skill to sustain a more than momentary engagement.

For present purposes we shall designate these stages as: 1. fictional acceptance, 2. the facilitation of reciprocal role-taking around a normalized projection of self, and 3. the institutionalization in the relationship of a definition of self that is normal in its moral dimension, however qualified it may be with respect to its situational contexts. As we shall indicate, the unfolding of these stages comprises what may be thought of as a process of deviance disavowal or normalization,[12] depending on whether one views the process from the vantage point of the deviant actor or his alters.[13]

Fictional Acceptance

In Western society the overture phases of a sociable encounter are to a pronounced degree regulated by highly elastic fictions of equality and normalcy. In meeting those with whom we are neither close nor familiar, manners dictate that we refrain from remarking on or otherwise reacting too obviously to those aspects of their persons which in the privacy of our thoughts betoken important differences between ourselves. In America at least, these fictions tend to encompass sometimes marked divergencies in social status as well as a great variety of expressive styles; and, it is perhaps the extreme flexibility of such fictions in our culture rather than, as is mistakenly assumed by many foreign observers, their absence that accounts for the seeming lack of punctiliousness in American manners. The point is nicely illustrated in the following news item:

NUDE TAKES A STROLL IN MIAMI

MIAMI, Fla., Nov. 13 (UPI)—A shapely brunette slowed traffic to a snail's pace here yesterday with a 20-minute nude stroll through downtown Miami. . . .

"The first thing I knew something was wrong," said Biscayne Bay bridgetender E. E. Currey, who was working at his post about one block away, "was when I saw traffic was going unusually slow."

Currey said he looked out and called police. They told him to stop the woman, he said.

Currey said he walked out of his little bridge house, approached the woman nervously, and asked, "Say, girl, are you lost?"

"Yes," she replied. "I'm looking for my hotel."

Currey offered help and asked, "Say, did you lose your clothes?"

"No," he said the woman replied, "Why?"

Currey said that he had to step away for a moment to raise the bridge for a ship and the woman walked away. . . .[14]

Unlike earlier societies and some present day ones in which a visible handicap automatically relegates the person to a castelike, inferior, status like that of mendicant, clown or thief—or more rarely to an elevated one like that of oracle or healer—in our society the visibly handicapped are customarily accorded, save by children,[15] the surface acceptance that democratic manners guarantee to nearly all. But, as regards sociability, this proves a mixed blessing for many. Although the polite fictions do afford certain entrée rights, as fictions they can too easily come to serve as substitutes for "the real thing" in the minds of their perpetrators. The interaction is kept starved at a bare subsistence level of sociability. As with the poor relation at the wedding party, so the reception given the handicapped person in many social situations: sufficient that he is here, he should not expect to dance with the bride.

At this stage of the encounter, the interactional problem confronting the visibly handicapped person is the delicate one of not permitting his identity to be circumscribed by the fiction while at the same time playing along with it and showing appropriate regard for its social legitimacy. For, as transparent and confining as the fiction is, it frequently is the only basis upon which the contact can develop into something more genuinely sociable. In those instances in which the normal fails or refuses to render even so small a gesture toward normalizing the situation, there exists almost no basis for the handicapped person to successfully disavow his deviance.[16] The following occurrence related by a young female informant is an apt, if somewhat extreme, illustration:

> I was visiting my girl friend's house and I was sitting in the lobby waiting for her when this woman comes out of her apartment and starts asking me questions. She just walked right up. I didn't know her from Adam, I never saw her before in my life. "Gee, what do you have? How long have you been that way? Oh gee, that's terrible." And so I answered her questions, but I got very annoyed and wanted to say, "Lady, mind your own business."

"Breaking Through"—Facilitating Normalized Role-Taking

In moving beyond fictional acceptance what takes place essentially is a redefinitional process in which the handicapped person projects images, attitudes, and concepts of self which encourage the normal to identify with him (take his role) in terms other than those associated with imputations of deviance.[17] Coincidentally, in broadening the area of minor verbal involvements, this also functions to drain away some of the stifling burden of unspoken awareness that, as we have seen, so taxes ease of interaction. The normal is cued into a larger repertoire of appropriate responses, and even when making what he, perhaps mistakenly, regards as an inappropriate response (for example, catching himself in the use of such a word as cripple or blind) the handicapped person can by his response relieve him of his embarrassment. One young informant insightfully termed the process "breaking through":

> The first reaction a normal individual or good-legger has is, "Oh gee, there's a fellow in a wheelchair," or "there's a fellow with a brace." And they don't say, "Oh gee, there is so-and-so, he's handsome" or "he's intelligent," or "he's a boor," or what have you. And then as the relationship develops they don't see the handicap. It doesn't exist any more. And that's the point that you as a handicapped individual become sensitive to. You know after talking with someone for awhile when they don't see the handicap any more. That's when you've broken through.

What this process signifies from a social psychological standpoint is that as the handicapped person expands the interactional nexus he simultaneously disavows the deviance latent in his status. Concurrently, to the degree to which the normal is led to reciprocally assume the redefining (and perhaps unanticipated) self-attitudes proffered by the handicapped person, he comes to normalize (i.e., view as more like himself) those aspects of the other which at first connoted deviance for him. (Sometimes, as we shall see, the normal's normalizing is so complete that it is unwittingly applied to situations in which the handicapped person cannot possibly function "normally" due to sheer physical limitations.) These dynamics might also be termed a process of identification. The term is immaterial, except that in "identifying" or "taking the role of the other" much more is implicated sociologically than a mere subjective congruence of responses. The fashioning of shared perspectives also implies a progressively more binding legitimation of the altered self-representations enacted in the encounter; that is, having once normalized his perception of the handicapped person, it becomes increasingly more compromising—self-discrediting, as it were—for the normal to revert to treating him as a deviant again.

The ways in which the visibly handicapped person can go about disavowing deviance are, as we have stated, many and varied. These range from relatively straightforward conversational offerings in which he alludes in passing to his involvement in a normal round of activities, to such forms of indirection as interjecting taboo or privatized references by way of letting the normal know that he does not take offense at the latter's uneasiness or regard it as a fixed obstacle toward achieving rapport. In the above quote, for example, the informant speaks of "good-leggers," an in-group term from his rehabilitation hospital days, which along with "dirty normals" he sometimes uses with new acquaintances "because it has a humorous connotation . . . and lots of times it puts people at their ease."[18]

Still other approaches to disavowing deviance and bridging fictional acceptance include: an especially attentive and sympathetic stance with respect to topics introduced by the normal, showing oneself to be a comic, wit, or other kind of gifted participant and, for some, utilizing the normalization potential inherent in being seen in in the company of a highly presentable normal companion.[19] These, and others too numerous to mention, are not of course invariably or equally successful in all cases; neither are such resources equally available to all handicapped persons, nor are the handicapped equally adept at exploiting them. As a class of corrective strategies however, they have the common aim of overcoming the interactional barrier that lies between narrow fictional acceptance and more spontaneous forms of relatedness.

Inextricably tied in with the matter of approach are considerations of setting, activity and social category of participants, certain constellations of which are generally regarded as favorable for successful deviance disavowal and normalization while others are thought unfavorable. Again, the ruling contingencies appear to be the extent to which the situation is seen as containing elements in it which: 1. contextually reduce the threat posed by the visible handicap to the rules and assumptions of the particular sociable occasion, and 2. afford the handicapped person opportunities for breaking through beyond fictional acceptance.

The relevance of one or both of these is apparent in the following social situations and settings about which my informants expressed considerable agreement as regards their preferences, aversions and inner reactions. To begin with, mention might again be made of the interactional rule violations frequently experienced at the hands of small children. Many of the informants were quite open in stating that a small child at a social occasion caused them much uneasiness and cramped their style because they were concerned with how, with other adults present, they would handle some barefaced question from the child. Another category of persons with whom many claimed to have difficulty is the elderly. Here the problem was felt to be the tendency of old people to indulge in patronizing sympathy, an attitude which peculiarly resists re-definition because of the fulsome virtue it attributes to itself. In another context several of the informants laid great stress on the importance of maintaining a calm exterior whenever the physical setting unavoidably exposed them to considerable bodily awkwardness. (At the same time, of course, they spoke of the wisdom of avoiding whenever possible, such occasions altogether.) Their attitude was that to expressively reflect gracelessness and a loss of control would result in further interactional obstacles toward assimilating the handicapped person to a normal status.

> It makes me uncomfortable to watch anyone struggling, so I try to do what I must as inconspicuously as possible. In new situations or in strange places even though I may be very anxious. I will maintain a deadly calm. For example, if people have to lift the chair and I'm scared that they are going to do it wrong, I remain perfectly calm and am very direct in the instructions I give.

As a final example, there is the unanimity with which the informants expressed a strong preference for the small, as against the large or semipublic social gathering. Not only do they believe that, as one handicapped person among the nonhandicapped, they stand out more at large social gatherings, but also that in the anonymity which numbers further there resides a heightened structural tendency for normals to practice avoidance relations with them. The easy assumption on such occasions is that "some other good soul" will take responsibility for socializing with the handicapped person. Even in the case of the handicapped person who is forward and quite prepared to take the initiative in talking to others, the organization and ecology of the large social gathering is usually such as to frustrate his attempts to achieve a natural, nondeviant place for himself in the group. As one young man, a paraplegic, explained:

> The large social gathering presents a special problem. It's a matter of repetition. When you're in a very large group of people whom you don't know, you don't have an opportunity of talking to three, four, or five at a time. Maybe you'll talk to one or two usually. After you've gone through a whole basic breakdown in making a relationship with one—after all, it's only a cocktail party—to do it again, and again, and again, it's wearing and it's no good. You don't get the opportunity to really develop something.

Institutionalization of the Normalized Relationship

In "breaking through" many of the handicapped are confronted by a delicate paradox, particularly in those of their relationships which continue beyond the immediate occasion. Having disavowed deviance and induced the other to respond to him as he would to a normal, the problem then becomes one of sustaining the normalized definition in the face of the many small amendments and qualifications that must frequently be made to it. The person confined to a wheelchair, for example, must brief a new acquaintance on what to do and how to help when they come to stairs, doorways, vehicle entrances, etc. Further briefings and rehearsals may be required for social obstructions as well: for example, how to act in an encounter with—to cite some typical situations at random—an overly helpful person, a waitress who communicates to the handicapped person only through his companion, a person who stares in morbid fascination.[20]

Generally, such amendments and special considerations are as much as possible underplayed in the early stages of the relationship because, as in the case of much minority group protest, the fundamental demand of the handicapped is that they first be granted an irreducibly equal and normal status, it being only then regarded as fitting and safe to admit to certain incidental incapacities, limitations, and needs. At some point however, the latter must be broached if the relationship to the normal is to endure in viable form. But to integrate effectively a major claim to normalcy with numerous minor waivers of the same claim is a tricky feat and one which exposes the relationship to the many situational and psychic hazards of apparent duplicity: the tension of transferring the special arrangements and understandings worked out between the two to situations and settings in which everyone else is behaving normally; the sometimes lurking suspicion of the one that it is only guilt or pity that cements the relationship, of the other that the infirmity is being used exploitatively, and of onlookers that there is something neurotic and unhealthy about it all.[21]

From my informants' descriptions it appears that this third, "normal, but . . ." stage of the relationship, if it endures, is institutionalized mainly in either one of two ways. In the first, the normal normalizes his perceptions to such an extent as to suppress his effective awareness of many of the areas in which the handicapped person's behavior unavoidably deviates from the normal standard. In this connection several of the informants complained that a recurring problem they have with close friends is that the latter frequently overlook the fact of the handicap and the restrictions it imposes on them. The friends thoughtlessly make arrangements and involve them in activities in which they, the handicapped, cannot participate conveniently or comfortably.

The other major direction in which the relationship is sometimes institutionalized is for the normal to surrender some of his normalcy by joining the handicapped person in a marginal, half-alienated, half-tolerant, outsiders orientation to "the Philistine world of normals."[22] Gowman[23] nicely describes the tenor and style of this relationship and its possibilities for sharply disabusing normals of their stereotyped approaches to the handicapped. *Épater le bourgeois* behavior is often prominently associated with it, as is a certain strictly in-group license to lampoon and mock the handicap in a way which would be regarded as highly offensive were it to come from an uninitiated normal. Thus, a blind girl relates how a sighted friend sometimes chides her by calling her "a silly blink." A paraplegic tells of the old friend who tries to revive his flagging spirits by telling him not to act "like a helpless cripple." Unlike that based on over-normalization, the peculiar strength of this relationship is perhaps its very capacity to give expressive scope to the negative reality of the larger world of which it is inescapably a part while simultaneously removing itself from a primary identification with it.

IMPLICATIONS

Two, more general, implications seem worth drawing from this analysis.[24]

First, in studies which trace the process wherein an actor who deviates comes to be increasingly defined as a deviant (e.g., the pre-mental patient, the pre-alcoholic, the pre-juvenile delinquent), unusual prominence is given to the normalizing behavior of those close to him (spouse, parents, friends, etc.). The picture that emerges is one of these persons assuming nearly the whole burden—by rationalizing, denying and overlooking his offensive acts—of attempting to reestablish a socially acceptable relationship with him. He is depicted typically as compulsively wedded to his deviance and incapable or uninterested in making restitutive efforts of his own. Finally, following some critical act of his, normalization fails in toto and community agencies are called in to relieve the primary group of its unmanageable burden.

There is much about this picture that is doubtlessly true and consonant with the ascertainable facts as we later come to learn of them from family, friends, police, courts and social agencies. We may question, however, whether it is a wholly balanced picture and whether, given the situational biases of these informational sources, all of the relevant facts have had an equal chance to surface. The perspective developed here suggests that it may be useful to consider whether, and to what extent, the deviator himself is not also engaged, albeit ineffectively, in somehow trying to sustain a normal definition of his person. Were research to indicate that such is the case, we might then ask what it is about his reparative efforts and the situations in which they occur that, as contrasted with the subjects of this study, so often lead to failure and an exacerbation of the troublesome behavior. (We probably will never know, except inferentially by gross extrapolation, of the possibly many cases in which some such interactive process succeeds in favorably resolving the deviating behavior.) In other words, as against the simplistic model of a compulsive deviant and a futile normalizer we would propose one in which it is postulated that both are likely to become engaged in making corrective interactional efforts toward healing the breach. And, when such efforts fail, as they frequently do, it is as important in accounting for the failure to weigh the interactional dynamics and situational contexts of these efforts as it is the nature of the deviant acts and the actor.

Second, we would note that the interactional problems of the visibly handicapped are not so dissimilar from those which all of us confront, if only now and then and to a lesser degree. We too on occasion find ourselves in situations in which some uncamouflageable attribute of ours jars the activity and the expectations of our company. We too, if we wish to sustain—and, as is typically the case, our company wishes us to sustain—a fitting and valued representation of ourselves, will tacitly begin to explore with them ways of redressing, insulating, and separating the discrepant attribute from ourselves.[25] Our predicament though is much less charged with awareness and is more easily set to rights than that of the visibly handicapped person and his company. But it is precisely this exaggeration of a common interactional predicament that affords us an added insight into the prerequisites and unwitting assumptions of sociable behavior in general. Put differently, it can be said that our understanding of a mechanism is often crude and incomplete until it breaks down and we try to repair it. Breakdown and repair of interaction is what many of the visibly handicapped experience constantly in their lives. In studying this with them we are also studying much about ourselves of which we were heretofore unaware.

NOTES

[1]Following Lemert, as used here the term deviant (or deviance) refers 1) to a person's deviation from prevalent or valued norms, 2) to which the community-at-large reacts negatively or punitively, 3) so as to then lead the person to define his situation largely in terms of this reaction. All three conditions must be fulfilled for it to be said that deviance exists (secondary deviation, in Lemert's definition). In this sense the Negro, the career woman, the criminal, the Communist, the physically handicapped, the mentally ill, the homosexual, to mention but a few, are all deviants, albeit in different ways and with markedly different consequences for their life careers. Edwin M. Lemert, *Social Pathology*, New York: McGraw-Hill, 1951, 75–77.

[2]Comprehensive and excellent reviews are to be found in R. G. Barker et al., *Adjustment to Physical Handicap and Illness: A Survey of the Social Psychology of Physique and Disability*, New York: Soc. Sci. Res. Council, 1953, Bulletin 55, 2nd ed. and Beatrice A. Wright, *Physical Disability, A Psychological Approach*, New York: Harper, 1960.

[3]Six were orthopedically handicapped, three blind, and two facially disfigured. Additional detailed biographical and clinical materials were secured on one blind and four facially disfigured persons, making for a total of sixteen records.

[4]Throughout this paper, whether or not the term "handicap" or "handicapped" is joined by the qualifier "visible," it should be read in this way. Unfortunately, it will not be possible to discuss here that which sociologically distinguishes the situation of the visibly handicapped from that of persons whose physical handicaps are not visible or readily apparent, and how both differ from what is termed the 'sick role.' These are though important distinctions whose analysis might illuminate key questions in the study of deviance.

[5]In the sections that follow the discussion draws heavily on the framework of dramaturgic analysis developed by Erving Goffman. See especially his "Alienation from Interaction," *Human Relations,* 10 (1957), 47–60; "Embarrassment and Social Organization," *American Journal of Sociology,* 62 (November, 1956), 264–71; *Presentation of Self in Everyday Life,* New York: Doubleday and Co., Inc., 1959.

[6]Cf. Anselm Strauss, *Mirrors and Masks,* Glencoe, Ill.: Free Press, 1959, 31–43.

[7]Kurt H. Wolff, ed., *The Sociology of Georg Simmel.* Glencoe, Ill.: Free Press, 1950, 45–46.

[8]Cf. R. K. White, B. A. Wright and T. Dembo, "Studies in Adjustment to Visible Injuries," *Journal of Abnormal and Social Psychology,* 43 (1948), 13–28.

[9]In a forthcoming paper. "Fun in Games: An Analysis of the Dynamics of Social Interaction," Goffman discusses the relationship between spontaneous involvement in interaction and the manner in which "external attributes" —those which in a formal sense are not situationally relevant—are permitted to penetrate the situation's boundaries.

[10]Cf. Goffman on "other-consciousness" as a type of faulty interaction, "Alienation from Interaction," *op. cit.*

[11]Everett C. Hughes, *Men and Their Work,* Glencoe, Ill.: Free Press, 1958, 102–106.

[12]As used here the term "normalization" denotes a process whereby alter for whatever reason comes to view as normal and morally acceptable that which initially strikes him as odd, unnatural, "crazy," deviant, etc., irrespective of whether his perception was in the first instance reasonable, accurate or justifiable. See Charlotte G. Schwartz, "Perspectives on Deviance—Wives' Definitions of Their Husbands' Mental Illness," *Psychiatry*, 20 (August, 1957), 275-91.

[13]Because of the paper's focus on the visibly handicapped person, in what follows his interactional work is highlighted to the relative glossing over of that of the normal. Acutally, the work of normalization calls for perhaps as much empathic expenditure as that of deviance disavowal and is, obviously, fully as essential for repairing the interactional breach occasioned by the encounter.

[14]*San Francisco Chronicle*, November 14, 1960.

[15]The blunt questions and stares of small children are typically of the 'Emperor's Clothes' variety. "Mister, why is your face like that?" "Lady, what are you riding around in that for? Can't you walk?" Nearly all of my informants spoke of how unnerving such incidents were for them, particularly when other adults were present. None the less, some claimed to value the child's forthrightness a good deal more than they did the genteel hypocrisy of many adults.

[16]On the other side of the coin there are of course some handicapped persons who are equally given to undermining sociable relations by intentionally flaunting the handicap so that the fiction becomes extremely difficult to sustain. An equivalent of the "bad nigger" type described by Strong, such persons were (as in Strong's study) regarded with a mixture of admiration and censure by a number of my informants. Admiration, because the cruel stripping away of pretenses and forcing of issues was thought morally refreshing, especially since, as the informants themselves recognized, many normals refuse to grant anything more than fictional acceptance while at the same time imagining themselves ennobled for having made the small sacrifice. Censure, because of the conviction that such behavior could hardly improve matters in the long run and would make acceptance even more difficult for other handicapped persons who later came into contact with a normal who had received such treatment. Cf. Samuel M. Strong, "Negro-White Relations as Reflected in Social Types," *American Journal of Sociology*, 52, (July, 1946), p. 24.

[17]George H. Mead, *Mind, Self and Society*, Chicago: University of Chicago Press, 1934. See also the discussion on interaction in Strauss, *op. cit.*, 44-88.

[18]Parallel instances can easily be cited from minority group relations as, for example, when a Jew in conversation with a non-Jew might introduce a Yiddish phrase by way of suggesting that the other's covert identification of him as a Jew need not inhibit the interaction unduly. In some situations this serves as a subtle means of declaring, "O.K., I know what's bothering you. Now that I've said it, let's forget about it and move on to something else."

[19]Alan G. Gowman, "Blindness and the Role of the Companion," *Social Problems*, 4 (July, 1956).

[20]Gowman, *op. cit.*

[21]The rhetoric of race relations reflects almost identical rationalizations and "insights" which are meant among other things to serve as cautions for would-be transgressors. "Personally I have nothing against Negroes [the

handicapped], but it would be bad for my reputation if I were seen socializing with them." "She acts nice now, but with the first argument she'll call you a dirty Jew [good-for-nothing cripple]." "Regardless of how sympathetic you are toward Negroes [the disabled], the way society feels about them you'd have to be a masochist to marry one."

[22]Students of race relations will recognize in this a phenomenon closely akin to "inverse passing" as when a white becomes closely identified with Negroes and passes into a Negro subculture.

[23]Gowman, op. cit.

[24]I am indebted to Sheldon Messinger for his valuable comments in these connections.

[25]Goffman, "Embarrassment and Social Organization."

Part V

THE ROLE OF
PEOPLE PROCESSING
INSTITUTIONS

10

Police Discretion in Emergency Apprehension of Mentally Ill Persons

EGON BITTNER

The official mandate of the police includes provisions for dealing with mentally ill persons. Since such dealings are defined in terms of civil law procedures, the mandate of the police is not limited to persons who for reasons of illness fail to observe the law. Rather, in suitable circumstances the signs of mental illness, or a competent allegation of mental illness, are in themselves the proper business of the police and can lead to authorized intervention. The expressed legal norms governing police involvement specify two major alternatives. On the one hand, policemen may receive court orders directing them to locate, apprehend, and convey named persons to specified hospitals for psychiatric observation and/or sanity hearings. On the other hand, policemen are authorized by statute to apprehend and convey to hospitals persons whom they perceive as ill, on an emergency basis. The first form parallels the common procedures of serving court warrants, while the second form involves the exercise of discretionary freedom that is ordinarily associated with making arrests without a warrant.[1]

The study reported in this paper concerns the rules and considerations underlying the exercise of discretion in emergency apprehensions.

Reprinted from *Social Problems,* 14 (1967), pp. 278–292, by permission of the Journal of Social Problems and the Institute for the Study of Social Problems. This research was supported in part by Grant 64-1-35 from the California Department of Mental Hygiene. The author gratefully acknowledges help from Sheldon L. Messinger in preparing this paper.

The findings are based on ten months of field work with the uniformed police patrol of a large West Coast city, and on psychiatric records of the hospital receiving all police referrals.[2] We shall first consider certain attitudinal and organizational factors involved in making emergency apprehensions. Next, we shall discuss the manifest properties of cases in which emergency apprehensions are frequently made. Finally, we shall deal with procedures directed toward recognized mentally ill persons who are not referred to the hospital. In the conclusion, we shall argue that the decision to invoke the law governing emergency apprehensions is not based on an appraisal of objective features of cases. Rather, the decision is a residual resource, the use of which is determined largely by the absence of other alternatives. The domain of alternatives is found in normal peace-keeping activities in which considerations of legality play a decidedly subordinate role. We shall also allude to the fact that our interpretation has important bearing on the problem of police discretion to invoke the law in general.[3]

ORGANIZATIONAL AND ATTITUDINAL FACTORS INFLUENCING EMERGENCY APPREHENSIONS

The statutory authorization under which apprehensions of the mentally ill are made provides that an officer may take steps to initiate confinement in a psychiatric hospital when he believes "as the result of his own observations, that the person is mentally ill and because of his illness is likely to injure himself or others if not immediately hospitalized."[4] It is fair to say that under ordinary circumstances police officers are quite reluctant to invoke this law. That is, in situations where, according to their own judgment, they are dealing with an apparently mentally ill person they will generally seek to employ other means to bring the existing problem under control. This does not mean that they attempt to deal with the problem as if it did not involve a mentally ill person or as if this person's illness were none of their business. It merely means that they will try to avoid taking him to the hospital.

The avoidance of emergency apprehensions has a background that might be called doctrinal.[5] To take someone to the hospital means giving the facts of his illness formal recognition and using them as grounds for official action. The police, however, disavow all competence in matters pertaining to psychopathology and seek to remain within the lines of restraint that the disavowal imposes. Accordingly, the diagnosis they propose is not only emphatically provisional but also, in a sense, incidental. From their point of view it is not enough for a case to be serious in a "merely" psychiatric sense. To warrant official police action a case must also present a serious police problem.

As a general rule, the elements that make a case a serious police matter are indications that if a referral is not made, external troubles will proliferate. Among these, danger to life, to physical health, to property, and to order in public places are objects of prominent concern. Estimating the risk of internal deterioration of the psychiatric condition as such is perceived as lying outside of the scope of police competence and thus not an adequate basis for making emergency apprehensions.

While a narrow construction of the police mandate might have the consequence of eliminating certain cases from the purview of official police interest, it does not eliminate the possibility of liberal use of the authorization. Thus, it might be expected that officers would tend to refer relatively few persons who are merely very ill psychiatrically but many persons who are troublesome without being very ill. This expectation seems especially reasonable since the police recently have been denied the use of certain coercive means they have employed in the past to control troublesome persons.[6] On a practical level such procedures would simply follow considerations of expediency, with the law providing a particular method and justification for taking care of matters that need be taken care of.[7] Indeed, given the heavy emphasis that mental hygiene receives in police training, it would be scarcely appropriate to attribute devious motives to the police if they were to use the "narrow construction" of the law "widely," for in many instances of untoward, but not necessarily illegal, behavior, the evidence of more or less serious psychopathology is close to the surface.[8] In fact, however, policemen do not make such use of the law. Instead, they conform in practice very closely to the views they profess. To make an emergency apprehension they require that there be indications of serious external risk accompanied by signs of a serious psychological disorder. There exist several attitudinal and organizational factors that help to explain the reluctance of the police to take official steps on the basis of the assumption or allegation of mental illness.

First, the views and knowledge of the police about mental illness are in close agreement with the views and knowledge of the public in general. Policemen, like everyone else, appear to have a correct conception of the nature of mental illness, in terms of standards of modern psychiatry, but like everyone else they avail themselves of various forms of denial when it comes to doing something about it.[9] The facts come into consciousness, as it were, without implying practical consequences; or, at least, the import of the facts is set aside in view of other considerations. Since the police almost always act on fragmentary information, their reasons for not taking any official steps are posted, among others, in the undetermined aspects of the case that must be presumed to have some undefined relevance. For example, one of the possibilities that officers must always consider is the chance that their involvement could be exploited by unknown persons for unknown reasons. Since they are not expert in symptoms of psychopathology, their desire to avoid possible future embarrassment is quite strong.

Second, policemen confront perversion, disorientation, misery, irresoluteness, and incompetence much more often than any other social agent. They can readily point to a large number of persons who, to all appearances, are ready for the "booby hatch," but who nevertheless seem to lead such lives as they can without outside aid or intervention. Against this background the requirement that one should have a good brain and an even temper belong to the same category of wishes as that one should have a large and steady income. Thus, making emergency apprehensions is, among others, a matter of economy. Lower the standards somewhat and the number of apprehensions might be multiplied by a substantial factor. Similar considerations apply to making various types of arrests. Though the police could readily multiply the number of arrests for some petty offenses, they somehow manage to produce just the right number to keep the courts busy and the jails full. With the same uncanny instinct they burden the hospital just to the limit of its capacity.

Third, though policemen readily acknowledge that dealing with mentally ill persons is an integral part of their work, they hold that it is not a proper task for them. Not only do they lack training and competence in this area but such dealings are stylistically incompatible with the officially propounded conception of the policeman's principal vocation. It involves none of the skills, acumen, and prowess that characterize the ideal image of a first-rate officer. Given the value that is assigned to such traits in furthering a man's career, and as grounds for esteem among his co-workers, it is a foregone conclusion that conveying a "mental case" to the hospital will never take the place of catching Willie Sutton in the choice of worthwhile activities. The opportunities for making spectacular arrests are not so widely available to the uniformed patrolman as to compete for attention with the emergency apprehensions of mentally ill persons, but the established ways of collecting credits with one's superiors work against the development of voluntary interest with patients.

Fourth, officers complain that taking someone to the psychiatric service of the hospital is a tedious, cumbersome, and uncertain procedure. They must often wait a long time in the admitting office and are occasionally obliged to answer questions of the admitting psychiatrist that appear to place their own judgment in doubt. They must also reckon with the possibility of being turned down by the psychiatrist, in which case they are left with an aggravated problem on their hands. The complaints about the hospital must be understood in the light of a strong and widely respected rule of police procedure. The rule demands that an officer bring all cases assigned to him to some sort of closure within reasonable limits of time and effort. The ability to take care of things in a way that avoids protracted and complicated entanglements and does not cause repercussions is, in fact, a sign of accomplished craftsmanship in police work that runs a close second to the ability to make important arrests. Relative to this standard, contacts with the hospital and the attitudes of psychiatrists are a source of endless frustration. Policemen are often puzzled by the hospital's refusal to lend its resources to help in keeping life outside free of violence and disorder; and, though they are relatively rarely turned down by admitting psychiatrists, many officers can cite cases in which persons who were not accepted into the hospital brought grief upon themselves and others.

Fifth, in addition to these experiences, certain other facts about the hospital exercise a restraining influence upon the making of emergency apprehensions. All officers are explicitly aware that taking someone to the hospital is a civil rather than a criminal matter. They are continually reminded of this distinction, and they employ the appropriate linguistic conventions in referring to such cases and in talking with ill persons and their relatives. The actual situation belies all this euphemizing and officers are unavoidably aware of this too. Ill persons are, indeed, arrested on account of being ill. They are not taken to the jail, to be sure, but they are nevertheless locked up. The knowledge that the mental hospital is a place in which to lock people up is inferentially prior to the making of emergency apprehensions. It is only natural that officers would infer from witnessed hospital procedures with mentally ill patients the conditions that presumably warrant them. To think otherwise would impugn the whole system, which operates not only under medical supervision but also under the auspices of the courts. Thus, in making an emergency apprehension the officer has to consider whether the person in question presents risks of such magnitude as warrant his confinement together with the rest of the "crazy" people who apparently require this sort of treatment.[10]

CONDITIONS SURROUNDING
EMERGENCY APPREHENSIONS

Despite the strong reluctance of the police, emergency apprehensions of mentally ill persons are quite frequent. Indeed, officers of the uniformed patrol make them about as often as they arrest persons for murder, all types of manslaughter, rape, robbery, aggravated assault, and grand theft, taken together; and more than one-fifth of all referrals to the receiving psychiatric service of the public hospital come from this source.[11]

In only a very few instances does the emergency apprehension involve the use of physical coercion. In most cases patients are passively compliant or at least manageable by means of verbal influence.

At times patients go willingly, or perhaps even voluntarily.[12] In approximately half of the cases policemen encounter the patient without any warning. This happens either when officers run into the person in the course of patrolling or when they are dispatched to some address by radio, without any indication of the nature of the problem they will have to deal with. In the other half, officers are informed that they will have to deal with a possible "mental case."[13] Though the observations on which this account is based do not permit a firm inference in this matter, it appears that prior labeling does not play a role in the formation of the policeman's decision to make an apprehension.

Five types of circumstances in which emergency apprehensions are made anywhere from often to virtually always can be isolated. It is important to define the nature of this inventory. Policemen typically do not reach the conclusion that an apprehension should be made by searching for, or finding, such features as we shall enumerate. Thus, these are not, in any real sense, criterion situations. Furthermore, each of the five types encompasses cases that are linked by the rule of analogy rather than by the rule of identity.[14] By this we do not mean merely that actual instances differ over a wide range of permissible variations. Rather, we propose that the membership of any particular case in a class, or in the scheme of classes in general, is based less on the presence or absence of specific characteristics than on the judgment that the case *amounts* to being of this or that class. If such a conclusion is to be reached, the case must not be allowed to dissolve into its particulars. Instead, the conclusion is reached as much by attending to the case as such, as it is reached by attending to its contextual background.

The following three horizons of context appear to matter in cases of referable mental illness: First, the *scenic* horizon, consisting of all the more or less stable features of the background that can be brought into play as employable resources to handle the problem, or that may assume the character of added reasons for making the emergency apprehension. Second, the *temporal* horizon, including both the changing nature of the problem as it is being attended to and what can be known or surmised about its past and future. Third, the *manipulative* horizon, which consists of considerations of practicality from the standpoint of the police officer. For example, an officer may encounter a mentally ill person in some such circumstances as we shall presently describe. He may learn that the person is a member of a stable and resourceful kinship group and that relatives can be mobilized to take care of him. In addition, there is information that the person has been in a similar state before and that he received outpatient psychiatric attention at that time. Whether this person will be moved to the hospital might then depend on whether others can take over within the limits of time the officer can allocate to waiting for them to arrive on the scene. The manipulative horizon is of particular interest and we shall discuss it more extensively in the section of the paper dealing with persons who are not referred to the hospital.

One further explanation—our description of the five categories of cases does not imply that officers themselves employ subcategories to classify mentally ill persons when they refer them to the hospital on an emergency basis. Rather, we propose the inventory as a scheme of prototypes to which policemen analogize in practice when they are confronted with a mentally ill person.

1. When there is evidence that a person has attempted, or is attempting, suicide he is virtually always taken to the hospital. Occasionally officers have doubts about the genuineness of the attempt, but such doubts do not seem to weigh significantly against making the apprehension. In some instances the evidence in support of the presumption that an attempt has been made, or is contemplated, is ambiguous. In such cases the prevailing practice is to act on the basis of positive indications. Furthermore, the information that an attempt has been made appears to be a sufficient indication in itself for an emergency apprehension. Not only is it not necessary for the victim to exhibit other signs of a mental disorder but there is no way in which a person can demonstrate that he is not in need of psychiatric attention, once the facts of the attempt have been adequately established. Both the most playful and the most rationally considered suicide attempts are treated as suggesting serious morbidity. The only circumstance under which officers can be dissuaded from taking a potential victim to the hospital is when a physician officially assumes responsibility for the case. Finally, when officers confront a person who shows patent signs of a mental disorder and they learn that this person has in the past attempted suicide, this information is apt to contribute significantly to the decision to make an emergency apprehension, even if the earlier attempts are not clearly connected with the present episode. In short, suicide presents the "ideal" combination of serious psychopathology and serious police business.

2. When the signs of a serious psychological disorder, i.e., expressions of radically incongruous affect or thought, are accompanied by distortions of normal physical appearance, the person in question is usually taken to the hospital. Such things as injuries of unknown origin, seizures, urinary incontinence, odd posturing, nudity, extreme dirtiness, and so on, all tend to augment the import of psychological indications. All such features are perceived as signifying loss of control over one's appearance and as adequate grounds to expect a further proliferation of external problems. An apprehension will not be made, however, if the situation contains features indicating a mere momentary lapse of control. For example, in a case in which the police were summoned to deal with a severely retarded person living with her parents, the officers helped in restoring the normally functioning restraint and supervision. Scenically, the home environment offered a sufficient

guarantee of control; historically, the situation was known to have been managed adequately in the past; and, manipulatively, the disruption could be remedied within reasonable time and with the cooperation of all parties who had a legitimate stake in the case.

3. When the signs of serious psychological disorder are expressed in highly agitated forms, and especially when they are accompanied by incipient or actual acts of violence, the person is often taken to the hospital. Two further conditions must be met, however, before the apprehension is seriously considered. The violence or the threat of violence must be nontrivial. For example, a feeble and senile old woman assaulting her normally healthy son will not be taken to the hospital, but the son may be advised about the availability of hospitalization. Furthermore, the agitated person must be largely unresponsive to efforts to pacify him.

4. Persons who appear to be seriously disoriented, or who by acting incongruously create a nuisance in a public place, are often taken to the hospital. Ordinarily policemen will make an effort to induce the person to leave the scene while helping him on his way to his normal habitat. Only when it becomes clear that such a person cannot be expediently returned to a sheltered place, or remanded to some caretaker, and when he is in danger of suffering injury due to accident or exposure, will he be taken to the hospital.

5. In the cases named so far the police act mainly on the basis of firsthand observation. Though there is always a certain amount of received information present, it plays a secondary role in the decision-making. The fifth category, however, is based primarily on received information. When requests for police aid come from complainants who stand to the allegedly mentally ill person in some sort of instrumental relationship, i.e., from physicians, lawyers, teachers, employers, landlords, and so on, the police generally, though by no means always, move the patient to the hospital.[15] It is usually assumed that the instrumentally related persons have exhausted their power and duty to help before calling the police and that there is little else left to do but to make an emergency apprehension. Interestingly, however, similar requests, in quite similar circumstances, made by family members, friends, roommates, or neighbors are usually not honored. Thus, for example, a severely depressed person may be taken to the hospital from his place of employment, on the urging of a doctor or his employer, both of whom presumably have already attempted alternative solutions, while he would be left in the care of his parent with the advice that the parent seek hospitalization for the patient.

The five types of circumstances in which emergency apprehensions are typically made are, of course, not mutually exclusive. Indeed, most actual cases are, in terms of their external circumstances, over-determined. The general impression one gets from observing the police is that, except for cases of suicide attempts, the decision to take someone to the hospital is based on overwhelmingly conclusive evidence of illness. The very stringency of criteria would lead one to expect that the police often deal with persons who are also seriously ill but whom they do not take to the hospital. In our description of the five types we have already alluded to the fact that this is in fact so. We have also mentioned earlier that such persons do not fall outside the purview of police interest once it is decided that they need not be apprehended. We now turn to the description of alternative methods of handling mentally ill persons, about which no records are kept.

NON-OFFICIAL WAYS OF DEALING WITH MENTALLY ILL PERSONS

The following description of police dealings with mentally ill persons concerns cases in which formal emergency apprehensions are not made. We shall concentrate on encounters in which officers explicitly recognize signs of mental illness and in which they treat the illness as the primary and, in most instances, the only business at hand. That is, we will not be dealing with cases such as, for example, those involving an offender about whom policemen say, after they have arrested him, "What a nut!" Nor will we deal with cases involving various types of troublesome persons who are perceived to be, among other things, "slightly crazy." To be sure, in actual police work there exists no clear-cut dividing line segregating persons who are blatantly mentally ill from persons who are "slightly crazy." For clarity, however, we shall concentrate on extreme cases.

De Facto Emergency Apprehension

To begin, we must consider certain types of police involvement that straddle the borderline between making and not making apprehensions. In such cases the patient usually ends up in the hospital but the police manage to avoid taking formal action. Insofar as the officers have no official part in the decision and thus no responsibilities, these cases might be considered de facto but not de jure emergency apprehensions. Occasionally policemen are summoned to aid in the move of a recalcitrant patient. The move is actually under way and the officers are merely expected, in their own words, to "do the dirty work." Though officers cannot readily avoid responding to such requests they typically do not employ coercive means. Instead, they remain in the background as a safety precaution against the possibility that the situation might get out of hand. Beyond that, they disperse curious onlookers, and at times provide help such as calling for an ambulance or a taxi. By and large they do nothing that will change the course of the ongoing development. They interpret their presence as having the value of making something that is already fully determined as peaceful and painless as possible. Insofar as they speak to the patient at all, they restrict their remarks to indicating that the move is legitimate and in his best interest. In fact, the officers are usually the only persons on the scene who listen attentively to the patient and who use the leverage of trust to facilitate the move. Though such cases do not involve police initiative and involve no police decisions, the successful accomplishment of these referrals actually does depend on the availability of police aid. The very fact that the person who made the decision solicited help is an indication that he could probably not have prevailed by himself, or at least not on that occasion. Generally, police officers do not accompany the patient to the hospital and their involvement is not a matter of record.

Another form of de facto apprehension occurs when officers transport a person whom they recognize as mentally ill to a medical emergency service. In such cases it is necessary, of course, that there be present some sort of physical complaint in addition to the psychiatric complaint. It is generally expected that the admitting physician will make the further referral to the psychiatric service. By this method policemen avoid taking formal action on account of mental illness and also, incidentally, avoid having to deal with psychiatric staff, which they find much more cumbersome than dealing with medical staff. Only rarely are records kept of these cases; such records as do exist identify the interventions as aiding a sick person rather than making an emergency apprehension.

Restitution of Control

By far the larger number of police encounters with mentally ill persons results neither in de jure nor in de facto emergency apprehensions. Rather, the involvements begin and end in the field. No other social agency, either legal or medical, participated in these cases and the policeman acts as the terminal, all-purpose remedial agent.

While discussing typical emergency apprehension situations we mentioned that officers often try to find competent persons to whom they may relinquish the care of the patient, or they try to return the ill person to his normal habitat in which he presumably can manage his affairs with minimal adequacy. Only in rare instances is this a simple "lost persons" problem. In these relatively rare cases, persons with stable social ties and fixed positions in the community escape the normally functioning controls or suffer a breakdown away from home. Whenever circumstances indicate that this is the case, the police will bring their technical communication and transportation facilities into play to locate caretakers for the patient. Though this is by no means always easy, it is a relatively simple problem. It may not be possible to find the caretakers within the time that can be allocated to the search, but the problem at least has a solution. In fact, when the caretakers cannot be expediently located, and the ill person is taken to the hospital, the search for the caretakers continues for the sake of informing them where the patient is. As a last resort, the identity of the lost mentally ill person is entered in the lost persons record to make it possible to respond to inquiries of caretakers. In general, however, the police are ready to devote a good deal of effort to returning persons to circumstances in which they are sheltered. As might be expected, however, persons with stable social ties and fixed positions in the community only rarely depend on the aid of the police and in many such instances the fact that the person is abroad is known before he is located because of inquiries of frantic relatives.

Much more difficult are cases in which the ill person cannot be presumed to be someone's responsibility in a structured sense, and whose living arrangements are unstable. In such cases the high proficiency of the police in tracing leads and in locating viable support are noteworthy. To solve such problems the officer invokes his detailed knowledge of people and places in the district he patrols. This knowledge, as often as not, permits him to guess who the person is and where he normally belongs. Failing this, the officer will know where to look and whom to ask for information. Bits and fragments of evidence have high informational value because the officer can fill in the missing parts out of past experiences in the same locale and with related persons.

This informational advantage is useful not only in the search for caretakers but also functions as the context for the considered transfer of responsibility. For while it is true that officers generally welcome opportunities to be rid of a mentally ill person, they are not uncritical about whom they will yield to. In one observed instance, for example, a young woman in agitated distress was taken to the hospital in part because her fiancé arrived on the scene and proposed to take over. Prior to his arrival the officers were about ready to leave the patient in the care of her mother and a neighbor who appeared to have a soothing influence on her. The entry of the fiancé seemed quite innocuous to the observer, but the officers gathered from his remarks that the arrangements he had in mind were not only not feasible but even destructive. The evaluation was possible because the officers knew many factual details about the places, persons, and arrangements the man envisioned. It is important to emphasize that the critical approach is not pursued by deliberate inquiry and scrutiny of all aspects of cases and decisions. Rather, the informational advantage of the officers automatically raises the level of demand for plausibility. That is, they can judge whether some proposed solution is practical and acceptable with reference to empirical details of particular known places, at specified times, and in known social contexts. In the instance cited, this background information persuaded the officers that the patient could not be left safely unattended.

Among the types of persons to whom policemen most readily transfer responsibilities are family members and physicians. It is, however, not unusual to find neighbors, hotel clerks, landlords, bartenders, or shopkeepers entrusted with someone who is mentally ill. Especially in blighted parts of the city such persons are known to "keep an eye" on certain others. In such areas the policeman often stands in the midst of a referral and information system that is unstable and informally fluid, but the network of connections is so rich and ramified that an accredited member of the system is scarcely ever completely at a loss. For example, an officer might learn from a news vendor that a certain bartender might know someone who knows something about a senile old lady. If the bartender does not happen to be on duty, some patron in the bar, or the pawnbroker across the street might know. Here is it important to emphasize that news vendors and bartenders are not so much good sources of information, as that they become good sources of information, and incidentally also good resource persons, when the officer knows them personally and is personally known to them. The officer's superior competence is to a large extent dependent on the fact that he is accepted as a powerful and in certain ways uniquely authoritative member of a system of mutual aid.

Unfortunately, we know very little about the ways in which people in blighted areas of the city corroborate each others' identities and augment each others' feeble powers. But there is no doubt that the policeman is the only social agent who has some access to the functioning of this arrangement, and the only one who can employ it knowledgeably for the protection and aid of its members. The unique effectiveness of the officer as a quasi-member of this community hinges on the fact that he can invoke the powers of coercion; the effectiveness of this resource would be, however, drastically reduced if he were not also an insider who understands the dominant interests and attitudes of the denizens. It is the officer's grasp of the stable aspects of the social structure of life in slums, in rooming house sections, and in business districts—aspects that often elude the attention of outside observers— that permits him to find alternatives to the emergency hospitalization of mentally ill persons. In certain ways, dealing with persons who inhabit blighted parts of urban areas is an easier task for a seasoned foot patrolman than dealing with persons who have stable addresses and social ties, although, of course, once the latter are located a more permanent solution is guaranteed.

The relative stability of circumstances to which a mentally ill person can be returned is, of course, distributed on a continuum. At one extreme there are those patients who need only be conveyed to worried relatives, and at the other extreme there are those who can only be returned to a status of inconspicuous anonymity. With the latter, as with those who have some tenuous ties, the problem of letting the patient slip back into his normal groove is adumbrated with questions whether the normally working controls can be entrusted with "taking care of the problem." In terms of the policeman's own standards of proper procedure it is scarcely ever sufficient to remove the patient from sight. What is intended, instead, is the achievement of a solution of some degree of permanency. Although the officer's own altruism is the main acknowledged motivational impetus for this activity, the achievement of this goal is also a practical necessity. To settle for less than an adequate solution is apt to result in repeated calls and more work.

"Psychiatric First Aid"

The involvement of the police with mentally ill persons who are not taken to the hospital is not confined to finding responsible caretakers for them, or to taking them to their normally sheltered place. Nor is this always the problem at hand, for quite often the very person who is most eligible for this role is the one who solicited police intervention. In these cases officers always administer some sort of direct "psychiatric first aid," even though they repudiate this designation. It is extremely rare that officers encounter a patient who is too passive or too withdrawn for interaction of some sort. In fact, most of the patients the police encounter are in states of relatively high agitation and can be drawn into an exchange. From the officer's point of view, his task consists of monitoring the transition of a state of affairs from its dangerous phase to a phase of relative safety and normalcy.

Although police training and literature have come to include references to the handling of mentally ill persons, it is fair to say that officers are not instructed in anything that deserves to be called a technique. With no more to go on than the maxims of kindness and caution, officers tend to fall back on being formally correct policemen. To start, seasoned officers invariably remove the patient from the immediate context in which they find him. In this they merely follow good police practice in general, applicable to all types of persons who attract police attention. The object is to establish boundaries of control and to reduce the complexity of the problem.[16] When it is not feasible to move the patient, the context is altered by removing others. The result in either case is the envelopment of the subject by police attention.

In direct dealings with the patient the policeman tries to establish and maintain the pretense of a normal conversational situation. All of the patient's remarks, allegations, or complaints are treated in a matter-of-fact manner. Policemen do not attempt to suppress or eliminate the absurd and bizarre, but rather leave them aside while concentrating verbal exchanges on the ordinary aspects of things. By this method every situation acquires a certain sense of normalcy. For example, in one observed instance a middle-aged lady complained, in highly agitated panic, that she was pursued by neighbors with an unheard-of weapon. Without questioning the lady's beliefs about what is possible in the domain of weaponry, or what might be reasonably assumed about the motives of angry neighbors, the officers went through the motions of dealing with the situation as if it involved a bona fide complaint. They searched the premises for nonexistent traces of impossible projectiles. They carefully took note of mundane particulars of events that could not have happened and advised the lady to be on the alert for suspicious occurrences in the future. The intervention, which lasted approximately one hour, terminated when the lady came to equate her predicament with the predicament of all other persons who were under some sort of threat and who apparently survive under police protection. She was visibly calmed and expressed the belief that the officers understood what she was facing and that it was within their capacity to ensure her safety. In the end, the conversation turned to such practical matters as how to summon the police quickly in situations of imminent danger and how to make doubly sure that locks on windows and doors were secure. Throughout the conversation the officers gave no hint that they doubted any part of the story. They did not challenge the statement that a projectile may travel through walls, furniture, and clothes without leaving any traces but be, nevertheless, fatal to persons. They also took pains to convince the lady that it would be tactically unwise and impractical to arrest or even interview suspected neighbors at this stage of the case.

Although the method of field work, as employed in this study, does not permit the formulation of reliable estimates of frequencies, it can be said that neither the observations nor the interviews with policemen suggested that the distribution of "psychiatric first aid" is anything but random, relative to social class. Furthermore, such interventions sometimes involve patients exhibiting signs of very serious psychopathology. In general, agitated patients receive much more careful and protracted attention than patients who are overtly passive, which accords with the fact that officers give high priority to risks of proliferation of external troubles. Finally, although the police occasionally encounter the same patient repeatedly, they tend to treat each confrontation as a separate emergency. Every precinct station has a fund of knowledge about persons who have been the subjects of past "psychiatric first aid," but there is no sustained concern for these persons. Whenever certain known persons come to the attention of officers, it is said that they are "acting up again." The avoidance of sustained concern and attention is part of the official posture of the police and an expression of the fact that the illness as such is of little interest and that it acquires relevance only through its unpredictable exacerbations.

The attitudes and procedures of "psychiatric first aid" are in a general sense representative of the overall involvement of the police with mental illness. The attitudes and procedures also play a role in cases in which emergency apprehensions are made. In the latter instances they provide, in part, the background for the decision, in the sense that if these measures do not succeed in reducing the potential of the external risk, the patient will be taken to the hospital. Thus, the practice of "psychiatric first aid" and the skill that it involves represent the core of what we earlier identified as the manipulative horizon of relevance in the decision-making process. The point to be emphasized about these interventions is that they involve no basic modification of police posture but rather its use for the particular purposes of dealing with patients. Though the officers are fully aware that they are dealing with mentally ill persons, they do not act in the manner of quasi-mental-health-specialists.

Continuing Care

After having placed proper emphasis on the generally prevalent pattern of the episodic, emergency, and ad hoc involvement of policemen with mentally ill persons, we turn to a significantly less frequent type of activity practiced by a limited number of patrolmen. In contrast with "psychiatric first aid," foot patrolmen, especially when they work in the slum, tenderloin, business, or rooming-house districts of the city, know some mentally ill persons with whom they have established a more or less regularized pattern of running into each other. Some of these persons are apparently chronic schizophrenics, others seem mentally defective, and others are senile. Many have a history of past hospitalization. Though the officers do not attempt to diagnose these persons, they recognize the presence of substantial psychological handicaps. Indeed, the officer's interaction with and interest in these people is basically structured by the consideration that they suffer from serious disorders.

The encounters are so highly routinized that they scarcely have an event-character of their own. It is part of the ordinary routine for a foot patrolman to meet people and to engage them in conversations. Each encounter is in its own way thematized. The themes occasionally are determined in terms of the prevailing contingencies of situations. For the most part, however, the exchanges are better understood, and often can only be understood, as episodes in long-standing relationships, with past exchanges furnishing the tacit background for presently exchanged remarks. This format of meetings holds also for the encounters with known mental patients, except that in these cases the encounters are thematized by the person's psychological handicap.

Officers acknowledge that their approach and manipulation of the patient is deliberately organized around this concern.

In one observed instance a young man approached an officer in a deteriorating business district of the city. He voiced an almost textbook-type paranoid complaint. From the statements and the officer's responses it could be gathered that this was a part of a sequence of conversations. The two proceeded to walk away from an area of high traffic density to quieter parts of the neighborhood. In the ensuing stroll the officer inspected various premises, greeted passersby, and generally showed a low level of attentiveness. After about twenty-five minutes the man bade the officer good-bye and indicated that he would be going home now. The officer stated that he runs into this man quite often and usually on the same spot. He always tried to lead the man away from the place that apparently excites his paranoid suspicions. The expressions of inattentiveness are calculated to impress the person that there is nothing to worry about, while, at the same time, the efforts the man must make to hold the officer's interest absorb his energies. This method presumably makes the thing talked about a casual matter and mere small talk. Thus, the practices employed in sustained contacts involve, like the practices of "psychiatric first aid," the tendencies to confine, to disregard pathological material, and to reduce matters to their mundane aspects.

CONCLUSION

Certain structural and organizational restraints leading to an apparent reluctance on the part of the police to invoke the law governing emergency apprehensions of mentally ill persons were discussed. Next we described the external properties of situations in which the law is often invoked. This approach left a seemingly residual category of cases in which persons are judged to be mentally ill but are not taken to the hospital. The category is residual, however, only in conjunction with one particular conception of the nature of police work. According to this conception the police act with competence and authority only when their actions can be subsumed under the heading of some legal mandate. If the conditions for making an arrest or an emergency apprehension are not satisfied, then, presumably, an officer has no further legitimate business with the case. It is universally accepted that the police could not possibly conform fully to this rule. Not only is it inevitable, but it has been said to be desirable that officers use a variety of means in keeping the peace.

In real police work the provisions contained in the law represent a resource that can be invoked to handle certain problems. Beyond that, the law contains certain guidelines about the boundaries of legality. Within these boundaries, however, there is located a vast array of activities that are in no important sense determined by considerations of legality. In fact, in cases in which invoking the law is not a foregone conclusion, as for example in many minor offenses or in the apprehension of mentally ill persons, it is only speciously true to say that the law determined the act of apprehension, and much more correct to say that the law made the action possible. The effective reasons for the action are not located in the formulas of statutes but in considerations that are related to established practices of dealing informally with problems.[17]

The important point about the relevance of established practice is that it contains the means and considerations in terms of which judgments are made whether there is any need to invoke the law. The practices are, of course, responsive to influences from the courts, from prosecutors, and from the public. They also stand in some relationship of correspondence to the intent of the law. Some problems are routinely handled by invoking the law, in other cases it is merely one of the available alternatives. In these latter cases it is possible that an officer who merely complies with the law may nevertheless be found to be an incompetent practitioner of his craft. About him it may be said that he should have been able to handle the problem in some other way. The other ways of handling are not explicitly codified and they undoubtedly depend on personal ingenuity on the part of the officer. Their foundation, however, is in a transmittable skill.

When one defines these established practices as the focal point of reference of police function, instead of ministerial law enforcement, then the cases of mentally ill persons who are not referred to hospitals do not constitute a residual category. Instead, "psychiatric first aid" appears as the standard practice that contains within the realms of its possibilities the emergency apprehension. In certain cases, as for example in cases involving suicide attempts, the apprehension is virtually a foregone conclusion, but in general it is viewed as merely one of several ways of solving problems. It happens to be the only visible alternative, but this is an artifact resulting from existing police recording systems that note only those actions that involve ministerial law enforcement. Indeed, it can safely be said that the proper understanding of recorded interventions hinges on the knowledge of cases for which there is no official record. When, for example, we say that one of the necessary conditions for the emergency apprehension is the discernment of the risk of proliferation of external troubles, then we must add that these are such perceived risks as cannot be controlled by the ordinarily available means contained in the standard practices. Thus, to understand the perception of risk it is necessary to know the structure of what can be, and is normally done to control it.

In this paper we have tried to describe briefly certain practices of dealing with mentally ill persons and we have argued that the structure and means contained in these practices determine who will be re-

ferred to the hospital on an emergency basis. The external characteristics of cases are not irrelevant to the decisions, but their import is
always mediated by practical considerations of what can and need be
done alternatively. We should like to propose that such procedures as
finding responsible caretakers who will look out for the patient, or
"psychiatric first aid," or the sustained interest in some patients by
foot patrolmen, are part of a larger domain of police work. We further
propose that this work, which has been called "keeping the peace,"[18]
in differentiation from "enforcing the law," consists of occupational
routines with particular procedures, skills, standards, and information,
in short, of craft, that meets certain tacit public expectations.[19]
Chances are that when police decisions are viewed from the perspective of the requirements of this craft, rather than with an interest in
seeking to discover how well they correspond to the conventional
formalities of the law, they may appear quite a bit less adventitious
than they are generally perceived to be. To say, however, that there
exists a body of methodically organized routines for keeping the peace,
which in some sense influence police decisions to invoke the law, in no
way settles the question whether the currently prevailing patterns of
police discretion are desirable or not. It merely urges that the study of
it will furnish a more realistic basis for appraisal.

NOTES

[1]See, for example, *Welfare and Institutions Code*, State of California,
Division 6, Part 1, Chapter 1.

[2]The city has a population of approximately .75 million inhabitants and
is patrolled by a uniformed police force of approximately 1,000 men. The receiving hospital is a public institution. Its psychiatric inpatient service registered a demand population of 7,500 during the period of the study, July 1,
1963–June 30, 1964. Eighty-eight percent of this population has been accepted
for observation and such short-term care as is ordinarily associated with it.
The average length of stay of patients is just short of five days, with a distribution that is heavily skewed toward shorter stays. The hospital also houses
a department of the court that holds sanity hearings.

[3]The problem referred to is treated in Joseph Goldstein, "Police Discretion Not to Invoke the Criminal Process," *Yale Law Journal*, 69 (1960), pp.
543–594; W. R. LaFave, "The Police and Non-enforcement of the Law," *Wisconsin Law Review* (1962), pp. 104–137, 179–239; S. H. Kadish, "Legal Norms
and Discretion in the Police and Sentencing Process," *Harvard Law Review*, 75
(1962), pp. 904–931; I. Piliavin and S. Scott, "Police Encounters with Juveniles," *American Journal of Sociology*, 70 (1964), pp. 206–214; Nial Osborough,
"Police Discretion Not to Prosecute Students," *Journal of Criminal Law,
Criminology and Police Science*, 56 (1965), pp. 241–245.

[4]California *Welfare and Institutions Code*, Section 5050.3.

[5]The term "doctrinal" is perhaps too strong, but only in the sense that the scheme of reasoning and justification lacks explicit formulation.

[6]The literature on this topic is voluminous and heavily polemical. For a general overview, see Wayne R. LaFave, *Arrest*, Boston: Little, Brown & Co., 1965; W. T. Plumb, Jr., "Illegal Enforcement of the Law," *Cornell Law Quarterly*, 24 (1939), pp. 337–393; Jim Thompson, "Police Control over Citizen Use of the Public Streets," *Journal of Criminal Law, Criminology and Police Science*, 49 (1959), pp. 562–568; R. C. Donnelly, "Police Authority and Practices," *Annals of the American Academy of Political and Social Science*, 339 (1962), pp. 90–110; Arthur H. Sherry, "Vagrants, Rogues and Vagabonds," *California Law Review*, 48 (1960), pp. 557–573.

[7]I have dealt with the practice of invoking official rules of procedure to legitimize various "necessary" activities, as a general problem in formal organizations, in "The Concept of Organization," *Social Research*, 32 (1965), pp. 239–255.

[8]The problem of the devious and exploitative use of the determination of mental illness in the administration of justice is dealt with by Thomas Szasz in a number of publications. See especially his *Psychiatric Justice*, New York: Macmillan, 1965.

[9]Shirley Star, "The Public's Ideas About Mental Illness," paper presented to the National Association of Mental Health, Indianapolis, 1955 (mimeo); "The Place of Psychiatry in Popular Thinking," paper presented to the American Association of Public Opinion Research, 1957 (mimeo).

[10]We propose that the degradation ceremony of the mental patient, to which Erving Goffman refers in his work, presents itself to the policeman as a justified necessity with certain patients.

[11]During the period of the study policemen apprehended and referred to the hospital approximately 1,600 patients. The total number of arrests for the mentioned offenses, by the uniformed patrol, was exactly 1,600, according to published statistics of the police department. However, the study covered the period from July 1, 1963, to June 30, 1964, while the published statistics of the department cover the calendar year of 1964.

[12]This observation is frankly judgmental; no one can estimate reliably the extent of covert coercion standing behind compliance. It is, however, not startingly unusual for patients to ask policemen to take them to the hospital.

[13]The information comes to the officer through radio code. The code contains special designations to indicate that an assignment involves a mental case, a suicide attempt, or an assignment of unknown nature.

[14]Edward H. Levi has argued that reasoning by analogy prevails generally in the administration of justice; see his *Introduction to Legal Reasoning*, Chicago: University of Chicago Press, 1949. Since policemen must be attuned to the style of proof and inference that is used in courts, it would not be unreasonable to assume that they might assimilate some of this pattern of thinking.

[15]In general, policemen insist on getting a fairly detailed story from the complainant and also on seeing the patient before they decide to make an emergency apprehension. One physician who was interviewed in the course of the study complained about this with a good deal of chagrin. From his point of view the police should take the word of a doctor without questioning him. Officers, however, maintain that the doctor's judgment would not protect them in the case of future complaints; they prefer making an "honest mis-

take." Policemen are generally acutely aware of the requirement of personal knowledge in finding "adequate grounds" for any action.

[16]One police lieutenant explained that one of the major stresses of police work has to do with the fact that officers are often forced to reach difficult decisions under the critical eye of bystanders. Such situations contain the simple hazard of losing physical control of the case as well as the risk that the officer's decision will be governed by external influence or provocation.

[17]We are talking about practice, of course, but the problem stands in the midst of a debate in legal theory. If it is maintained that the substance of the law is that it contains a system of rules of conduct, informing people what they must not do, and providing sanctions for violations, then neither the policeman nor the judge has any legitimate powers to exculpate a violator. If, however, it is maintained that the substance of the law is that it contains a system of rules limiting the powers of the institutions of the polity with respect to certain offenders and offensive types of conduct, then alternative means of control are not out of order, provided that they are not explicitly forbidden. The former position is expressed in Jerome Hall, *General Principles of Criminal Law,* Indianapolis: Bobbs-Merrill, 1947; an exposition of the latter view is contained in Norberto Bobbio, "Law and Force," *The Monist,* 49 (1965), pp. 321–342.

[18]Michael Banton proposed and discussed the distinction between peacekeeping and law-enforcement functions in his book, *The Policeman in the Community,* New York: Basic Books, 1965.

[19]Elaine Cumming and her co-workers define the policeman engaged in activities that do not relate to "keeping the law from being broken and apprehending those who break it" as an "amateur social worker." They do not consider, however, that their conception of the role of the policeman, that is, as being limited to law enforcement and restrictive control, may have been correct only "by definition and by law," and not in reality. Our own contention is that keeping the peace contains elements of control *and* support in a unique combination and that its pursuit has nothing amateurish about it. See Elaine Cumming *et al., "Policeman as Philosopher, Guide and Friend," Social Problems,* 12 (1965), pp. 276–286.

11

The Selection of Clients
by Social Welfare Agencies:
The Case of the Blind

ROBERT A. SCOTT

The purpose of social welfare is to promote the social betterment of a class or group of people who are defined as disadvantaged, handicapped, or deprived. A set of common problems are attributed to such persons based upon the nature of the trait or quality which sets them apart from the rest of society. Programs of social welfare are then planned to meet the needs which arise out of these problems.

It is believed that the form and content of such programs should be determined by the needs of the client. As his needs change, the programs themselves must change; conversely, the welfare of the client should be the primary factor to consider in making any policy decisions about changes in such programs.

In reality, other factors also exert a determining influence on social welfare programs. These factors are at least as important for setting policy as the clients' welfare and at times may even supersede it. Many such factors have been identified by other investigators.[1] Two are especially important. First, welfare services are characteristically distributed in our society through private philanthropy or government at its federal, state, and local levels. These programs are ordinarily

Reprinted from *Social Problems*, 14 (1967), pp. 248–257, by permission of the Journal of Social Problems and the Institute for the Study of Social Problems. Materials for this paper were gathered while the author was a member of the Research Staff of Russell Sage Foundation. The author wishes to acknowledge Russell Sage Foundation and the New York Association for the Blind for Supporting the project from which these materials were obtained.

incorporated in large-scale bureaucratic structures. As such, they are subject to the pressures and forces common to all complex bureaucracies. The preservation of the organization itself is a vital factor in setting program policy; and standardization based upon the criteria of efficiency, production, and costs is often applied to services which are intended to meet highly personal human needs.

Second, welfare programs must rely upon the public for their support, whether through legislative appropriation or private fund raising efforts. The availability of services depends, at least in part, upon the kinds of support which the benefactors of welfare are willing to provide. When the benefactors are the body politic, funds will ordinarily be made available for only those programs which the legislators believe are politically tenable to support. When the benefactors come from the private sector of society, the kinds of programs they are willing to support depend upon their personal conception of the nature of the problems of disadvantaged groups, and what they imagine constitutes a desirable and moral solution. In either case, such conceptions are generally responsive to broad cultural themes and values, especially those of youth, work, hope, contentment, and personal fulfillment.

At times, the personal welfare of the client, the needs of the bureaucratic structures through which services are supplied, and the benefactors' definition of the problems of the disadvantaged persons will coincide. Ordinarily these factors will coincide when the client possesses valued cultural attributes (e.g., youth, intelligence) and when valued cultural goals (e.g., employment, independence) are realistically attained for him. More often, however, these forces do not coincide; they may even conflict. Consequently, the public, whether through legislative bodies or private donations, may be unwilling to support programs for individuals with personal characteristics which are culturally devalued, although such individuals may be the majority of the disadvantaged group. From the point of view of organizational maintenance, it may be untenable to undertake extensive service programs for persons who, by virtue of their disability and other characteristics, may be unable to make a productive contribution to the society, even though they represent a majority of those who need service programs.

Social welfare programs are, therefore, set within and responsive to a variety of organizational and community pressures, which are highly determinative. By contrast, the problems of the recipient group ordinarily are caused by factors which are entirely unrelated to those which work upon the welfare agencies. The causes of the specific problems, and therefore the needs of a handicapped person, are not the same factors which determine what kinds of welfare services are offered to them. Clients' needs and the kinds of available welfare services run in two separate orbits, which may coincide only at certain points. It cannot be assumed, therefore, that the services which are offered apply to all persons who belong to the disadvantaged group, nor can it be assumed that the persons who receive services are necessarily benefited by them.

These facts suggest a number of questions for research about the relationships between social welfare service programs and the welfare problems of persons to whom the services are directed. First, it is necessary to determine the amount of congruence between services required by a disadvantaged group and those available to them. Second, it is necessary to determine the amount of congruence between persons who are in need of services and those who in fact receive them through existing structures. Finally, it is necessary to determine the consequences for a disadvantaged person of receiving services in existing welfare programs.

The purpose of this paper is to provide data related to the latter two questions, by examining one type of social welfare program: services for the blind. I will compare existing services in this field to the population of blind persons, in order to identify what, if any, discrepancies exist in the present distribution of services. This will be done by describing the demographic properties of the blind population of the United States at the present time; and the corresponding distribution and properties of agencies which serve it. From these data, I will also examine some of the consequences for an individual, both for himself and in relation to the community, of receiving welfare services through existing agencies.

While the remainder of this discussion will specifically deal with agencies for the blind, my remarks apply with equal cogency to many types of welfare agencies, and especially to those which provide social services to persons possessing stigmatized and unimprovable deviant qualities.[2]

DEMOGRAPHIC CHARACTERISTIC OF THE BLIND

Approximately 955,000 persons in the civilian, noninstitutionalized population of the United States under the age of 80 are blind.[3] There are a number of significant facts about the blind population. First, a majority of them are elderly. Sixty-six percent are between the ages of 55 and 80; another 15 percent are in the age group of 45–54; 17 percent of all blind persons are in the age group of 18–44; and only about 2 percent are children under 18. According to these data, two-thirds of all blind persons are in age groups where retirement is either pending or a reality, and only a small minority of blind persons are in age groups where either employment or education is realistic.

Second, blindness is much more common in women than in men.[4] Seven out of ten cases of blindness occur in women, and in all age groups there are more blind women than blind men, although the sex difference is greatest in the older age groups. Taking the factors of age and sex together, one-half of all cases of blindness are among women 55 years of age and older; another 20 percent of the cases of blindness occur among women in the age group of 18–54. Elderly men account for 18 percent of all cases, and only 12 percent of the cases of blindness occur among men 18–54.[5]

Third, blindness is comparatively rare among children. There are estimated to be only about 27,000 blind children in the United States at the present time.[6] The blindness rate among children is only .35 per 1,000 of the population. In contrast, the rate for elderly persons is about 33 per 1,000 of the population.

Finally, the term "blindness" refers both to those who are completely without vision and to those who have severe visual impairments but who can see. Only a small number of blind persons are in fact totally blind; a majority of them have some measurable visual acuity. The available data suggest that there is a direct relationship between the amount of visual loss and age.[7] The older a blind person is, the more serious his visual loss is likely to be.

The adequacy and effectiveness of welfare programs can be judged in many ways. One such measure, which will be used in this paper, concerns their completeness. By this I mean the degree to which welfare services are provided for all or most segments of the population in need. From this point of view, service programs for the blind may be regarded as adequate insofar as they reflect, in a general way, the composition of the blind population; correspondingly, they may be regarded as inadequate insofar as they apply only to special segments of the blind population.

It is recognized that this point of view is not commonly accepted among workers for the blind. They have argued that it is more worthwhile to supply services to those blind persons for whom there is the greatest expectation of success. Accordingly, it is held that resources are more wisely devoted to the education and training of blind children than to the care of elderly blind adults; and that it is more logical to aid the employable blind than those who are not employable. This argument is based on the assumption that resources for supporting service programs are limited, and that it is therefore necessary to establish these priorities. In reality, this assumption is generally incorrect in view of the fact that enormous sums of money are expended annually for services to the blind (for further information on this point see footnote 16). The argument also contains an erroneous implication: that there is a correspondence between the way in which an individual experiences problems of blindness and the priority which his problems are assigned by the criteria of real or imagined economic and social factors. Because there are economic and social reasons why the problems of blind children might receive priority in service programs, we cannot assume that the older blind person experiences his problems as less serious.

If services for the blind roughly reflect the age and sex distribution of the blind population, then we would expect to find a major portion of the financial and manpower resources of this field invested in programs designed to meet the needs of those who are not expected to be self-supporting, and more particularly of the elderly. Conversely, we would expect that only a small portion of those resources would be invested in programs for educating and training children and employable adults. An analysis of services for the blind in this country reveals that the situation is exactly the opposite.

I made a study of the programs of all direct service agencies listed in a substantially complete directory of agencies for the blind in this country.[8] Seven hundred and ninety-eight separate agencies were identified, 274 of which are private and 520 governmental. Only 9 percent (71) of these agencies are concerned exclusively with elderly blind persons. By contrast, 67 percent (529) of the agencies have programs intended primarily for children and employable adults. The remaining 23 percent (187) are "mixed" agencies, which offer services to blind persons of all ages. The remaining 1 percent (11) do not offer direct services to the blind.

An analysis was made of programs in the 71 agencies and organizations which serve elderly blind persons exclusively. There are 21 domiciles which house and care for about 1,000 elderly blind persons. The remainder of these organizations are state offices responsible for administering the federal-state program of aid to the needy blind. In the mixed agencies, programs for the elderly are almost exclusively recreational, ranging from organized recreational programs to drop-in daytime clubs.

One hundred and thirty-four separate agencies serve blind children exclusively, and 395 agencies have programs primarily concerned with vocational rehabilitation and employment. Although mixed agencies do offer some recreational services to elderly blind persons, the primary emphasis of their programs is unmistakably on children and employable adults. Of the 187 mixed agencies, only a few have a separate division for the elderly blind; by contrast there are almost none which do not have a children's division or a division for employable adults.

These data show a clear bias in work for the blind in favor of children and employable adults and against elderly blind persons. About 90 percent of agencies in work for the blind place exclusive or primary emphasis upon serving less than one-third of the blind population; and only 9 percent of the agencies are seriously concerning themselves with the bulk of blind persons.

Another important fact is not apparent from these data. Existing programs are not geared to serve all blind persons in a given age group.

Numerous services are available for the child who is educable, but there are almost no services for the multiply handicapped child. There are many services for the blind person who is thought to be employable, but few for the one who is thought to be untrainable or for whom employment is an unrealistic goal. Recreation programs for elderly blind persons are located in the agency itself, so that only those older blind persons who are mobile and independent enough to travel can take advantage of them. In effect, programs are geared to serve selected blind persons, and usually those who enjoy the highest probability for success; conversely, most service programs are ill-equipped to assist those for whom success is unlikely.

This systematic bias of work for the blind in favor of young blind children and employable blind adults, and the corresponding neglect of older blind persons, is reflected in another way—in the literature of work for the blind. An analysis was made of all articles which appeared in the *New Outlook for the Blind* (the principal professional journal of that field) from 1907 to 1963. This study showed that out of 1,069 articles, 36 percent dealt with children, 31 percent with rehabilitation, 15 percent with braille reading, 17 percent with specific services such as mobility, 21 percent with employment, and only 2 percent with geriatric problems. In short, 70 percent of the blind population (the elderly) received only 2 percent of the attention of writers in the major professional journal in work for the blind; whereas less than 30 percent of the population (children and employable adults) were discussed in 98 percent of the analyzed articles.

The reasons for the proliferation of services for a limited segment of the blind population are numerous and complex. I will try to discuss the most significant ones here. First, the same concepts which guided the pioneers of work for the blind 125 years ago make up a large part of contemporary theory. The demographic characteristics of the blind population then differed in several important ways from the present population. The number of persons in the general population who survived childhood and lived to old age was low, and the number of elderly blind persons was therefore correspondingly small.[9] A major cause of blindness in the adult population at that time was industrial accidents.[10] Ordinarily the eyes were the only organs involved, so that adult blind persons were healthy working people whose only handicap was blindness. Substantial numbers of children were blinded at birth because of diseases which specifically affected the eyes.[11]

Because a majority of the blind in the late nineteenth century were children and adults of working age, the concepts in this field stressed education and employment. Through the years, these concepts have not changed in response to changing social, economic, and public health conditions. In addition, workers for the blind have implicitly assumed that these problems of education and employment are inherent to the condition of blindness. They have mistaken these concepts for the problem of blindness itself. The blind to whom the concepts cannot be easily applied are viewed by workers as marginal to the "real work" in services for the blind. This work is believed to be educational and vocational; services for elderly, unemployable, or uneducable blind individuals are regarded as marginal activities. Education and employment are viewed as the only alternative solutions to the problems of the blind. If a person cannot benefit from either service, his problems are defined as unsolvable, and his case is closed. Consequently, elderly blind persons, the multiply handicapped and the unemployable are considered apart from the "real problems" of blindness, because workers for the blind continue to employ archiac concepts in their service approach.

This tendency to employ archaic concepts can be viewed as a specific instance of a more general tendency by workers for the blind to resist any innovation or change in service programs. In the history of this field, there has been a characteristic and stubborn resistance to the adoption of any mechanical aids, educational devices, or concepts which in any way deviate from the status quo.[12] This tendency is itself a function of a complex set of factors, the nature of which can be only briefly delineated in this article. Essentially work for the blind is a low-prestige profession, one of that category of occupations called "dirty work."[13] Because the stigma associated with blindness may inadvertently rub off on workers for the blind,[14] this field is unable to attract the top persons in such fields as social work, psychiatry, psychology, education, ophthamology, and rehabilitation. In fact, in work for the blind, there is an unusual opportunity for individuals with very little formal training to attain positions of great power and responsibility.

This phenomenon has had many consequences for the field, one of which is a tendency to resist change. Many leaders in this field have power which derives from the agencies they control, and from their acquired expertise in certain specific service programs such as braille, mobility, rehabilitation, employment, or education. They lack generic professional training; consequently, it is difficult for them to move from one type of service program for the blind to another, or from services for the blind to services for other types of handicapped persons. Their expertise is highly specialized and is acquired by hard experience. Because of these limitations, little is transferable from traditional services to new ones which are proposed. Consequently, when changes are attempted in existing programs and agencies, such persons are faced with a major loss in power, status, and income. It would be impossible for them to secure comparable positions outside agencies for the blind because assignment to such positions would be based upon formal credentials such as education, rather than upon their specialized skills and acquired status in the field. The person with only a high school education who holds a powerful position in an agency for the blind stands to lose a great deal if that agency changes in any substantial way. Therefore, workers for the blind have traditionally had more intense commitment to the agencies they have built than to the persons whom they serve.[15] Concomitantly, they have tried to maintain the traditional base upon which their power rests and to rationalize these efforts by traditional concepts and theories of the field.

Another cause of client selectivity in service programs for the blind is the fact that agencies are dependent upon the public for financial support. All but a few private agencies rely upon fund-raising appeals to finance their programs, and public agencies are entirely dependent upon annual appropriations from state legislatures and from Congress. In either case, agencies for the blind are in stiff competition with one another, and with hundreds of other charities, for a share of the public's philanthropic dollars.

In this competitive situation, the success of fund-raising campaigns depends upon strong emotional appeals on behalf of the needy. In their fund-raising campaigns, agencies for the blind exploit a certain number of cultural stereotypes in our society. These stereotypes concern blindness, youth, work, and hope. The images of blind persons which are projected in these campaigns are either those of educable children, or of young, employable adults, who can be helped to overcome a serious handicap to become materially productive.[16] These appeals, therefore, leave the unmistakable but erroneous impression that blind people are young, intelligent persons who can be educated and employed. The public has come to expect results which are measurable in these terms. This consequence intensifies the agencies' search for the few blind people who in fact have these personal attributes.

At the same time, agencies are extremely reluctant to begin programs for other groups of blind persons unless there is good reason to believe that these programs will be supported by the public. It is assumed that appeals for funds to help persons from whom only modest gains can be expected, such as elderly blind persons and multiply handicapped children or adults, will not succeed in offsetting the costs of such programs. It has been argued by the agencies that funds obtained through appeals on behalf of blind children and employable adults can be partly diverted to support programs for other groups of blind persons. However, programs for children and employable adults involve enormous capital investments. These investments require increasing sums of money annually for maintenance and growth purposes. One consequence, therefore, of successful fund raising has been that more and more money is needed simply to keep programs going.

I have compared the distribution of services for the blind in this country to the demographic characteristics of the blind population, and I have tried to indicate some of the reasons there is such a discrepancy between them. Now I want to consider another question—the avowed purpose of all programs for the blind to help the individual blind person to function as independently as he can. The question therefore arises, "What is the actual impact of agency programs upon those blind persons who do receive services?"

Since there are only about 950,000 blind persons in the entire country, the number of visually impaired individuals living in any particular geographical area is usually quite small. It is estimated that there are only about 40,000 to 50,000 blind persons in all of New York City, only about 10,000 in Philadelphia, and only about 140,00 blind persons in the Boston metropolitan area.[17] Yet, there are over 700 separate agencies and organizations for the blind in this country, a majority of which are situated in large urban areas. New York City has 50 separate organizations for the blind, 38 of which offer direct services; Philadelphia has 14 major direct agencies; and there are 13 major agencies in the greater metropolitan area of Boston.[18] Since a majority of these agencies offer services only to children and/or employable adults, there is obviously a very high ratio of agencies to clients. In New York City, for example, three major agencies and six smaller ones offer direct social and educational services to an estimated 1,000 blind children living in the area. Even if we assume that none of these children are multiply handicapped (which we cannot), the agency-client ratio is very large indeed. Twenty-two different organizations and agencies provide direct rehabilitation and vocational services to an estimated 13,000 blind persons who are of working age. This figure is inflated somewhat when we consider that between 50 and 60 percent of blind persons 18–54 years of age are women, for whom employment is not always a realistic or appropriate objective. Eleven other organizations specialize in the production and distribution of braille books and recordings for the blind. In addition, a number of state and federal services are available to the blind of New York City.

The disproportionately large number of agencies offering services has many consequences for blind persons, agencies for the blind, and for the community which supports them. One consequence is an intense and often highly spirited competition for clients among agencies for the blind. In some instances, this competition has become so keen that outside parties have had to intervene to protect the welfare of those involved. The pirating of clients is not unknown,[19] and great conflict between agencies ordinarily occurs in urban areas which have not been previously assigned to the competing agencies.

The intense and sometimes ruthless competition between these agencies for clients who fit their programs affects the agency's relationship to its clients. When an agency has the opportunity to provide services to a blind person who is suitable for its program, it is reluctant to let him go. The chances of finding a replacement for the client who leaves are not always good, and without a substantial number of clients on hand, the agency may find it difficult to justify its expenditures to the supporting public. Clients are encouraged to organize their lives around the agency. Employment is secured for them in the agency's sheltered workshop, free recreational services are provided by the agency on an indefinite basis, and residential homes are maintained for them. Gradually a greater and greater portion of the client's contact with the larger community becomes mediated, and often determined by the agency, until the blind person is literally sequestered from the community.[20] At this point, the agency completely negates its original objective, which is to help the blind persons to become independent.

DISCUSSION

My analysis indicates that programs of services for the blind are often more responsive to the organizational needs of agencies through which services are offered, than they are to the needs of blind persons. Moreover, by sequestering certain blind persons from the community, agencies for the blind are actually contributing to the very problems which they purport to be solving. The sociological concept which most appropriately applies to this phenomena is "displacement of organizational goals." This concept describes a situation in which an organization "substitutes for its legitimate goals some other goals for which it was not created, for which resources are not allocated, and for which it is not known to serve."[21]

This phenomenon, which has been observed in a variety of organizational settings, has been attributed to a number of factors, including the selection of organizational means and policies which preclude implementation of the goals,[22] the effects of bureaucracy on the personality and motivation of those who work in it,[23] elimination of the problems for which the organization was originally established,[24] and the requirement of the bureaucratic structure for resources and manpower.[25] The findings of a larger study of work for the blind, of which the data of this paper are but one part, suggest that each of these factors plays a part in accounting for goal displacement in this field. In addition, another factor is suggested: the absence of any clear criteria by which to determine if the agency is or is not implementing its objectives.

It is generally agreed that the purpose of agencies for the blind is to help blind persons to maximize their ability to perform independently. Rehabilitation, which is a core service in any agency, seeks to restore the blind person, "to the fullest physical, mental, social, vocational, and economic usefulness of which he is capable." The phrase "of which he is capable" is a crucial modifier, since there is no consensus among workers for the blind regarding what a blind person can or cannot do. In practice, this definition is often used tautologically, since any level of performance which a blind person happens to attain is regarded as the one "of which he is capable." It is difficult, and at times impossible, to know if an agency for the blind is actually attaining its goals.

Using the definitions often employed by workers for the blind, every client they serve is a successful case. By other criteria, such as amount of independent employment or degree of participation in the larger community, the conclusions with respect to the implementation of goals are more modest. In addition, when a blind person performs in a manner which everyone agrees is his maximum level of independence, it is difficult to demonstrate concretely that his independence is a result of the services which he has received. By the same token, when he is not functioning at a level believed to be his maximum, it is not known if this is because services have been inadequate, or because he is a victim of the erroneous beliefs of the larger society about blindness and its effects on human functioning. There is, therefore, a great amount of uncertainty concerning whether an agency is or is not attaining its goals. Criteria of measurement are nebulous, and so many factors might explain success or failure that it is impossible to demonstrate conclusively that a given agency has in fact implemented its goals.

A preoccupation with organizational means is one of the responses to the uncertainty which is generated by this situation. Over the years an intense interest has developed in the refinement of administrative procedures of service programs. This interest has been accompanied by a growing disinterest in the more fundamental questions concerning the necessity for a particular service, or its impact upon the client.[26] This preoccupation with administrative procedures provides workers with a feeling of certainty and accomplishment which would not otherwise exist. Since most workers for the blind are not professionally trained, and their competency to help the blind is therefore continually being challenged, we can see that this uncertainty regarding goal attainment is intensified. As a defense against this situation, workers bury themselves in the administrative details of their jobs. This preoccupation ultimately leads to the displacement of the organizations goals.

Ironically, the tendency toward the displacement of goals is not entirely dysfunctional when viewed from the perspective of the general public. There is a general resistance among most "normals" to becoming involved with stigmatized persons such as the blind, and avoidance is the characteristic initial response.[27] The blind have always complained that they are segregated from the rest of society, and that they are assigned a marginal and unsatisfying social role.[28] The tendency of agencies for the blind to sequester certain clients (i.e., those for whom there is the greatest probability of integration into the larger community) is consistent with the desire of the public to avoid blind persons. This response, of course, is not unique in welfare services for the blind; it applies with equal cogency to other groups of persons who are defined as disabled, handicapped, or otherwise socially undesirable.[29] The very fact that agencies for the blind exist creates a repository into which the blind may be placed by the larger community. Consequently, the fact that goals are displaced may have unfortunate consequences for particular blind persons, but not necessarily for society at large.

Finally, it should be clear that there is no nationally or regionally coordinated effort to provide services for blind persons. Since agencies must compete with one another for funds and clients, they do not ordinarily coordinate their activities with respect to the problems of the entire population in need of them. Nor, for that matter, do they even possess a clear image of the parameters of that population. A deliberately coordinated national effort is clearly indicated as one important step to remedy the present unnecessary duplication of effort among agencies which are committed to the same general goals.

NOTES

[1]See, for example, Harold L. Wilensky and Charles N. Lebeaux, *Industrial Society and Social Welfare,* New York: Russell Sage Foundation, 1958, chs. VII and X.

[2]Eliot Freidson, "Disability as Social Deviance," in Marvin B. Sussman, ed., *Sociological Theory Research, and Rehabilitation,* American Sociological Association, 1966.

[3]This figure has been derived from data from two separate sources. For estimates of the prevalence of blindness in the noninstitutionalized civilian population of the U.S. between the ages of 18–79 see "Binocular Visual Acuity of Adults, United States, 1960–1962," National Center for Health Statistics, Series 11, #3. For estimates of the prevalence of blindness in children, see "Annual Report," American Printing House for the Blind (APHB), Louisville, Kentucky, 1962.

[4]National Center for Health Statistics, "Binocular Visual Acuity," Table 3, p. 16.

[5]National Center for Health Statistics, "Binocular Visual Acuity."

[6]This estimate is based upon the figures of the APHB for school-age children, and an educated guess by practitioners of works for the blind for preschool-age children.

[7]National Center for Health Statistics, "Binocular Visual Acuity."

[8]*Directory of Agencies Serving Blind Persons in the United States,* 14th ed., New York: American Foundation for the Blind, 1965.

[9]See Harry Best, *Blindness and the Blind in the United States,* New York: Macmillan Company, 1934, ch. XII.

¹⁰Best, *Blindness and the Blind*, New York: Macmillan Company, 1934, ch. I and IV.

¹¹Best, *Blindness and the Blind*, New York: Macmillan Company, 1934, ch. II and III.

¹²For discussions of resistance to the adoption of the Hoover cane, see Thomas Carroll, *Blindness*, pp. 134–135; for discussions related to braille, see Robert Erwin, *As I Saw It*, New York: AFB, 1966, pp. 1–36; for discussions related to seeing eye dogs, see W. H. Ebeling, "The Guide Dog Movement," in Paul A. Zahl, *Blindness: Modern Approaches to the Unseen Environment*, New York and London: Hofner Publishing Company, 1962; also see Hector Chevigny and Sydell Braverman, *The Adjustment of the Blind*, New Haven: Yale University Press, 1950, ch. IX.

¹³Marvin Sussman, "Sociology of Rehabilitation Occupations," *Sociological Theory, Research and Rehabilitation*, ch. II.

¹⁴Erving Goffman, *Stigma, Notes on the Management of Spoiled Identity*, Englewood Cliffs, N.J.: Prentice Hall, Inc., 1963, ch. 1.

¹⁵Chevigny and Braverman, *The Adjustment of the Blind.*, ch. IX.

¹⁶Such appeals have been enormously successful. I have estimated that in the state of New York alone, between $57 million, and $63 million is annually expended by public and private organizations for services to the blind. This figure was compiled from data from a variety of sources, including the routine annual reports of governmental-sponsored service programs, the annual reports of private agencies which are routinely filed with the Charities Registration Bureau of the State of New York, and private correspondence with the numerous other organizations who do not ordinarily make financial reports public.

¹⁷These estimates were derived by computing the blindness rate per 1,000 of the population and then multiplying them by the number of persons living in each city.

¹⁸For a listing of most of these agencies, see *Directory of Agencies Serving Blind Persons in the United States*, 1965.

¹⁹Chevigny and Braverman, *The Adjustment of the Blind*, ch. IX.

²⁰This situation also applies to other types of welfare organizations. See, for example, Erving Goffman, *Asylums, Essays on the Social Situation of the Mental Patient, and Other Inmates*, Garden City, N.Y.: Anchor Books, 1961: and Harold Orlans, "An American Death Camp," *Politics* (Summer, 1948), pp. 162–167.

²¹A. Etzioni, *Modern Organization*, Englewood Cliffs, N.J.: Prentice Hall, Inc., 1964, p. 10.

²²R. Michels, *Political Parties*, Glencoe, Ill.: Free Press, 1949; P. Selznick, *TVA and the Grass Roots*, Berkeley: University of California Press, 1949.

²³Robert K. Merton, *Social Theory and Social Structure*, rev. ed., Glencoe, Ill.: Free Press, 1957.

²⁴S. L. Messinger, "Organizational Transformation: A Case Study of a Declining Social Movement," *American Sociological Review*, 20 (February, 1955), pp. 3–10.

²⁵B. R. Clark, "Organizational Adaption and Precarious Values," *American Sociological Review*, 21 (1956), pp. 327–336.

²⁶One manifestation of this trend is the shifting focus of papers and discussions at meetings of workers for the blind. At the beginning of organized pro-

grams of services for the blind, papers at such meetings were largely devoted to basic discussions of the appropriate goals of work for the blind; at the present time they are concerned almost exclusively with perfection of the means. See *Annual Proceedings* of the American Association of Workers for the Blind.

[27]Goffman, *Stigma*, ch. 1.

[28]Alan Gowman, *The War Blind in American Social Structure*, New York: American Foundation for the Blind, 1957, pp. 5-9.

[29]Goffman, *Stigma*, ch. 1.

12

The Moral Career of a Bum

JAMES P. SPRADLEY

More arrests occur in the United States for public drunkenness than for any other crime; during 1965, of six million arrests, nearly two million were for this charge. The President's Commission on Law Enforcement and Administration of Justice has commented that this system of criminal justice "burdens police, clogs lower criminal courts and crowds penal institutions throughout the United States," an observation borne out in Seattle, where 70 percent of all police man-hours are spent on this type of offense and 80 percent of the jail population throughout the year are the chronic alcoholic offenders.

Any person arrested for public drunkenness in Seattle may post a bail of $20 and be released in a few hours, and most of those who post bail do not appear in court, preferring to forfeit their bail. Some chronic offenders spend hundreds of dollars each year in this manner. Those without sufficient funds to post bail must appear in Seattle Criminal Court, where it was reported that during 1967 nearly 65 percent of all cases were those charged with public drunkenness, or an average of about 70 persons per day. Ninety-seven percent of those appearing in court are found guilty and sentenced to serve time in the city jail for their crime.

The effect of this system upon the individual, especially those who cannot post bail, is often held to be partially therapeutic by many members of our society. On June 17, 1968 the Supreme Court of the United States rules, in the case of *Powell* v. *Texas,* to uphold the laws which make public drunkenness an offense in every state of the Union. One of the majority opinions stated the following reasons for this decision:

Jailing of chronic alcoholics is definitely defended as therapeutic, and the claims of therapeutic value are not insubstan-
tial. As appellees note, the alcoholics are removed from the
streets, where in their intoxicated state they may be in physical danger, and are given food, clothing, and shelter until
they "sober up" and thus at least regain their ability to keep
from being run over by automobiles in the street.

Not everyone agrees with this modestly positive evaluation, however, least of all the drunks themselves. They know they are caught in
a revolving door, and it is time to listen to their view of it. Consider
the case of Mr. John Hallman, a long-time resident of Seattle: he was
first arrested for public drunkenness in 1947 and two years later declared by the courts to be a "common drunkard;" during the 21-year
period from 1947 to 1968, he was convicted over 100 times for this
crime; he received many suspended sentences and posted $165 in bails
which he forfeited; and there were 74 charges of public drunkenness
during this period on which he was sentenced to jail. He was given a
total of 5,340 days for these convictions, or *more than 14 years*. If he
had posted $20 bail it would have cost him $1,480. In this man's experience, then, a year of his life was worth only about $100! During
1966 he received two six-month sentences which he could have avoided
for only $40.

MAKING THE BUCKET

Why do urban nomads encounter the police, get arrested, plead
guilty, and do time in an almost never-ending cycle? They do, of
course, violate local ordinances that prohibit drunkenness, drinking,
begging, sleeping, and urinating in public. But what they do is much
less significant than who they are. These men do their life sentences on
the installment plan because they have been discredited and stigmatized by other Americans.

No man begins life as a bum, nor were these men socialized into
the world of tramps as children. At one time in their adult life these
men had a variety of respected identities—they were fathers, husbands, students, sons, employers, and employees. Many attended high
schools; some went to college. One informant who had been a tramp
for several years was a graduate of Harvard University. Others had
owned businesses or worked at skilled trades. Nearly half of these men
had once maintained a family.

The conception a man has of himself and his place in the world is,
in part, socially constructed. Like the brick and mortar that go into
creating a building, so the edifice of the human self is constructed, one
building block at a time. While new dimensions of self-identity may be

acquired throughout the life span, dramatic change in personality can occur only if these former identities are subjected to radical manipulation.

The revolving jail house door is for the drunks "making the bucket;" it is a rite de passage, the actions, timing, and spatial ordering of which are intertwined in a complex array of symbolic meanings that ceremonially tell the urban nomad and those in his world who he is no longer and who he is becoming. We shall focus here upon the "stages of making the bucket," using the categories that tramps employ to order their experience throughout this rite and to anticipate and prepare for what is ahead.

STAGE 1: STREET

One of the most important ways in which members of any society learn a new identity is through a process of being labeled by others, especially by those who hold power over their lives. Not all labeling activity by others is significant of course, but when a man's concept of himself is shaken because of his own loss of control over those things that society considers important, he is especially vulnerable to the labels others use for him.

For the urban nomads, as I shall call them, the most significant "others" are the police. One man recalled, "That bull said I was just a wino and a bum that wasn't worth being tossed in a shit ditch." The label of tramp was often used in a manner which implied the inferiority of such an identity. "Get going, you fuckin' tramp. Can't you hear your own name, ass-hole?" Many other discrediting labels such as "you wino son-of-a-bitch," "dingbat," "fucking dehorn," "drunken bum," "cocksucker," "Skid Road bastard," "fuckin' tramp" and "phoney ass" were among those reported by my informants. Tramps are often threatened as well—"Shut up or we will put you in the pads and beat the shit out of you."

A man may also be stigmatized by the police by having other aspects of his identity thrown up before him as evidence that he is only a bum. There is, for example, a large population of Indians in the city of Seattle, and many find companionship in the Skid Road District and often get charged with being drunk in public. In many ways they are considered beneath all others. One man said, "That bull called me a fucked-up chief and stated that liquor rights should never have been given to these fuckin' Injuns." Another remembered an officer saying to him, "They didn't play cowboys and Indians long enough; they should have killed all of you bastards off."

Whatever the reasons for this labeling behavior, most tramps are aware that it goes on and come to the same conclusion as the man who stated, "In many cops' minds a drunk isn't human."

STAGE 2: CALL BOX

Personal and social identity are not only structured by the roles we play and the names we use, but also by objects of personal property. For the tramps, rings, watches, money, wallets, identification papers, address books, and clothing help to give form and structure to *who* one is, and their loss is significant. Although they may be robbed at any point during the entire ritual of making the bucket, the first fleecing often takes place at the call box.

When a man is arrested by a policeman on his beat, he is taken to the call box where a paddy wagon or police car is summoned to take him to jail. In the interim he undergoes a thorough search and may lose some of his belongings; in a sample of 100 men, 23 percent of the men indicated they had been robbed by a policeman while he was shaking them down at a call box.

Even if they make it to jail without being robbed, their possessions are not safe. When the wagon takes them off to jail, they hope against the odds that their possessions will be in their property box when they are released, but as one man recalled, "They took a watch and ring from me in 1968 and told me it would be in my property box at the jail. I never got them back."

In addition to being despoiled of his property, a man at the call box is almost always robbed of his autonomy at a deeper psychological level. His world has been invaded by someone with the authority to treat him in a manner designed to show him that he is utterly power-less, and certainly not that he is innocent until proven guilty. The street corners on Skid Road have a different meaning to tramps than they do to others in American society. They are not merely dingy public places, they are the living rooms and private meeting places for urban nomads. A man who has recently arrived in town will hang around a street corner hoping to meet an old friend or find a new one. Therefore, when a man is required to place his hands over his head and allow an officer to invade his clothing and other domains of privacy, while at the same time threatening him, it is done in full view of other tramps.

STAGE 3: PADDY WAGON OR POLICE CAR

Although the drive to the jail may involve only a few blocks, a man does not always get there after he is picked up in the paddy wagon; 23 percent of the sample reported the police had stopped them or picked them up, taken their money or other property, and then let them go. Because they are not arrested on such occasions, this form of shake-down is considered to be an involuntary payoff to the police. Only 6 percent of the sampe reported they had every made a *voluntary* payoff.

Some have stories such as this man's: "In 1968 they picked me up in a prowl car and took me down on Skid Road back in an alley and searched me, took my money, drove me around for awhile and then let me out way down on Skid Road in a back alley. They drove off without returning my money."

It is almost impossible to verify these incidents by legal means, but enough tramps have experienced this official thievery for it to have become part of their general cultural knowledge. The strategies tramps use to make themselves invisible when they sleep are also used to protect their personal property. They are careful to conceal any hint that they have valuable possessions. Some men reported they would dress in old clothes "like a bum" in order to avoid becoming a candidate for jackrollers and thieves.

STAGE 4: ELEVATOR

The elevator from the basement of Seattle's Public Safety Building to the sixth floor where the jail is located is especially dangerous for the tramp. He is entirely cut off from the view of everyone except the police—not even a disinterested passerby can influence what takes place. Although it is a short trip, the bull can easily push the stop button between floors. As the elevator slowly rises, the reality of imprisonment sweeps over the tramp with an immediacy that suffocates any self-assertive wishes he may still harbor. The two bulls at his side, like uniformed bars of a cell, cannot be seen as human beings to whom he can respond, for any reaction on his part other than a plastic passivity may be interpreted as resistance. The tramp may not himself have been worked over in the elevator, but he has certainly heard of it from his fellow urban nomads.

Although being clubbed or smashed against a wall symbolically reminds a man that his body, the most intimate dimension of his self-concept, is vulnerable, it also has another important meaning. Like a rehearsal before a dramatic performance, it forcefully instructs the tramp to play the part of a dependent and passive actor within the bucket. The longer a man has been in the world of tramps, the more he learns to respond as if he were an animal whose master had broken his will. Labels, threats, physical abuse, and thefts of property in themselves are hard for any man to take, but more significant is the implicit message in these actions: they clearly identify for the tramp those who hold power over his life then and during the coming months he may spend in jail. If he refuses to acknowledge his deferential role, further steps will be taken, as they were with the man who recalled:

> In 1967 he shook me down, took my wallet, looked in it, took $11. Put my wallet back, and I said, "Since when do you look

for a gun or a knife in a man's wallet?" He split my head, and it took four stitches.

STAGE 5: BOOKING

When the elevator door opens, a man sees to his left the gun rack where the officers deposit their weapons. Before him is a row of closely spaced steel bars that lurch into motion with the sound of a buzzer pressed from behind the booking desk. As the steel gate opens he is ushered across a waiting area of 20 or 30 feet in diameter to a high counter with several windows. For each man the officer fills out in quadruplicate a property record and booking sheet. Although there is space for the prisoner to sign and verify the property record, almost 70 percent of my informants indicated they were not usually allowed to do this, and 98 percent of the sample indicated they had never received a receipt.

When I questioned tramps about thefts from their property boxes, 40 percent reported their occurrence. One man recalled this story:

> I was in jail and had no money, and there was a fellow who owed me $12, and so I wrote and asked him for it and told him to send it registered letter. I got the letter, but the money wasn't in it. When I got out I didn't have no money in my property box. I said, "I've got a registered letter here saying I was sent $12. I'm not leaving until I get it." The bull said, "You don't have no money." The sergeant came by just then, asked what it was and looked at the letter and went back to the property box and then came out and said, "Oh, here's your $12. It was in the wrong property box."

One factor of which tramps are most keenly aware in the entire ritual of making the bucket is that at every point they receive different kinds of treatment than those they refer to as "citizens" or "uptown tramps." A well-dressed man is seldom robbed, beaten, or cursed because he is likely to cause trouble.

The booking desk has one further significant effect on these men who are undergoing an identity change, and that is creating a "record." This record becomes part of the court file on each man, and it is used to determine the severity of his sentence. Later it may be much more widely disseminated, as was noted in the study of the Seattle Police Department made by the International Association of Chiefs of Police in 1968. Any success at passing as an average citizen, whether it be for employment, housing, or friendship, may crumble when others discover a tramp's record. Although *he* may know that many of his arrests were simply due to his visibility in the Skid Road area, it is not easy to convince others that this was the case.

STAGE 6: PADDED DRUNK TANK

From the booking desk it is a short distance down a hallway to the padded drunk tank, so called because a thin layer of cork covers the floor, to cushion the men as they sleep off a drunk or await the next stage of the ritual. Most men have very few memories of this tank because they spend little time there or they are too drunk to remember what transpired. Only one of my informants got a second (sober) glimpse of the padded drunk tank. A young merchant seaman, who was 29, had arrived in Seattle and was arrested several times. While waiting for his appearance in court, the following incident occurred:

> I was in the cement drunk tank with about 40 guys. They had some visitors coming through the jail, and they took several of us out of the cement drunk tank and gave us each two blankets and put us in the padded drunk tank. It had a rubber floor. They brought us in food, they heaped our trays with stew for dinner at 4:30, and the visitors came through and everything looked great.

Tramps are aware of such subterfuge, and it is one of the reasons they believe no one can discover their plight and that you "can't change City Hall."

STAGE 7: MUG AND PRINT ROOM

Any man who has made the bucket more than once knows that here is the watershed at which the poor are separated from the not so poor. After a man is sober enough to be processed in this room, he is also sober enough to post a bail of $20, walk out of the jail a free man. He has bought his way out for $20. He has purchased a clean slate, a new sense of self, an *immediate* opportunity to assert himself and release all the pent-up hostility he may have felt toward the system—all for only $20. And he can continue bailing himself out forever if he has the resources or friends who will pay. But what does this say to the man who sees others post their bail, who tries to phone a friend or bondsman for the needed money, only to fail and enter the drunk tank with the knowledge that he could have been free if he had not been poor—a poverty which may have been incurred only a few hours earlier at the hands of his captors?

STAGE 8: CEMENT DRUNK TANK

Events have moved rapidly for the tramp who has gone through the first stages of the ritual. From the street to the call box, into a paddy wagon and up the elevator, through the booking desk process, and on into the padded drunk tank for a few hours of sleep. X-rays and pictures follow in quick succession. And then suddenly, as the heavy door closes on the cement drunk tank, time seems to wind backwards.

The cement drunk tank is not a comfortable place to spend several days, and 90 percent of my sample reported having spent two or more days there. There are no bunks in this room, meant to hold about 35 men, and only one toilet and washbasin. Only 3 percent of the sample reported ever receiving a blanket. The lights are left on 24 hours a day, and there is nothing resembling privacy; but the most abhorrent part of this experience is the crowding, which makes it impossible for a man to protect himself from being contaminated by others. One man described these conditions in graphic terms:

> That's all right if you're a young fellow, you can take it. It's miserable, but you can take it. Sometimes, I don't know what the reason for it is, it doesn't make sense for you at all, but I've been in there when there is standing room only, in one of those concrete cells, for two or three days. There's barely room to sit down. You certainly can't lie down without putting your face in someone's dirty socks or something like that. And this is when there are two or three other tanks available that are completely empty. There's no reason why they don't take half of them and put them in another one, except they don't want to bother to clean it up.

In fact, the physical discomfort in itself is not unbearable; after all, tramps have slept on cold hard cement before without a blanket. But now they have lost control of their lives, and as they lie there waiting for court, the drunk tank reminds them of this as nothing else could.

A man's most immediate needs are often for cigarettes, food, and information about the state of his property. He has lost the control over all of these items. Although food is served three times a day, it is never enough. If he has been able to smuggle some money into the drunk tank in his clothing, he can pay a trusty 50 cents or a dollar to "hustle" him a cup of coffee or get something from his property. But he can never depend on this. The trusties often steal, but the men cannot complain to the bulls since it is against the rules to have money. Moreover, the bulls will often not even protect them against other prisoners in the drunk tank. One man recalled:

I remember about three years ago I was working in a logging camp and had just come to town, and I ended up in the drunk tank. I woke up, and I caught some guy trying to steal my shoes in the drunk tank. He was taking them off my feet, see, so we got into it, and he had two or three buddies in the drunk tank, and I started hollering for the bull, the jailer, and they put the finger on me, see, that I started it. I tried to tell the jailer that the son-of-a-bitch was trying to steal my shoes. I'd sobered up by that time, and that big jailer, he says, "You come out here." He took me over into an empty tank, and I knew what was comin' then. He slammed the door shut, and he walks up to me and says, "You think you're pretty tough, huh?" I seen it coming, you know, and held my breath, and he hit me in the guts as hard as he could. He didn't even knock me down. I just stepped back two or three feet, and he kind of looked at me, you know, and that was it. He didn't knock me down the first time, so he left me alone, and I said, "What in hell did you do that for?" He didn't answer me, but if I had swung on him, which I could have done, well then they'd have brought in two or three more, you know, and really whipped my ass."

Even though he is already in the drunk tank, in principle a man may still contact a bondsman, attorney, employer, or friend who will help get him out of jail. But to contact the outside, he must of course use the phone. Eighty-five percent of my informants said they had been permitted to make one phone call, but the man who has no regular employment, family, or permanent address finds the privilege of a single telephone call next to useless. He may need to contact several people until he finds one who will bail him out, get his money, pay for his room, get his clothing, or assist him in some other way.

STAGE 9: COURT DOCKET

Time drags its feet in the drunk tank. The hours creep by, turning slowly into days and nights to be endured. The men think about food, count the hours until they will appear in court, rack their brains for someone who could bail them out, swap experiences of other jails, listen eagerly to newcomers with word from outside, and wonder where they will travel when they are released. Uppermost in the minds of most men are thoughts of "beating their drunk charge."

The heavy door of the drunk tank opens at about 8:00 A.M. each morning, Monday through Friday, for the drunks to file out, walk down the hallway, through the main lobby past the booking desk, up the stairs and through a maze of corridors to the court docket. This room is much like the cement drunk tank except that it is smaller and filled with rows of steel benches where the men await court. On most days, just before court begins, a counselor for the alcoholism treatment center appears to explain their program and how a person can qualify for it. Most men are sitting sleepily on the benches or lying on the floor, some still fighting the pains of a hangover or withdrawal from a long drunk. They move out, then, in groups of about 25 into the small area to the right and front of the judge's bench, barricaded from the rest of the courtroom by a railing. They are crowded into this cramped space and told where to stand by the officer, where they remain, lined up three deep, pressed together, holding their hats in their hands, heads down, waiting for the judge to speak.

STAGE 10: COURTROOM

> You men have all been charged with drinking in public, drunk in public or begging which are in violation of the ordinances of the city of Seattle. The maximum penalty for these crimes is $500 fine and/or 180 days in jail. You have a right to plead guilty or not guilty. You have a right to consult a lawyer before you enter a plea of guilty or not guilty. If you want to consult a lawyer you must pay for your own attorney. The court does not have provisions for this. If you wish a continuance, please indicate when you return to court. On a plea of guilty you waive your rights to appeal to a higher court. On a plea of not guilty your case will be continued for trial at a later date. Now return to the court docket and when you are called in you will enter a plea of guilty or not guilty. If you wish to make a statement you may do so.

The "rights spiel," as one man fondly dubbed it, takes less than a minute to complete. The group of men are then hurried back into the court docket to listen for their names again. When a man hears his name, he returns to the courtroom alone. He faces the judge's bench, separated by the railing and the prosecuting attorney for the city of Seattle who says, "You have been charged with the crime of public drunkenness, how do you plead?" If a man enters a plea of guilty, and over 90 percent of them do so, the prosecutor reads his prior record to the judge who will sentence him according to a preset formula based on his record. A man may plead guilty or not guilty, ask for a continuance, make a statement or request he be sent to the alcoholism treatment center.

The best way to beat a drunk charge is to have a good record, a strategy that has wide ramifications for the life style of tramps. In some courts there is a single sentence for anyone guilty of public drunkenness, but in Seattle, as in many cities, there is a sliding scale determined by a man's past record. A first offender, who may only be new to that court or who simply may have been out of action for six months or more, will get two days suspended. An eight-time loser may get as much as 90 days.

Whenever tramps discuss previous experiences in jail and court they explain them by making references to how many days they have "hanging" (the amount of time they know they will be sentenced to do). It is impossible to understand the actions a man takes, such as bailing out, asking for the treatment center or pleading guilty, unless it is also known how many days he had hanging.

The judge apparently gives sentences of increasing magnitude, with an occasional major suspended sentence, for two reasons: to reduce the recurrence of a man's drinking sprees and help him regain his health. Tramps, however, know they are arrested for many reasons besides their drinking behavior; it is their life style, only one feature of which involves drinking, that brings them into court. While the punishment of longer sentences may motivate some men to abstain from public drunkenness, it has a much more significant influence for most tramps: it motivates them to travel. In order to improve their record in court so as to reduce the amount of time they will do on their next conviction, tramps choose another alternative—leaving town. With each succeeding arrest in Seattle a person's record becomes more tarnished and the number of days he has hanging increases. But every tramp knows this slate could be completely erased by leaving town for six months.

The suspended sentence is an even more important stimulus to the mobility of tramps. When a tramp receives a suspended sentence of ninety days, he has escaped doing time, but only for the moment; back on the street he walks with the knowledge that he now has probably doubled the number of days he has hanging. If arrested again he may serve the suspended and the new sentence consecutively.

After a long period of incarceration, a man feels like "moving on" as an end in itself; he wants to enjoy his freedom to the utmost. But tramps also travel from one place to another because they become marked men who are arrested over and over again for their very presence in the Skid Road District.

There is an intimate relationship between mobility and other features of their life style which involve drinking: alcoholic beverages function as a social lubricant at all levels of American society, but they fulfill this need in a special way for urban nomads. Nomadism creates a unique kind of loneliness and sense of isolation in an individual, and when he arrives alone in a new town he seeks to find others of his own kind to reduce such anxieties. Almost the only place where he can find acceptance, friendship and sociability is on Skid Road and in the bars located there.

Bars are categorized among tramps in a variety of ways, but

especially in terms of what one may find there in the way of friends, female companionship, and work opportunities. For urban nomads, bars function as churches and clubs, employment agencies and dating centers, begging places, drinking and eating places, and flops. Most of all, they are a place to find friendship, even if it is only of a fleeting nature. In a Skid Road bar one is not restricted in his behavior; he can perform in ways appropriate to this subculture and know he will be accepted; he can find out important information about jail and court and employment which other tramps will freely give him. One tramp who wanted to control his drinking behavior clearly saw the relationship between mobility and drinking. As he was about to be released from the alcoholism treatment center he commented: "My biggest problem when I get out next week is traveling. When I get in a strange vicinity I head for a bar. If I want work, I go to a bar. That's where they come to hire a man." Skid Road and its bars, in addition to being a place to solidify new-found friendships with a drink, is also where most arrests for public drunkenness occur. And so we have come full circle: *urban nomads visit Skid Road and its bars because they travel; they are arrested because they live and drink in this area of town; and they travel because they are arrested.*

Some of the strategies used to beat a drunk charge are linked together. A man who requests a continuance does so in order to be able to bail out; similarly, a person who uses an alias does so to have a good record or escape the one he has created over the past months. As one informant stated, "If they have no previous arrest for a name they usually give a kickout. You've got to beat them some way." But few men use this dodge as it is too risky:

> One Friday Sanders gave the name Johnson, as he had time hanging. They called for Johnson many times Friday, Saturday and Sunday. Monday morning when they called Johnson for court the officer who knew him spotted Sanders and told him he ought to kick his teeth in. Sanders had forgot what name he'd used.

The most widely used way to beat a drunk charge is a passive one—plead guilty and hope for the best. Ninety-four percent of the sample reported they usually pleaded guilty to a drunk charge even when they felt sure they were not really drunk at the time of arrest. Nearly 97 percent of the drunk cases heard in the Seattle court result in convictions. Tramps firmly believe that "you can't beat the charge," "you can't win the case" and it doesn't make any difference what you plead—"you are guilty anyway." Most men feel they actually have no other choice, and some believe they will get a lighter sentence.

Twenty-seven percent of the sample had, however, entered a plea of not guilty at one time or another, although only four men reported they had been acquitted. One stated, "The judge told me if I didn't think I was guilty to plead not guilty, which I did. He moved my case ahead 30 days, and I spent 30 days in jail, was found guilty and sentenced to 30 days." It is important to remember how these men feel about the drunk tank and the sense of isolation there. It is an almost unbearable thought to stand in court and know that if you plead not guilty you will return to that place. A man pleads guilty because he can be sentenced sooner and start "doing my time." The uncertainty of waiting for the outcome of trial and the fact that the days you wait for trial may be "dead time," not even counted as part of the sentence you finally receive, are perceived as punishments for entering an honest plea, and they provide sufficient motivation to enter a plea of guilty. One who pleads not guilty also runs the risk of offending the arresting officers who must take time to appear in court as witnesses. One man recalled: "If you plead not guilty you have the arresting cops against you, so you can't win anyway."

Finally, men plead guilty most of the time because they believe the courts are in collusion with the police against them. "All a cop has to do is say you were drunk—the judge never goes against a cop."

Tramps not only know the principles and rules of our legal system, they also know that the law enforcement agencies violate these rules as far as they are concerned: they are assumed to be guilty rather than innocent; they are rewarded for pleading guilty even when they are innocent; they have no way to provide themselves with a defense attorney; and they are punished if they go against the system by pleading not guilty. The network of protections for the innocent is stripped away from the process of criminal justice for these men, and in its place is an overwhelming pressure coercing them into violating their own integrity by agreeing with the verdict of the system.

One option usually open to a man attempting to beat a drunk charge is to make a statement. Only 16 percent of the sample reported they had ever asked to make a statement in court and not been allowed to do so. The tramp learns which factors influence the judge as he sentences a man to jail for public drunkenness, and the statement he makes will reflect these concerns.

Equal justice for all under the law is the maxim of this court, yet when we consider whom the judge sentences and who escapes, we must conclude that some men are more equal than others. The man who still has family responsibilities may talk of family ties in an effort to get a suspended sentence. He is aware that being a responsible family man is one of the things that separates urban nomads from the rest of society, and any indication that he is still trying to keep from being a bum will carry weight with the judge.

Many men indicate they have a job, but unless it is a rather permanent one or unless there are some other extenuating circumstances, they are still apt to get a sentence. The most effective kind of statement may be a promise to get out of town. In these cases, the men are offering the judge the only thing they have left in life—their mobility:

Prosecutor: Mr. Brown, you have been charged with drunk in public. How do you plead?

Mr. Brown: Guilty.

Judge: When were you released?

Mr. Brown: Last Saturday morning. Could I have a break? I want to go pick apples. Last time, I got out of jail and walked around to where the bus to the apples was and when I got to the bus I was waiting in line to get on and the patrol car picked me up.

Judge: Will you go pick apples if I give you an opportunity?

Mr. Brown: Yes, I will.

Judge: Thirty days suspended.

Such claims as "I was asleep in my car" or "I just got out of the hospital, and I've been taking pills. I had a couple drinks and fell asleep, but it was the pills that made me fall asleep" are commonly heard in court, but they do not often lead to a suspended sentence. At the least they offer a meager opportunity for a man to attempt to restore his damaged self-respect for having given in to the system and pleaded guilty.

During the past couple of years in Seattle, a new strategy for beating drunk charges has been added to the list: request the alcoholism treatment center. When the judge considers a man to be a good candidate, he then continues his case, and waits for him to be psychologically and medically examined and finally recommended by the treatment center staff for acceptance. If he is acceptable, he will then be sentenced to the treatment center for a period of four months. Sometimes a man is anxious for treatment but does not indicate appropriate interest and goes to jail instead, as in the following case:

Prosecutor: Mr. Pace, you have been charged with drunk in public. How do you plead?

Mr. Pace: Guilty.

Judge: Do you have a drinking problem?

Mr. Pace: We all have drinking problems, but I've worked on mine.

Judge: Have you had any help?

Mr. Pace: Yes, I went to Alcoholics Anonymous, but their rules are too stringent. They wouldn't allow working any night job or overtime. I talked to the probation officer, and he said try to take their advice.

Judge: Do you want assistance, or do you want to continue as you are?

Mr. Pace: It depends on how strong the treatment would be.

Judge: We have a new treatment center, but it's only for those who want help and will cooperate with the program. If you don't want to, you can go back to the city jail.

Mr. Pace: Well, I would like to go if their program isn't too stringent.

Judge: There can be no conditions on your going there. The sentence is 30 days in the Seattle city jail.

The treatment center is viewed by some men, however, as an easier place to do time than jail, and in a sense they "beat their drunk charge" by going there. Very few tramps have become totally immune to the norms and values of American culture, and they often feel guilty, especially when they are arrested for a long drunk. Some men reported that the worst aspect of court was the way it intensified their feelings of shame and guilt without any opportunity to express this. One said, "It hurts my pride. It's degrading. You are on exhibition for everyone to see, not being able to express how sorry you really are for being drunk." In all these experiences—the public humiliation, the waiting, facing the judge without any means of defense, the physical discomfort involved—tramps feel that underlying the whole process they are looked upon by the officials of the society as objects to be manipulated, as something less than human. The worst thing about court is being "herded around like a bunch of cattle—dumb animals."

STAGE 11: HOLDING TANK

Men who receive a sentence walk back into the seventh-floor section of the jail and are placed in the holding tank after the court session is completed. The trusty officer joins them there, and a decision is made regarding the future role they will have in jail: trusty or lockup. This decision is probably the most significant factor in determining whether a man does hard time or easy time, since trusties have many advantages that lockups do not. They are put in several different kinds of tanks that are unlocked during the day. Some have freedom to move throughout most of the jail, and others may even go outside to work. Their greater freedom allows them to watch TV at certain times, and, most important, they have access to food and other resources in and out of the jail. It is difficult to determine the reasons why an individual may not become a trusty, but often there are not enough jobs, or a man may be too old and sick, while another may have run away the last time he was a trusty.

STAGE 12: DELOUSING TANK

The men spend several hours in the delousing tank, and most of them felt it was the worst part of the entire process of making the bucket. As soon as the assignments are made in the holding tank, all inmates, both trusties and lockups, are taken a few feet down the hall to be deloused. There are 16 bunks in this tank with a small passageway between the bunks, a shower, and toilet. The men are crowded in and ordered to strip off all of their clothing. The nakedness that the men must now endure is felt to be degrading in itself, but the men also feel they may be contaminated by each other. And their clothes, if not lousy before, certainly will be after the treatment they get.

> One machine with 30 men's clothes for delousing—some guys are better than looking at carnivals, wearing a couple of union suits, couple pair of pants. The clothes should be turned inside out where the seams show so the greybacks can't hide; some guys are filthy. If they're lousy and guys are so crowded together, everybody's contaminated. Them clothes should really be in that machine for maybe three hours so nobody gets lousy.

Many men reported that they felt very keenly about their clothing, and they are perfectly aware that the designation of bum is used for them largely because of their appearance. While they were in court, after lying in the drunk tank for several days, the state of their clothing caused them great embarrassment and concern. But all these feelings about clothes reflect the fact that as the self crumbles, men cling more desperately to the last vestige of any material objects which symbolize, in some sense, their personal identity and the world outside. Not only is the men's clothing stripped from their backs, but the best articles are sometimes stolen by trusties, and almost everything comes out of the heating machine in worse shape than when it went in.

STAGES 13 AND 14:
TIME TANK AND TRUSTY TANK

For the lockup nothing so increases the amount of hard time a man does as much as hunger. One man said, "You can do hard time any place especially if there's poor grub or if you're sleeping on the steel," and almost everyone agreed that in Seattle jail the grub was poor indeed and everyone was continually hungry.

The experience of doing hard time as a trusty or lockup is related to many other facets of life in the bucket besides food, however. It results, in part, from failure to maintain a compliant attitude towards the social and physical environment, failure to live a day at a time, losses of personal property and jobs on the outside and losses of clothing in the delousing process. In addition, a system of rewards and punishments within the jail contributes directly to the experience of doing hard or easy time.

While rewards are sought and favors are gratefully accepted from many policemen, the men are aware that these are granted only if one maintains a submissive attitude, and even at that, are few and far between. The men are much more alert to the possibility of punishment, which may come in the form of withheld privileges, extra physical torment or being busted. In jail men have the privilege of writing letters, making a phone call each week, getting out of their cell for a brief period of exercise, and using the money in their property to purchase candy and cigarettes through the weekly commissary. These privileges are not equally available to all men, and their withdrawal by the police is felt as a terrible loss.

The bulls may also punish more directly. The men usually refer to this as being put on "the bull's shit list" or having "a cop on your ass." One man recalled, "Even a trusty may do hard time if a cop is on his ass." Fifteen percent of the sample reported that they had been put on the bull's shit list for various reasons—"I refused to polish a cop's shoes," or "I told them I was going to call the Civil Liberties Union about the sadistic treatment," or "I didn't call him 'officer.'"

The final kind of punishment is being busted. Almost any person, whether lockup or trusty, can be busted to another less desirable place within the jail. There are six distinct places within the jail to which a man may be busted for misbehavior, for getting on the bull's shit list, or for some unknown reason: trusty tank, time tank, padded cell, drunk tank, stand-up cell, and the hole. One man reported being busted to the drunk tank because he kept asking for medical treatment: "This is what I received to keep me quiet." Another said, "The nurse had this man busted on word from another trusty which was not true pertaining to his work in the dispensary, and he did 35 days there."

A few men will go to the drunk tank at their own request in order to do easy time. They want the extra food which those who are too ill and cannot eat will leave there for them, or they may want to avoid having to control their behavior as carefully as they must when they are lockups or trusties. But no one goes voluntarily to the stand-up cell or the hole. Many men did not know of these places, but one man described the hole this way:

> There was a small Indian man who I knew, and he got in a fight with a bull at the booking desk. They cuffed his hands behind his back and worked him over and then put him in the hole and left him there for two days. He said he passed his time by doing pushups. They stripped him naked, he had no clothing, and the hole is a little concrete cell about six-foot square. There was no light, and he was fed bread and water.

But overarching the concrete results of the rewards and punishment used to control the tramp's behavior are two other factors. A man summed up one, the dread of loss:

> Well, one thing a man does not do in jail is talk unless he is spoken to. There is a constant fear of loss, because loss is a penalty. One way to penalize a man is simply to ignore him

as he rattles the bars of his cage or the cell. For instance, a man might be going into DTs and need some medical attention, and so attract the attention of the guard he will shake the cell bars very loudly, because he is desperate for some kind of help, and he'll be penalized by simply ignoring him.

Second, it should be pointed out that most men felt there was a great deal of unpredictability in the punishments they might receive. Everything depended on the vagaries of the officers' moods and especially which officer one encountered.

STAGE 15: THE STREET AGAIN

Whether a man is a lockup or trusty the days do pass until the inmate is doing short time—only a few days remain on his sentence. For some, the last few days are easy time, filled with the knowledge and expectation of release. For others, as their minds become filled with memories of the outside and they plan for the days ahead, it is not so easy. But eventually the morning arrives when a man knows he will be escorted from his cell, lay aside his identity as a lockup or trusty and become, if only for a few hours, a kickout. After being discharged he walks to the elevator and rides quickly to the ground floor, walks out of the building—a free man who will now take up his life as an urban nomad in other scenes of that world.

But jail is perhaps the most important scene in that world. Here the remaining shreds of respectable identity have been stripped away as the nomads became participants in the elaborate ritual of making the bucket. Society, which has swept them out of sight and in the process cut them off from their former selves, now views them as bums or common drunkards. But in jail there has developed in these men an identity vacuum, along with powerful motivations to fill it, not only because of their material losses, but because inactivity, restraint and oversensitivity to the staff create pressures to act, to become and to gain a new sense of personal identity and a new set of values to replace what has been lost.

The novice who repeats this experience several times may first seek to escape it by travel to a new town, but once there he usually goes to Skid Road for ready acceptance. Sooner or later, for many men, the world and culture of the tramp become a viable alternative to replace what has been lost in the ritual of making the bucket. In that culture he may still be alienated from the rest of society—but *not from himself* or others like him. He will find acceptance as well as adaptive strategies for survival as an urban nomad. But more importantly, something else has been going on simultaneously during the days in jail—he has been learning the attitudes, values and skills which are required for survival in this new culture.

LETTERS FROM THE TANK

Mr. William R. Tanner, the writer of these letters and notes, is 49 and unmarried. He arrived in Seattle in 1967 and stayed for less than a year, during which time he was arrested nine times for public drunkenness and served nearly 200 days in jail. The author has lost contact with Mr. Tanner, who may well be languishing in jail somewhere. His story is common to thousands of men, the urban nomads of America.—J. P. S.

Somewhere in Seattle, August 14, 1967

Dear Jim,

In all sincerity (as far as I'm able to be so) I'll be happy to write my own thoughts and you can sift thru the garbage and use whatever you wish. My only desire is that it would perhaps help some other in this bedlam. My background is peculiar: I was born in Minnesota, December 15, 1918. Father was a miner, mother a housewife. My brother Wayne, eight years my senior, was class valedictorian, a West Point nominee, a salesman and compulsive gambler. Died in 1951—second heart attack. My "namesake Tanner," or my father, died of TB somewhere when I was born. Mother remarried my stepfather. We were pretty tight; he said I was his true son. Several older people have as much as said so. I had a grand childhood. I now have a nephew and a sister-in-law who is remarried. I took my frustrations and self-anger out on her at my step-dad's funeral so thus far she has understandably refused to forgive. Thru a priest I found out that she does not wish to hear from me. Perhaps in fear that I may contaminate my nephew. I still expect to make amends if time will permit. I was tested by a psychologist a year ago in Minneapolis, the Minnesota Multiphasic Personality Inventory. He said I didn't belong in jail at all, my IQ was 131. He said I indicated that I liked people and said he wished I'd go back to college and get a degree in anything and get into social work.

Well, I was pinched last Friday and they threw me in the drunk tank where I stayed until court time this morning. . . . The general consensus amongst the jail population is that this is the hungriest jail in the country—even the southern jails give of quantity if not quality. All seems to revolve around the pleasure-pain process. But why penalize the homeless, tortured, the ill? I reiterate, and Jim you're aware that in truth, none of us were slapped for being exuberant, jocose, morose, bellicose, or comatose, but because of lack of a lousy $20 bail. My own stand is that booze has been with us as long as the "oldest profession." Since humanism is being back-seated (not without a struggle), money is what's respected! The good judge gave me a kickout. I'm now going to seek work and try once again to get a period of sobriety. . . . It's 2:00 p.m.—I just sold a pint of plasma for five skins. I thank you much for your friendship and interest.

49er Bill

Tank # 709—Seattle City Jail, August 15, 1967

I entered a plea of guilty to the good judge—no other way to do it— and I'm on the steel for another ten days. There's no chance of beating a drunk charge. . . .

Tank # 709—Seattle City Jail, August 29, 1967

I was busted last Saturday and got twenty days this time. Walked out on Friday and back in on Saturday. Some towns in California pay $1 a day and smokes for work done by inmates. Most state pens pay a little and give a man "gate money." This bit of turning a man loose at 10:00 a.m. or later, stone-broke and hungry, with parting shots like "See you tomorrow!" First you must hustle pad, food, minus carfare— too late to seek work . . . rough. It's always easy to spear drink or promote a jug of apple wine. In emaciated condition it's very easy to get loaded and then back to the "ballroom" and equal justice. Only it's not equal unless you got $20.

A lad of 71 was released Monday and is back today. Out for a day-and-a-half. Slept most of the time he was here, slightly deaf and senile. The judge should have his head examined. The man's harmless! So he got drunk . . . I suspect he probably got robbed too. Doesn't weigh 90 pounds. They let us walk ten minutes in the corridor tonight and I looked in on him—he was conked out on the ballroom floor with a hangover. . . .

Alcoholism Treatment Center, October 4, 1967

The program here isn't started yet—this place just opened up a couple weeks ago with the first patients. The program isn't doing any of us any good. Of course they feed us well and they're building us up, but 30 days is enough to do that. It's not necessary for them to keep us in as long as they're going to keep us out here. It will take a lot of money to get this program off the ground. It may never get off the ground.

Alcholism Treatment Center—Seattle, October 9, 1967

We had a meeting this afternoon and a lot of patients were angry about there not being much of a program out here. Alcoholics Anonymous meetings, lectures, vitamins and work—most of the time we work! Routine and monotonous though it's a lot better than the jail.

I had planned to bring up some questions—even typed them out on paper, but didn't even ask them. When do we get out of here? When does the training program and treatment program begin and what does it consist of? Who is going to decide about our release? Several patients asked why we had to be in here for six months and they said we could get out earlier if we had a job and a place to stay. So I guess I'll have to wait it out. I work every day cleaning up one of the dormitories. I have to mop and wax the floors, clean the commodes and sinks and mirrors. It doesn't take all day—but it is supposed to be work therapy. If I have to do this very long I'll become a zombie. . . .

Holding Tank—Seattle City Jail, November 3, 1967

Jim, I'm back again. Released from the treatment center on October 30. It was done in a casual manner. Given a letter to the president of Local # 6 for a job. They dropped me off at a half way house for alcoholics at 5:00 p.m. The assistant manager said they weren't interested in the fact that I'd been at the treatment center, I had to get on their program. I couldn't work for two weeks, had to attend Alcoholics Anonymous meetings seven nights a week, be in by 11:00 p.m. and do work at the half-way house. I felt as if I'd been transferred from one institution to another. When he stated, "The door swings both ways," I swung out—blew cool—ready for a drunk. When I presented letter to Local # 6, he said, "Oh yes, the alcoholism treatment center, quite a place. I'll put you on the list." Sounded like, "Don't call us, we'll call you!" When I said I could wax, burr, strip, he said, "Well, maybe I can get you on right now," and made a call and did. I never showed. Had a beer. While in the rest room had a bag with two pairs of slacks stolen, so off to the races. I don't know why I got drunk. I didn't intend to drink. It was really a combination of things. A long bus wait, plus the desire to drink. The pure fact is, I did hard time even at the treatment center. Hadn't made a dime, no smokes, and a sense of anxiety because I was broke. But, facilities like that are an improvement over jail in that they will restore the body at least with food and rest. The compulsion to drink—I would think the proper approach would be to try and find out what is lacking, what the person needs to help fill his needs. Myself, I had a small taste of sobriety in the five and a half months I wasn't drinking. Haven't been happy drinking since. Maybe that is all anyone needs—plus the ability to remember past miseries caused by booze.

 # 709 City Jail—Seattle, Washington, November 18, 1967

Greetings! I trust you are still pursuing your studies of the inebriates with tenacity and dedication.

Now to get to the toils and travails of Tanner. I pleaded guilty

Thursday (November 16)—was sentenced to 35 days. I handed the judge a Writ of Habeas Corpus directed to the Superior Court. Gave notice of intent to appeal and appeal bond set at $50. I don't have 50 cents. The bailiff told me my time does not start until after my appeal. Now, he must be wrong, or else I may languish here for a year waiting trial. The theory of "Equal Protection" is a myth. Possibly it is idiotic of me but I do feel more strongly than I can state that it is futile to jail a drunk—cruel and purposeless. I probably do not possess the ability, stamina, or wherewithal to successfully contest the sentence and I realize I do not possess even the minimal virtues but I am curious to see the outcome.

Tank # 709—Seattle City Jail, December 14, 1967

Jim, do me a favor and call the ACLU for me. I was sentenced to 35 days on 11/16/67 on public drunk. Given credit for time served from 11/8/67. My time has been served the hard way—purely because I tried to exercise my rights. I'm sending this note with another inmate who is being transferred to the treatment center from the jail. Please explain to the ACLU attorney that I have no means of communication other than this. This is absolutely the rottenest setup I've ever seen. Thanks a lot, Your Friend. . . .

Somewhere in Seattle, December 19, 1967

Again—your bewildered, dismayed, bemused, delerious, bedazzled, defunct scribe salutes you with some gossamerlike, misty caperings. Yesterday they took me to court and the judge said, "Well, since your time is served, your case has been remanded from Superior Court to me." I said, "Your Honor, I served 40 days!" Judge said, "You will be released today." As I walked away a fat cop says, "Get back in there!" I told him the judge said I was released. "Oh no," he says, "It is the jailor who has to release you." I thought they were going to give me 35 more days. Like the sergeant said, "You broke your pick with us— don't expect any favors." I'm afraid I'm becoming paranoid. When I got out the letter you wrote me on December 8 with writing material and stamps was in my property!

I'm gradually trying to introduce myself to society and regain my civilian bearings. If you can trail me along this devious track, you've a much better acumen than I. After 30 days in jail you owe yourself a drunk.

10:00 a.m., "Hotel Flea-Bag-On-The-Sound," December 20, 1967

I will not even attempt to justify my "smart bastard" self-projection of yesterday. I think I have the drunk out of my system. It does seem, at least to me, that I do seem to be able to communicate (with some false bravado) when loaded, which same I seem to lack when sober. I finally got to bed last night—first time since release. Such fun being amongst people again, even though I'm still leaning on alcohol to lubricate my communicational office.

My only intention in this writ and appeal bit was purely to see what a person without a dime could do. I wish almost that I'd stayed in until January 9. But, let's face it—appearance and reality. The latter I've always dodged.

Tank # 709—Seattle City Jail, January 21, 1968

My last day—kickout tomorrow a.m. I think I'd better get back to Minneapolis or anywhere. The alcoholic treatment center kills you with kindness and boredom. This place is a pressure chamber and then some. Audio system plays some taped melancholic crap either so low you can't hear the news or so loud you can't hear each other or think—a sort of brainwashing—torture. Understand ballroom is loaded. The circle continues, where she stops no one knows. . . .

Edgecliff Sanitarium, Spokane, Washington, March 29, 1968

. . . now a TB suspect. Have been on a marathon drunk. I was pinched in Seattle on March 10 and the good judge gave me 60 days suspended. Next time in his court I would have gotten that 60 plus additional so I blew town.

Division of Corrections, Minneapolis, Minnesota, May 20, 1968

Greetings! Heavy, heavy hangs the time. I must have an urge to seek self-punishment—But like a homing pigeon I returned here—knowing damn well I'd wind up here. Slightly mellow, I walked or ran a red light—Damn if I do not get accosted by the most dedicated cops (I use the term loosely).

I hope you're not getting the impression that I'm getting a father complex writing you (bugging you). I've already got a "mother" complex as far as institutions are concerned. Everything was going good. Had a job, pad, clothes, etc.

Perhaps I'd better volunteer for a cure or start a flood of writs to bug the judge or judges. I guess I'm involved with about three. . . .

Part VI

IMPLICATIONS OF THE INTERACTIONIST FRAMEWORK

13

Conceptions of Deviant Behavior: The Old and the New

JACK P. GIBBS

The ultimate end of substantive theory in any science is the formulation of empirical relations among classes of phenomena, e.g., X varies directly with Y, X is present if and only if Y is present. However, unless such propositions are arrived at by crude induction or sheer intuition, there is a crucial step before the formulation of a relational statement. This step can be described as the way the investigator comes to perceive or "think about" the phenomena under consideration. Another way to put it is the development of a "conception."

There is no clear cut distinction between, on the one hand, a conception of a class of phenomena and, on the other, formal definitions and substantive theory. Since a conception emphasizes the predominant feature of a phenomenon, it is not entirely divorced from a definition of it; but the former is not identical with the latter. Thus, for example, the notion of exploitation looms large in the Marxian conception of relations among social classes; but exploitation is or may be only one feature of class relations, and it does not serve as a formal definition of them. Further, in certain fields, particularly the social sciences, a conception often not only precedes but also gives rise to operational definitions. As the case in point, if an operational definition of social class relies on the use of "reputational technique," the investigator's conception of social class is in all probability non-Marxian.

"Conceptions of Deviant Behavior: The Old and the New" by J. P. Gibbs is reprinted from *Pacific Sociological Review*, Volume 9, Number 2 (Spring 1966) pp. 9–14, by permission of the Publisher, Sage Publications, Inc.

What has been said of the distinction between definitions and conceptions holds also for the relation between the latter and substantive theory. A conception may generate a particular theory, but it is not identical with it. For one thing, a conception contains definitional elements and is therefore partially tautological, which means that in itself a conception is never a clear-cut empirical proposition. Apart from its tautological character, a conception is too general to constitute a testable idea. Nonetheless, a conception may generate substantive theory, and it is certainly true that theories reflect conceptions. Durkheim's work is a classic illustration. His theory on suicide clearly reflects his view of society and social life generally.

In a field without consensus as to operational definitions and little in the way of systematic substantive theory, conceptions necessarily occupy a central position. This condition prevails in most of the social sciences. There, what purports to be definitions of classes of phenomena are typically general and inconsistent to the point of lacking empirical applicability (certainly in the operational sense of the word). Moreover, what passes for a substantive theory in the social sciences is more often than not actually a loosely formulated conception. These observations are not intended to deride the social sciences for lack of progress. All fields probably go through a "conceptions" stage; it is only more apparent in some than in others.

Of the social sciences, there is perhaps no clear-cut illustration of the importance of conceptions than in the field identified as criminology and the study of deviant behavior. As we shall see, the history of the field can be described best in terms of changing conceptions of crime, criminals, deviants, and deviation. But the purpose of this paper is not an historical account of major trends in the field. If it is true that conceptions give rise to formal definitions and substantive theory, then a critical appraisal of conceptions is important in its own right. This is all the more true in the case of criminology and the study of deviant behavior, where conceptions are frequently confused with substantive theories, and the latter so clearly reflect the former.

OLDER CONCEPTIONS

In recent years there has been a significant change in the prevailing conception of deviant behavior and deviants. Prior to what is designated here as the "new perspective," it commonly was assumed that there is something inherent in deviants which distinguishes them from nondeviants.[1] Thus, from Lombroso to Sheldon, criminals were viewed as biologically distinctive in one way or another.[2] The inadequacies of this conception are now obvious. After decades of research, no biological characteristic which distinguishes criminals has been discovered, and this generalization applies even to particular types of criminals (e.g., murderers, bigamists, etc.). Consequently, few theorists now even toy with the notion that all criminals are atavistic, mentally defective, constitutionally inferior. But the rejection of the biological conception of crime stems from more than research findings. Even casual observation and mild logic cast doubt on the idea. Since legislators are not geneticists, it is difficult to see how they can pass laws in such a way as to create "born criminals." Equally important, since most if not all "normal" persons have violated a law at one time or another,[3] the assertion that criminals are so by heredity now appears most questionable.

Although the biological conception generally has been rejected, what is here designated as the analytic conception of criminal acts largely has escaped criticism. Rather than view criminal acts as nothing more or less than behavior contrary to legal norms, the acts are construed as somehow injurious to society. The shift from the biological to the analytical conception is thus from the actors to the characteristics of their acts, with the idea being that some acts are inherently "criminal" or at least that criminal acts share intrinsic characteristics in common.

The analytical conception is certainly more defensible than the biological view, but it is by no means free of criticism. Above all, the "injurious" quality of some deviant acts is by no means conspicuous, as witness Durkheim's observation:

> . . . there are many acts which have been and still are regarded as criminal without in themselves being harmful to society. What social danger is there in touching a tabooed object, an impure animal or man, in letting the sacred fire die down, in eating certain meats, in failure to make the traditional sacrifice over the grave of parents, in not exactly pronouncing the ritual formula, in not celebrating holidays, etc.?[4]

Only a radical functionalism would interpret the acts noted by Durkheim as literally injuring society in any reasonable sense of the word. The crucial point is that, far from actually injuring society or sharing some intrinsic feature in common, acts may be criminal or deviant because and only because they are proscribed legally and/or socially. The proscription may be irrational in that members of the society cannot explain it, but it is real nonetheless. Similarly, a law may be "arbitrary" in that it is imposed by a powerful minority and, as a consequence, lacks popular support and is actively opposed. But if the law is consistently enforced (i.e., sanctions are imposed regularly on violators), it is difficult to see how it is not "real."

The fact that laws may appear to be irrational and arbitrary has prompted attempts to define crime independently of legal criteria, i.e., analytically. The first step in this direction was Garofalo's concept of natural crime—acts which violate prevailing sentiments of pity and probity.[5] Garofalo's endeavor accomplished very little. Just as there is probably no act which is contrary to law universally, it is equally true that no act violates sentiments of pity and probity in all societies. In other words, cultural relativity defeats any attempt to compile a list of acts which are crimes universally. Also, it is hard to see why the violation of a rigorously enforced traffic regulation is not a crime even though unrelated to sentiments of pity and probity. If it is not a crime, what is it?

The search for an analytic identification of crime continued in Sellin's proposal to abandon legal criteria altogether in preference for "conduct norms."[6] The rationale for the proposal is simple. Because laws vary and may be "arbitrary" in any one society, a purely legal definition of crime is not suited for scientific study. But Sellin's observations on the arbitrariness of laws apply in much the same way to conduct norms. Just as the content of criminal law varies from one society to the next and from time to time, so does the content of extra-legal norms. Further, the latter may be just as arbitrary as criminal laws. Even in a highly urbanized society such as the United States, there is evidently no rationale or utilitarian reason for all of the norms pertaining to mode of dress. True, there may be much greater conformity to conduct norms that to some laws, but the degree of conformity is hardly an adequate criterion of the "reality" of norms, legal or extralegal. If any credence whatever can be placed in the Kinsey report, sexual taboos may be violated frequently and yet remain as taboos. As a case in point, even if adultery is now common in the United States, it is significant that the participants typically attempt to conceal their acts. In brief, just as laws may be violated frequently and are "unreal" in that sense, the same applies to some conduct norms; but in neither case do they cease to be norms. They would cease to be norms if and only if one defines deviation in terms of statistical regularities in behavior, but not even Sellin would subscribe to the notion that normative phenomena can or should be defined in statistical terms.

In summary, however capricious and irrational legal and extra-legal norms may appear to be, the inescapable conclusion is that some acts are criminal or deviant for the very simple reason that they are proscribed.

THE NEW CONCEPTION

Whereas both the pathological and the analytical conception of deviation assume that some intrinsic feature characterizes deviants and deviant acts, an emerging perspective in sociology flatly rejects any such assumption. Indeed, as witness the following statements by Kitsuse, Becker, and Erikson, exactly the opposite position is taken.

Kitsuse:
> Forms of behavior *per se* do not differentiate deviants from nondeviants; it is the responses of the conventional and conforming members of the society who identify and interpret behavior as deviant which sociologically transform persons into deviants.[7]

Erikson:
> From a sociological standpoint, deviance can be defined as conduct which is generally thought to require the attention of social control agencies—that is conduct about which "something should be done." Deviance is not a property *inherent in* certain forms of behavior; it is a property *conferred upon* these forms by the audiences which directly or indirectly witness them. Sociologically, then, the critical variable in the study of deviance is the social *audience* rather than individual *person,* since it is the audience which eventually decides whether or not any given action or actions will become a visible case of deviation.[8]

Becker:
> From this point of view, deviance is *not* a quality of the act a person commits, but rather a consequence of the application by others of rules and sanctions to an "offender." The deviant is one to whom that label has successfully been applied; deviant behavior is behavior that people so label.[9]

The common assertion in the above statements is that acts can be identified as deviant or criminal only by reference to the character of reaction to them by the public or by the official agents of a politically organized society. Put simply, if the reaction is of a certain kind, then and only then is the act deviant. The crucial point is that the essential feature of a deviant or deviant act is *external* to the actor and the act. Further, even if the acts or actors share some feature in common other than social reactions to them, the feature neither defines nor completely explains deviation. To take the extreme case, even if Lombroso had been correct in his assertion that criminals are biologically distinctive, the biological factor neither identifies the criminal nor explains criminality. Purely biological variables may explain why some persons commit certain acts, but they do not explain why the acts are crimes. Consequently, since criminal law is spatially and temporally relative, it is impossible to distinguish criminals from noncriminals (assuming that the latter do exist, which is questionable) in terms of biological characteristics. To illustrate, if act X is a crime in society A but not a crime in society B, it follows that, even assuming Lombroso to have been correct, the anatomical features which distinguish the criminal in society A may characterize the noncriminal in society B. In both societies some persons may be genetically predisposed to commit act X, but the act is a crime in one society and not in the other. Accordingly, the generalization that all persons with certain antomical features are criminals would be, in this instance, false. True, one may assert that the "born criminal" is predisposed to violate the laws of his own society, but this assumes either that "the genes" know what the law is or that the members of the legislature are geneticists. (i.e., they deliberately enact laws in such a way that the "born criminal" will violate them). Either assumption taxes credulity.

The new perspective of deviant behavior contradicts not only the biological but also the analytical conception. Whereas the latter seeks to find something intrinsic in deviant or, more specifically, criminal acts, the new conception denies any such characterization. True, the acts share a common denominator—they are identified by the character of reaction to them—but this does not mean that the acts are "injurious" to society or that they are in any way inherently abnormal. The new conception eschews the notion that some acts are deviant or criminal in all societies. For that matter, the reaction which identifies a deviant act may not be the same from one society or social group to the next. In general, then, the new conception of deviant behavior is relativistic in the extreme.

CRITICISM OF THE NEW PERSPECTIVE

The new perspective of deviant behavior is much more consistent not only with what is known about deviant behavior but also with contemporary sociological principles generally. However, while containing a fundamentally sound idea, the new perspective leaves some crucial questions unanswered. For one thing, it is not clear whether the perspective is intended to be a "substantive theory" of deviant behavior (i.e., an explanation of the phenomenon) or a conceptual treatment of it. Consider, again, statements by Becker, Kitsuse, and Erikson:

Becker:
    . . . *social groups create deviance by making the rules whose infraction constitute deviance,* and by applying those rules to particular people and labeling them as outsiders.[10]

Kitsuse and Cicourel:
    . . . *rates of deviant behavior* are produced by *the actions taken by persons in the social system* which define, classify and record certain behaviors as deviant.[11]

Erikson:
> . . . transactions taking place between deviant persons on the one side and agencies of control on the other are boundary maintaining mechanisms. They mark the outside limits of the area in which the norm has jurisdiction, and in this way assert how much diversity and variability can be contained within the system before it begins to lose its distinct structure, its unique shape.[12]

Now these statements appear to be something more than definitions. However, if regarded as explanations of deviant behavior, these and other similar observations do not provide adequate answers to three major questions: 1. Why does the incidence of a particular act vary from one population to the next? 2. Why do some persons commit the act while others do not? 3. Why is the act in question considered deviant and/or criminal in some societies but not in others?

The assertion that deviation is created or produced by the character of reactions to behavior (see statements by Becker and Kitsuse above) implies an answer to the question on incidence. But are we to conclude that the incidence of a given act is in fact a constant in all populations and that the only difference is in the quality of reactions to the act? Specifically, given two populations with the same kind of reaction to a particular type of act, can the new perspective explain why the incidence of the act is greater in one population than in the other? Not at all! On the contrary, even if two populations have the same legal and social definition of armed robbery and even if instances of the crime are reacted to in exactly the same way, it is still possible for the armed robbery rate to be much higher in one population than in the other. Reaction to deviation may influence the rate of deviation in that certain kinds of reaction may have a deterrent effect, but the deterrent quality of reaction has not been examined systematically by Becker, Kitsuse, or Erikson, primarily because they view reaction in terms of *identifying* deviant behavior. Actually, apart from identifying deviation, the new conception presents a sophisticated framework for the study of deterrence as an aspect of reaction to deviant behavior. All three of the advocates are sensitive to the importance of the deviant's response to reaction, and it would not be inconsistent for them to devote more attention to the possibility that some kinds of reaction have consequences beyond identifying behavior as deviant.

What has been said of the new perspective with regard to explaining variation in the incidence of deviant acts also applies to the second major question: Why do some persons commit a given act while others do not? The point is that the new perspective does not generate an answer to this question. For example, the fact that the reaction to armed robbery may involve incarceration hardly explains why some but not all persons commit the act. Again, the quality of reaction (or the probability of reaction) may have a differential deterrent effect, a possibility which is relevant in attempting to answer the question; but, as noted before, the new perspective exhibits little concern not only with deterrence but also with etiological factors generally. The lack of concern with etiological factors suggests that Becker, Erikson, and Kitsuse actually are seeking a theory not about deviant behavior *per se* but rather about reactions to deviant behavior (i.e., why does the quality of reaction vary from place to place and time to time?). In any event, the three persons closely associated with the perspective have not explicitly stated that they are seeking such a theory.

It is not at all clear whether Becker is pursuing a theory about deviant behavior or a theory about reactions to deviation. If it is the latter, then his focus on deviants rather than reactors is puzzling. Kitsuse is concerned with reaction to deviant behavior as a process, but he views reaction not only as a criterion of deviant behavior but also (evidently) as the decisive factor in relation to incidence. As such, he is apparently seeking a theory about deviant behavior and not reactions to it. Erikson's "functionalist" position could be construed as a theory about deviant behavior, or reactions, or both. However, even if reactions to deviation do serve a "function"—boundary maintenance —a functional interpretation hardly explains why the quality of reaction varies from one society to the next. Further, with reference to incidence, are we to conclude that social boundaries are maintained or demarcated if and only if the rate of deviant behavior is high?

Even if deviant acts are defined in terms of reactions to behavior, the identification does not and cannot explain why a given act is considered deviant and/or criminal in some but not all societies (the third major question). After all, a certain kind of reaction may identify behavior as deviant, but it obviously does not explain why the behavior is deviant.

The danger in evaluating the work of Becker, Erikson, and Kitsuse is that of prematurely rejecting what is a most promising approach to the study of deviant behavior. The danger can be avoided if it is clearly understood that they have formulated what is essentially a conception. As such, it contains both definitions and elements of substantive theory, and the development of the latter would be furthered considerably by making the distinction explicit. Finally, since a conception precedes substantive theory, it would be most unrealistic to demand testable empirical propositions at this stage. The only justifiable criticism on this point is that the three men have not specified their goal adequately, i.e., whether they are seeking an explanation of deviant behavior or of reaction to it. The fact that it may be both testifies to the fertility of the conception, but it is all the more reason to treat the distinction seriously.

REACTION AS A CRITERION OF DEVIATION

The point stressed continually by the new perspective is that acts are identified as deviant by the character of reactions to them. Whatever the merits of this position, it is not free of criticism. For one thing, Becker, Erikson, and Kitsuse have never specified exactly what kind of reaction identifies deviant acts. Becker constantly refers to deviants as persons labeled "outsiders," but this term is Becker's, not that of the man on the street. For that matter, the public may be more familiar with the meaning of the term "deviant" than with "outsider."

When we turn to concrete cases of reactions supposedly indicative of deviant acts, there are some rather curious results. Kitsuse, for example, found reactions of students to persons identified by the students as homosexuals to be "generally mild."[13] These reactions may or may not be representative of the public generally; nonetheless, two significant questions are posed. First, are we to conclude, because of the mildness of the reaction, that homosexuals are not deviants after all? Second, how "harsh" must the reaction be before the behavior is to be construed as deviant? More generally, since "mild" and "harsh" are subjective terms, exactly what "kind" of reaction identifies deviant acts or deviance? Some of Becker's observations are puzzling in this connection. As a case in point: "Whether an act is deviant, then, depends on how other people react to it. You can commit clan incest and suffer no more than gossip as long as no one makes a public accusation. . . ."[14] Why is it that gossip does not qualify as a reaction which identifies deviant behavior?

The failure of Becker, Erikson, and Kitsuse to specify the kind of reactions which identify deviation is further complicated by the contradictions in their own position. The contradictions stem from the fact that a deviant act can be defined as behavior *which is contrary to a norm or rule*. One type of norm is simply what the members of a social unit think conduct "ought" or "ought not" be. For example, on this basis it is probably true that the act of joining the Communist party is "deviant" in American society, even though the quality of reaction to it in a particular instance may be problematical. This conception of deviation enables one to treat deviant acts and reactions to them as conceptually distinct. But this is not so from the viewpoint of Becker, Erikson, and Kitsuse, because deviant behavior for them *is defined in terms of reactions to it*. On the other hand, while advocates of the new perspective do recognize the "norm" conception of deviation, they do not consistently reject it. Witness, for example:

Becker:
An even more interesting kind of case is found at the other extreme of *secret deviance*. Here an improper act is

committed, yet no one notices it or reacts to it as a violation of the rules.[15]

Kituse and Cicourel:
We wish to state explicitly that the interpretation of official statistics proposed here *does not* imply that the forms of behavior which the sociologist might define and categorize as deviant (such as Merton's modes of adaptation) have no factual basis or theoretical importance.[16]

Erikson:
There are societies in which deviance is considered a natural pursuit for the young, an activity which they can easily abandon when they move through defined ceremonies into adulthood. There are societies which give license to large groups of persons to engage in deviant behavior for certain societies in which special groups are formed to act in ways "contrary" to the normal expectations of the culture.[17]

Now all of these statements admit, in one way or another, that deviant behavior can be identified in terms of norms, but the authors do not come to grips with the problem and take a consistent stand on the issue. Thus, if deviant behavior is defined in terms of reactions to it, then Becker cannot speak properly of "secret deviance." If behavior defined as deviant by sociologists in reference to the prevailing social norms is "real," then in what sense can one maintain, as Kitsuse does elsewhere, that behavior is deviant if and only if there is a certain kind of reaction to it. Finally, in the case of Erikson, how can the behavior of "large groups of persons" be identified as deviant when they have been given a "license" to engage in it? To be consistent, Becker, Kitsuse, and Erikson would have to insist that behavior which is contrary to a norm is not deviant unless it is discovered and there is a particular kind of reaction to it. Thus, if persons engage in adultery but their act is not discovered and reacted to in a certain way (by the members of the social unit), then it is not deviant! Similarly, if a person is erroneously thought to have engaged in a certain type of behavior and is reacted to "harshly" as a consequence, a deviant act has taken place!

The extreme position of Becker, Erikson, and Kitsuse is also apparent when attempting to explain why reaction or deviant behavior is not purely random and idiosyncratic. One could argue that a satisfactory explanation cannot be given without making reference to norms, but this concept evidently is not altogether welcome in the new perspective. Finally, apart from the issue of norms, the new perspective negates a significant empirical question: Why do reactions to deviant behavior vary from place to place and time to time? An answer to this question from the new perspective necessarily would be at least partially tautological because deviant behavior is defined in terms of reactions to it.

As the tone of the above criticism suggests, this writer differs with Becker, *et al.*, on the issue of identifying deviant behavior. My preference is to identify deviant acts by reference to norms, and treat reaction to deviation as a contingent property. However, this preference reflects nothing more than opinion, and the ultimate evaluation of the new conception on this point must await an assessment of substantive theory generated by it. Accordingly, no claim is made that Becker, Erikson, and Kitsuse are "wrong." Rather, the criticism is that (1) they have not specified exactly what kind of reaction identifies behavior as deviant, and (2) they have failed to take a consistent stand on a particular conceptual issue.

OVERVIEW

The major trend in the study of crime and deviant behavior has been in the direction of a distinctly "social" conception of the subject matter. Whereas Lombroso thought of criminals in biological terms and later positivists sought to discover intrinsic features of criminal acts, the new perspective conceives of both in terms of the quality of social reaction to behavior. Accordingly, whether or not a person or an act is criminal or deviant is a matter of the way in which the public and/or officials react.

The relativistic criterion of deviation introduced by the new perspective is in keeping with contemporary sociological principles. Further, a social conception of the phenomenon promises to generate substantive theories that are distinctly sociological in outlook. But the new conception has left at least four crucial questions unanswered. First, what elements in the scheme are intended to be definitions rather than substantive theory? Second, is the ultimate goal to explain deviant behavior or to explain reactions to deviation? Third, is deviant behavior to be identified exclusively in terms of reaction to it? Fourth, exactly what kind of reaction identifies behavior as deviant?

No claim is made that the advocates of the new conception are unable to answer the above questions, nor that their answers would be wrong. The only point is that the questions must be answered if the new conception is to develop and receive the constructive attention that it deserves.

NOTES

[1]Throughout this paper crime is treated as a subclass of deviant behavior. Particular issues may be discussed with reference to crime, but on the whole the observations apply to deviant behavior generally.

[2]Although not essential to the argument, it is perhaps significant that the alleged biological differentiae of criminals have been consistently viewed as "pathological" in one sense or another.

[3]See Edwin H. Sutherland and Donald R. Cressey, *Principles of Criminology*, 6th ed., Chicago: J. B. Lippincott, 1960, p. 39.

[4]Emile Durkheim, *The Division of Labor in Society*, George Simpson, trans., Glencoe, Ill.: The Free Press, 1949, p. 72.

[5]Raffaele Garofalo, *Criminology*, Boston: Little, Brown, and Co., 1914, Chapter I.

[6]Thorsten Sellin, *Culture Conflict and Crime*, New York: Social Science Research Council, Bulletin 41, 1938.

[7]John I. Kitsuse, "Societal Reaction to Deviant Behavior: Problems of Theory and Method," *Social Problems*, 9 (Winter, 1962), p. 253.

[8]Kai T. Erikson, "Notes on the Sociology of Deviance," *Social Problems*, 9 (Spring, 1962), p. 308.

[9]Howard S. Becker, *Outsiders*, New York: The Free Press of Glencoe, 1963, p. 9.

[10]Becker, *Outsiders*, p. 9.

[11]John I. Kitsuse and Aaron Cicourel, "A Note on the Uses of Official Statistics," *Social Problems*, 11 (Fall, 1963), p. 135.

[12]Erikson, "Notes on the Sociology of Deviance," p. 310.

[13]Kitsuse, "Societal Reaction to Deviant Behavior," p. 256.

[14]Becker, *Outsiders*, p. 11.

[15]Becker, *Outsiders*, p. 20.

[16]Kitsuse and Cicourel, "A Note on the Uses of Official Statistics," pp. 138–139.

[17]Erickson, "Notes on the Sociology of Deviance," p. 313.

Deviance, Deviant Behavior, and Deviants: Some Conceptual Problems

JOHN I. KITSUSE

In recent years the growing interest in the study of deviance has been at the center of a more general development of sociological theory. The impetus for this development has come from two major sources —the social psychology of G. H. Mead and the phenomenological sociology of Alfred Schutz. Theory and research in the sociology of deviance more directly and explicitly reflect the former than the latter, particularly the line of inquiry that has come to be associated with the term "labeling." In this paper, I want to examine the development of the labeling approach, some of its characteristics, some criticisms that have been made of it, and the problems raised by these criticisms.

Ironically, we immediately face the problem of labels. Proponents as well as critics have referred to the approach by several names from the straightforward "the labeling approach to deviance" and "the new conception of deviance" to the more grandiose "labeling theory of deviance." Labeling, in its many variations, is an unfortunate term that has more confused than clarified the distinctive perspective that has developed around this approach. The most unfortunate aspect of the term is that it invites if not encourages a vulgar acceptance as well as rejection of the approach; for example, the simple-minded ways in which Howard S. Becker's definition of deviant and deviant behavior has been used and misused (see Clinard, 1968, and Rushing, 1969).

This article was originally prepared for a symposium on deviance at the University of Minnesota, Minneapolis, May 21–22, 1971. It is published here for the first time. Copyright 1972 by John I. Kitsuse.

It is worth commenting in passing that a curious and instructive comparison can be made between the development of this approach to deviance and the "value-conflict approach" to the study of social problems. Willard Waller's "Social Problems and the Mores" (Waller, 1936) contains the provocative statement: "Value judgments are the formal causes of social problems, just as the law is the formal cause of crime." Waller's article was followed by another by Fuller and Myers (1941) in which the authors wrote: *"Social problems are what people think they are* and if conditions are not defined as social problems by the people involved in them, they are not problems to those people, although they may be problems to outsiders or to scientists. . . ."

I find the comparison between the developments of these two approaches curious and instructive because almost forty years after Waller's statement, Merton (1971) writes a spirited, and, in my judgment, wrong-headed, criticism of the value-conflict perspective on social problems. Perhaps the most cogent response to Merton's criticism, informed by what is still the dominant view of the sociology of social problems, is that Waller's (1936) observation on the state of theory remains a pertinent commentary today: "Although sociologists have studied social problems for many years, they have produced astonishingly little systematic thought concerning them." That this should be so is, I think, a consequence of the fact that the manifold implications of Waller's view have not been explored systematically. There are now clear indications that this exploration has begun—for example in Becker's introduction to *Social Problems* (1966), Horowitz and Liebowitz's formulation of social and political marginality (1968), and Turk's (1966) and Quinney's (1970) recent formulations of crime, and so forth. (It might be noted that the work of the late George Vold, 1958, has had an influence on "the new criminology" paralleling that of Waller's on the sociology of social problems.)

As it turns out, the comparison between the development of these two approaches in our discipline is more than a case for the sociology of sociology. They contain very similar theoretical issues that have been the source of confusions and difficulties; for example, the distinction between social conditions and social problems, behavior and deviant behavior, and the independence of the scientist's definition from those of community members.

But we should return to the term "labeling" as applied to this approach to the study of deviance. Consider the collection of sociologists who frequently find themselves identified as proponents of "labeling." First, Tannenbaum is claimed by some to have fathered this view by a short statement concerning the "process of tagging" contained in his *Crime and the Community* (1938). Tannenbaum certainly had the germ of the idea, but he did not develop it. The more interesting part of his statement has to do with the "dramatization of evil," which links his use of Thomas' definition of the situation to the notion of the self-fulfilling prophecy.

After Tannenbaum one usually cites the works of Lemert (1951), Becker (1963), Erikson (1962), Kitsuse (1962), Cicourel (1963, 1968), Schur (1965), Scheff (1966), sometimes Goffman (1961), the redoubtable Garfinkel (1956), and more recently even Matza (1969). Now, whatever is common to them, the term "labeling" does not begin to indicate the diversity of their concerns.

Similarly, the term "societal reaction," which is frequently used as an alternative designation, masks the differences by pointing to an ambiguous common ground. Although "social interactionist" is so broad as to provide little focus on what is distinctive about the approach, it does underline the emphasis on process common to those associated with this development in the study of deviance. For want of a better term, then, I propose to refer hereafter to the interactionist approach, a practice adopted by Becker in his most recent discussion of this subject (1971).

In the following discussion, I should like to focus on the *sociological* issues contained in the interactionist approach to deviance. I make this statement to guard against the strong tendency for such discussions to move directly to social psychological questions, thus obscuring some of the distinctive features of this approach. The tendency to which I refer here is particularly expressed in the charge most of the critics make against it: it does not deal with the "etiology of deviant behavior." That this charge is raised so persistently is more than what some counter-critics have characterized as the amelioristic, welfaristic perspectives which have dominated the sociology of deviance. Even though Lemert and Becker have expressed their views explicitly, their statements have contained strategic ambiguities that have led even some of their followers to confuse the issue of the definition of deviant behavior.

In Lemert this ambiguity is contained in the first three postulates of his theory of sociopathic behavior. In these postulates, he moves from a statement about the differentiation and distribution of behavior in the statistical sense to "deviations from the modalities" of those distributions in the normative sense. He proposes that these deviations are functions of "culture conflict which is expressed through social organization." Since Lemert states in his third postulate that there are societal reactions to these deviations, the reader is left to make the inference that deviations from the statistical norms are perceived, defined, and treated as deviations from social norms by the reacting agents.

There are many implications of such an interpretation of Lemert's postulates, but one especially concerns me here: that the differentiated behavior in the statistical sense is conceived to be *deviant* behavior in the normative sense. Given such an interpretation, it is not surprising that proponents as well as critics should examine Lemert's theory for the implications it contains for the etiology of "deviant behavior."

However, in his discussion of this issue, Lemert (1951: 75) clearly does not consider the question of etiology a productive line of investigation. He says:

> There has been an embarrassingly large number of theories, often without any relationship to a general theory advanced to account for various specific pathologies in human behavior. . . . This has been occasioned in no small way by the preoccupation with the origins of pathological behavior and by the fallacy of confusing *original* causes with *effective* causes. All such theories have elements of truth, and the divergent viewpoints they contain can be reconciled with, the general theory here if it is granted that original causes or antecedents of deviant behaviors are many and diversified. . . . From a narrower sociological viewpoint the deviations are not significant until they are organized subjectively and transformed into active roles and become the social criteria for assigning status. The deviant individuals must react symbolically to their own behavior aberrations and fix them in their sociopsychological patterns. The deviations remain primary deviations or symptomatic and situational as long as they are rationalized or otherwise dealt with as functions of a socially acceptable role.

This statement, following a wide-ranging exploration of the origins of sources of deviant behavior (under such topic headings as "American Culture Conducive to Deviation," "Cultural Discontinuities as Critical Points Where Deviation Arises," "Anomie as a Source of Deviation," and so forth) might understandably come as a surprise to the reader. However, Lemert has further elaborated this view in his paper "The Concept of Secondary Deviation" (1967). In this work he makes clear that his theory was not and is not intended to be a theory of primary deviation.

Howard Becker's readers are presented in another way with the possibilities of misinterpretation on the issue of the etiology of deviant behavior. The problem is created by the definition of deviant and deviant behavior that has now become the citation separating the critics from the proponents of the approach. Once again, I find Merton's views instructive and useful for my purposes. In his most recent statement on deviance, he quotes the following passage from Becker (1963: 8–9):

> Deviance . . . is created by society. I do not mean this in the way it is ordinarily understood, in which the causes of deviance are located in the social situation of the deviant. . . . I mean rather that *social groups create deviance by making the*

rules whose infraction constitute deviance, and by applying those rules to particular people and labeling them as outsiders. From this point of view, deviance is not a quality of the act the person commits, but rather a consequence of the application by others of rules and sanctions to an "offender." The deviant is one to whom that label has successfully been applied; deviant behavior is behavior that people so label.

Merton (1971: 827) then opens his criticism of this view with the following:

This passage puts forward a variety of theoretical claims. The first, which it shares with every other theory of deviance, is blatantly true and trivial: namely, the statement that behavior cannot be considered "deviant" unless there are social norms from which that behavior departs. It seems banal and safe to stipulate: no rule, no rule-violating behavior.

Given Becker's statement, Merton's criticism is not without foundation. The confusion is imbedded in the conception of social rules as they function in the process by which "groups create deviance." The passage quoted by Merton clearly implies that a more or less coherent system of rules exists in social groups, that its members know what those rules are, that they know what behaviors are appropriate to those rules, and that conversely, they know what behaviors are infractions of them. If this is indeed all Becker is saying, not only in the quoted passage but in the rest of his book, one can only agree with Merton that it is blatantly true, trivial, and banal. Then we are left to wonder how it is that Becker's statement has commanded such attention.

It seems to me that the confusion is created, as in Lemert's discussion, by the subtle shift in Becker's statement of his argument. Note that after he makes the point that (1) "social groups create deviance by making rules whose infraction constitutes deviance and by applying those rules to particular people and labeling them as outsiders," he makes point (2) that "From this point of view, deviance is *not* a quality of the act the person commits, but rather a consequence of the application by others of rules and sanctions to an 'offender.'" Now, for point 1 to be a revelation to a sociologist, he would have to believe that rules are somehow given in the world; point 2 suggests that this staement is directed to such a sociologist. Deviance is *not* a quality of an act, but it is the rule that assigns the quality of deviance to the act. But of course!

So what more is there to say? There is this: Can the sociologist specify a priori the social rules or social norms, the behaviors they prescribe or proscribe, the situations in which those norms govern behavior, and the sanctions prescribed as reactions to nonconformance? If the answer to this series of questions is "Yes," then Merton is certainly justified in saying that this approach is not distinguishable from others. But on what basis can the question be answered "No"?

When we examine the works of the interactionists concerned with deviance, we find a variety of conceptions of social norms that inform their research. The common element in these conceptions is that social norms are problematic as they are invoked by members of the community to identify, define, judge, and treat persons as deviant. Sometimes the problematic character is expressed in terms such as "negotiated," "the social construction of reality," "emergent definitions of the situation," and the like. However, it is expressed, the view that social norms *are* problematic has led them to examine the commonly held sociological assumptions that find expression in the literature in conceptions of "normative systems," "cultural prescriptions," "social roles," and so forth. The focus and emphasis on the practiced and enforced rules of conduct as they are revealed in interaction rather than on abstract sociological formulations of "normative behavior" is characteristically reflected in the participant observational method of the interactionist approach to deviance.

We note also the apparent preference of the interactionist for the term "rules" rather than norms, which is related to their interest in problems in the sociology of knowledge. The conception of social interaction as organized by the invocation and application of rules by parties to the interaction leads the interactionist to investigate how those members decide that a rule has been broken, how they assign significance to that violation, how they decide what to do about it, and so on. This is turn has led to the stance common to most of the interactionists that interaction must be viewed from the perspectives of the members, which includes discerning their categories of thought, the rules by which events are classified into these categories, how treatment is differentiated by the classification of objects, and so forth. In short, there is much in this approach that can be characterized as a focus on decision-making processes "from within," whether those decisions are examined in the organization of everyday activities or in relatively more formally institutionalized organizational settings.

Examing Lemert in this light, we find the following statement about social norms (1951: 31):

> In the context of our theory norms refer to limits of variation in behavior explicitly or implicitly held in retrospect by members of a group, community, or society. The assertion that norms are seen in retrospect is another way of saying that few people, unless they are professional social scientists, are conscious of the standards of behavior in their culture. On the whole, people tend to be aware of norms only when they are breached, and only projectively, that is people dis-

cuss the action of others after it takes place, from the stand-point of its specific appropriateness and what "ought to have been done" in the situation.

It is clear enough in this statement that these members are conceived to be able to provide sociologists with norms they apply to identify norm violations *after the fact.* For the purposes of the sociologist concerned with the etiology of deviant behavior, however, an a priori specification of norms is required. He wants to investigate how those social norms do or do not determine the behavior of members, and to test the hypothesis that norm-violation *will in fact* be defined and treated as deviant. Given such a conception of social norms, discrepancies between norm-prescribed and observed behavior directs the sociologist to specify in greater detail the prescriptions that cover the contingencies of norm violation and sanctions. In contrast, when norms are viewed as problematic, the conditions that make for the problematic character of interaction are social psychological on the one hand (for example, perceptual processes such as normalization, neutralization, and denial) and sociological on the other (for example, the status relations that obtain between the "norm violator" and others, the ambiguities of the situational activities, and the integration of the "norm violating behavior" within a new definitional concensus).

The importance of the conception of norms or rules as problematic for the interactionist approach is reflected in Becker's recent clarification of his statement in *Outsiders.* The "Typology of Deviant Behavior" presented in that work was ambiguous on this question and it has been the source of considerable confusion. Since one dimension of the typology is designated obedient/rule-breaking behavior, the implication is that the rules *can* be specified a priori by the sociologist —how else could he identify rule-breaking behavior independent of the labeling of that behavior as deviant by community members? This typology has, of course, also been that basis for the criticism that in terms of Becker's definition of deviant and deviant behavior, the "secret deviant" type is a logical contradiction (Gibbs, 1966).

Acknowledging the confusion created by his original formulation, Becker (1971: 4) states:

> The distinction implied the prior existence of a determination that rule-breaking had occurred though, of course, it was just that the theory proposed to make problematic. I think it better to describe that dimension as the commission or non-commission of a given act. . . . It is useful to have a term for such activities that indicates that they are likely to be defined as deviant by others without making that a scientific judgment that the act is in fact deviant. I suggest we call them "potentially deviant."[1]

In this clarification, Becker has in effect divided the problem into (1) whether or not a given act has occurred, and (2) whether or not that act is rule-breaking. With this division, it is now possible to ask and to answer the question within the same framework: Assuming that an act has occurred, how do we (sociologists) know whether or not it is rule breaking? We know it is rule breaking if others (community members) perceive it to be so.

This answer, in turn, is of course, the target of much criticism from the perspective of the "old conception of deviant behavior." Gibbs (1966) clearly defines the issue in his criticism that it precludes treating deviant acts and reactions to them as conceptually distinct. Without entering here into a detailed examination of Gibbs' critique, I would state my agreement with his view that if the proponents of the interactionist approach are not concerned with the "etiology of deviant behavior," they might reasonably be expected to develop a theory of the reaction process.

I am being careful about my language here: I have said the proponents of the approach might be expected to develop a theory of the reaction process, without specifying the processes of reaction to *what*. The *what* consistent with the logic of the approach is first and foremost *persons*, not acts or behavior, whether deviant or not. In saying this, I am proposing that conceptual distinctions be made between "differentiated behavior" (in Lemert's sense), "norm-violating behavior" (in Gibb's sense), and "rule-breaking behavior" or "act" (in Becker's sense). With these distinctions in mind, I propose further that none of these conditions is necessary or sufficient to produce a *deviant*. Deviants are produced by the differential treatment of persons by others, and behavior or acts in any of the above sense may or may not be the occasion for such treatment. Which is to say that logically, the production of deviants *need not* have anything at all to do with their acts or behavior. Nor is it theoretically necessary that some act or behavior *even be imputed* to those who are socially differentiated as deviant by the treatment others accord him. He may be treated as deviant simply for what he is *conceived to be* (Katz, 1971). This is perhaps a more radical conceptual distinction than Gibbs had in mind, but it may help to disabuse us of the idea that the social differentiation of deviants necessarily presupposes acts or behaviors on the part of those who have been differentiated.

I mentioned earlier the tendency toward defining issues in social psychological terms in discussions of the interactionist approach to deviance. This is no less true of the proponents of the approach than of its critics. Although the former have turned away from etiological problems, they have tended to focus their concern on the effects or consequences of "labeling" and "societal reaction" for the shaping of the deviant's self-conceptions, behavior, associations, and careers. In my judgment, the problem of etiology as conventionally formulated is of minor importance for the sociology of deviance. On the other hand, I suggest that the investigation of "secondary deviation," which of course is a theoretically significant issue, is only one of two major lines of inquiry suggested by the interactionist perspective.

The second, and more neglected inquiry, concerns the social differentiation of deviants per se. If social differentiation is conceived as the processes by which persons, groups, and institutions, are *made different* through social interaction, it is clear enough that the differentiation of deviant populations are, as Lemert (1951: 21) has proposed, "a special phase of social and cultural differentiation." This sociological aspect of Lemert's conception of deviance has not been given the attention it deserves. Interest in his treatment of the processes of sociopathic individuation—the social psychological dimensions of secondary deviation—has tended to obscure the ways in which Lemert's early work has influenced our conceptions of the relation between "societal reactions" and the forms of social control.

There is, however, another more subtle aspect of the social control process that deserves attention. While the concept of secondary deviation directs attention to the relation between the reactions of the deviant to the reactions of others, there is also a concurrent, but not necessarily related, process in which members of the community react to *their own* reactions as well as to the deviants those reactions have produced. That is to say, the reactions that produce deviants generate "problems of adjustment" not only for the deviants but also for the so-called nondeviants. For example, if alcoholics are conceived to be weak-willed and irresponsible, how is one to acknowledge that one's spouse, friend, or colleague is an alcoholic; how is he to be engaged, judged, and treated in the routines of social interaction?

Such questions tend to be obscured by a bias, implicit in the sociology of deviance, that assumes that it is the *deviant's* behavior that finally must be explained. One of the points I have tried to make in this paper is that the logic of the interactionist approach enables us to uncover and examine this bias. In making this statement, I do not intend to join Bordua (1967) or Gouldner (1968) who have commented on this bias in ideological terms. I mean simply to say that on theoretical grounds, the systematic investigation of the "nondeviants'" perspectives, behavior, activities, "problems of adjustment," and so forth are as justified as an interest in the deviants they have created.

With the possible exception of Goffman's work on stigma, Matza's imaginative phenomenological analysis of the process of signification, and the works of some of the ethnomethodologists, no existing work attempts to articulate theoretically the deviant-defining processes with the *social interaction* by which nondeviants assign and maintain the deviant's defective social and moral status. Investigation of this interaction process would provide a theoretical and empirical link for studies of secondary deviation and formally organized social control activities. Within such a theoretical frame, we may then be in a position perhaps to examine and interpret the social differentiation of various categories of deviants as it is reflected in data generated by census and other social agencies.

NOTE

[1]It should be noted, however, that from the value-conflict perspective which characterizes Becker's formulation, to suggest that an act be called "potentially deviant" is not a significant clarification. The contingencies of what act becomes defined and treated as deviant are in the final analysis political, that is, they are essentially expressions of power differentials. In this sense, any act may theoretically be considered "potentially deviant."

REFERENCES

Becker, Howard S.
   1963   Outsiders. New York: Free Press.
   1966   (ed.) Social Problems: A Modern Approach. New York: Wiley. Introduction.
   1971   "Labelling Theory Reconsidered." Proceedings of the British Sociological Association, in process.
Bordua, David.
   1967   "Recent trends: Deviant behavior and social control." Annals of the American Academy of Political and Social Science 369 (January): 149–163.
Cicourel, Aaron V. and John I. Kitsuse
   1963   The Educational Decision-Makers. Indianapolis: Bobbs-Merrill.
Cicourel
   1968   The Social Organization of Juvenile Justice. New York: Wiley.
Clinard, Marshall B.
   1968   Sociology of Deviant Behavior, 3rd ed., New York: Holt Rinehart. Ch. 1.
Erikson, Kai T.
   1962   "Notes on the sociology of deviance." Social Problems 9 (Spring): 207–314.
Fuller, Richard G. and Russell R. Myers
   1941   "The natural history of social problems." American Sociological Review 6 (April): 320–329.
Garfinkel, Harold.
   1956   "Conditions of successful degradation ceremonies." American Journal of Sociology 61 (March): 420–424.

Gibbs, Jack P.
   1966   "Conceptions of deviant behavior: The old and the new." Pacific
          Sociological Review 9 (Spring): 9–14.
Goffman, Erving.
   1961   Asylums. New York: Anchor.
Gouldner, Alvin W.
   1968   "The sociologist as partisan: Sociology and the welfare state." The
          American Sociologist 3 (May): 103–116.
Horowitz, Irving Louis and M. Liebowitz.
   1968   "Social deviance and political marginality." Social Problems 15
          (Winter): 280–296.
Katz, Jack.
   1971   "Deviance and ontological labeling." unpublished manuscript.
Kitsuse, John I.
   1962   "Societal reaction to deviant behavior: Problems of theory and
          method." Social Problems 9 (Winter): 247–256.
Lemert, Edwin M.
   1951   Social Pathology. New York: McGraw-Hill. Chs. 1–4.
   1968   Human Deviance, Social Problems, and Social Control. Englewood
          Cliffs, N.J.: Prentice-Hall.
Matza, David.
   1969   Becoming Deviant. Englewood Cliffs, N.J.: Prentice-Hall.
Merton, Robert K. and Robert Nisbet.
   1971   Contemporary Social Problems. 3rd ed. New York: Harcourt Brace.
          Epilogue.
Quinney, Richard.
   1970   The Social Reality of Crime. Boston: Little, Brown.
Rushing, William A.
   1969   Deviant Behavior and Social Process. Chicago: Rand McNally.
          Ch. 1.
Scheff, T. J.
   1966   Being Mentally Ill. Chicago: Aldine.
Schur, Edwin.
   1965   Crime Without Victims. Englewood Cliffs, N.J.: Prentice-Hall.
Tannenbaum, Frank.
   1938   Crime and the Community. New York: Ginn. Ch. 1.
Turk, Austin.
   1966   "Conflict and Criminality." American Sociological Review 31
          (June): 338–352.
Vold, George.
   1958   Theoretical Criminology. New York: Oxford.
Waller, Willard.
   1936   "Social problems and the mores." American Sociological Review 1
          (December): 922–933.

15

A Note on the Uses
of Official Statistics

JOHN I. KITSUSE
AARON V. CICOUREL

Current theoretical and research formulations in the sociology of deviance are cast within the general framework of social and cultural differentiation, deviance, and social control. In contrast to the earlier moralistic conceptions of the "pathologies," the focus of description and analysis has shifted from the vagaries of morbid behavior to the patterning effects of the social-cultural environment on forms of deviant conduct. These forms of deviation are conceived as social products of the organization of groups, social structures, and institutions.

Three major lines of inquiry have developed within this general framework. One development has been the problem of explaining the rates of various forms of deviation among various segments of the population. The research devoted to this problem has produced a large body of literature in which individual, group, and areal (e.g., census tracts, regions, states, etc.) characteristics are correlated with rates of deviation. Durkheim's pioneer study of suicide is a classic example of this sociological interest. Merton's more general theory of social structure and anomie[1] may be cited as the most widely circulated statement of this problem.

The second line of investigation has been directed to the question

Reprinted from *Social Problems*, 12 (1963), pp. 131–139, by permission of the Journal of Social Problems and the Institute for the Study of Social Problems. The authors acknowledge the support of the Youth Development Program of the Ford Foundation in facilitating the preparation of this article. Footnotes have been renumbered.

of how individuals come to engage in various types of deviant behavior. From the theoretical standpoint, this question has been posed by the fact that although an aggregate of individuals may be exposed to the "same" sociogenic factors associated with deviant behavior, some individuals become deviant while others do not. Research into this problem has led some sociologists into the field of actuarial statistics and others to social and depth psychology to investigate differences in individual "adaptation" to the social-cultural environment. The search for the etiology of deviant behavior in individual differences has reintroduced the notion of "pathology," in the garb of "emotionally disturbed," "psychopathic personality," "weak ego-structure," and other psychological concepts, which has created an hiatus between sociological and social psychological approaches. Sutherland's differential association theory[2] represents a counterformulation which attempts to account for the etiology of deviant behavior within the general framework of "normal" learning processes.

A third line of inquiry has been concerned with the developmental processes of "behavior systems." Theory and research on this aspect of deviant behavior focuses on the relation between the social differentiation of the deviant, the organization of deviant activity, and the individual's conception of himself as deviant. Studies of the professional thief, convicts, prostitutes, alcoholics, hoboes, drug addicts, carnival men, and others describe and analyze the deviant subculture and its patterning effects on the interaction between deviant and others. The work of Lemert[3] presents a systematic theoretical and empirical integration of this interest in the sociology of deviance.

Although the three lines of investigation share a common interest in the organizational "sources" of deviant behavior, a theoretical integration between them has not been achieved. This is particularly apparent in the theoretical and methodological difficulties posed by the problem of relating the rates of deviant behavior to the distribution of sociogenic factors within the social structure. These difficulties may be stated in the form of two questions: 1. How is deviant behavior to be defined sociologically, and 2. what are the relevant rates of deviant behavior which constitute the facts to be explained? We shall propose that these difficulties arise as a consequence of the failure to distinguish between the social conduct which produces a *unit* of behavior (the behavior-producing processes) and the organizational activity which produces a unit in the rate of *deviant* behavior (the rate-producing processes.)[4] The failure to make this distinction has led sociologists to direct their theoretical and empirical investigations to the behavior-producing processes on the implicit assumption that the rates of deviant behavior may be explained by them. We shall discuss some of the consequences of this distinction for theory and research in the sociology of deviance by examining the problems of the "appropriateness" and "reliability" of official statistics.[5]

I

The following statement by Merton is a pertinent and instructive point of departure for a discussion of the questions raised above:

> Our primary aim is to discover how some *social structures exert a definite pressure upon certain persons in the society to engage in nonconforming rather than conforming conduct.* If we can locate groups peculiarly subject to such pressures, we would expect to find fairly high rates of deviant behavior in those groups, not because the human beings comprising them are compounded of distinctive biological tendencies but because they are responding normally to the social situation in which they find themselves. Our perspective is sociological. We look at variations in the *rates* of deviant behavior, not at its incidence.[6]

The central hypothesis that Merton derives from his theory is that "aberrant behavior may be regarded as a symptom of dissociation between culturally prescribed aspirations and socially structured avenues for realizing these aspirations."[7] The test of this general hypothesis, he suggests, would be to compare the variations in the rates of aberrant behavior among populations occupying different positions within the social structure. The question arises: What are the units of behavior which are to be tabulated to compile these rates of aberrant behavior?

Merton answers this question by discussing the kinds of rates which are "inappropriate," but he is less explicit about what may be considered "appropriate" data for sociological research. Discussing the relevance of his theory for research on juvenile delinquency, Merton presents two arguments against the use of "official" rates of deviant behavior. He asks:

> . . . to what extent and for which purposes is it feasible to make use of existing data in the study of deviant behavior? By existing data I mean the data which the machinery of society makes available—census data, delinquency rates as recorded in official or unofficial sources, data on the income distribution of an area, on the state of housing in an area, and the like . . .
>
> There is little in the history of how statistical series on the incidence of juvenile delinquency came to be collected that shows them to be the result of efforts to identify either the sources or the contexts of juvenile delinquency. These are social bookkeeping data. And it would be a happy coincidence if some of them turned out to be in a form relevant for research.

From the sociological standpoint, 'juvenile delinquency' and what it encompasses is a form of deviant behavior
for which the epidemiological data, as it were, may not be
at hand. You may have to go out and collect your own appropriately organized data rather than to take those which
are ready-made by governmental agencies.[8]

Our interpretation of this statement is that for the purposes of
sociological research, official statistics may use categories which
are unsuitable for the classification of deviant behavior. At best such
statistics classify the "same" forms of deviant behavior in different
categories and "different" forms in the same categories. Thus, the
"sources or the contexts" of the behavior are obscured.

Merton also argues against the use of official statistics on quite
different grounds. He states that such data are "unreliable" because
"successive layers of error intervene between the actual event and the
recorded event, between the actual rates of deviant behavior and the
records of deviant behavior."[9] In this statement, the argument is
that the statistics are unreliable because some individuals who manifest deviant behavior are apprehended, classified, and duly recorded
while others are not. It is assumed that if the acts of all such individuals were called to the attention of the official agencies they would
be defined as deviant and so classified and recorded. In referring to the
"unreliability" of the statistics in this sense, however, Merton appears
to suspend his "sociologically relevant" definition of deviant behavior
and implicitly invokes the definitions applied by the agencies which
have compiled the statistics. That is, the "unreliability" is viewed as
a technical and organizational problem, not a matter of differences
concerning the definition of deviant behavior.

Thus, Merton argues against the use of official statistics on two
separate grounds. On the one hand, official statistics are not appropriately organized for sociological research because they are not collected by the application of a "sociologically relevant" definition of
deviant behavior. On the other hand, he implies that official statistics
could be used if "successive layers of error" did not make them "unreliable." But if the statistics are inappropriate for sociological research on the first ground, would they not be inappropriate regardless
of their "unreliability"?

It is evident, however, that "inappropriate" or not, sociologists,
including Merton himself,[10] do make use of the official statistics after
a few conventional words of caution concerning the "unreliability" of
such statistics. The "social bookkeeping data" are, after all, considered to bear some, if unknown, relation to the "actual" rates of deviant
behavior that interest sociologists. But granted that there are practical
reasons for the use of official statistics, are there any theoretical
grounds which justify their use, or is this large body of data useless for

research in the sociology of deviance? This question directs us to examine more closely the theoretical and methodological bases of the two arguments against their use.

II

The objection to the official statistics because they are "inappropriate" is, as indicated above, on definitional grounds. The argument is that insofar as the definitions of deviant behavior incorporated in the official statistics are not "sociologically relevant," such statistics are *in principle* "inappropriate" for sociological research. What then is a sociologically relevant definition of deviant behavior and what are to be considered "appropriately organized data" for sociological research?[11]

We suggest that the question of the theoretical significance of the official statistics can be rephrased by shifting the focus of investigation from the processes by which *certain forms of behavior* are socially and culturally generated to the processes by which *rates of deviant behavior* are produced. Merton states that his primary aim is to explain the former processes, and he proposes to look at variations in the rates of deviant behavior as indices of the processes. Implicit in this proposal is the assumption that an explanation of the behavior-producing processes is also an explanation of the rate-producing processes. This assumption leads Merton to consider the correspondence between the forms of behavior which his theory is designed to explain and their distribution in the social structures as reflected in some set of statistics, including those commonly used official statistics "which are ready-made by governmental agencies."

Let us propose, however, the following: Our primary aim is to explain the *rates of deviant behavior*. So stated, the question which orients the investigation is not how individuals are motivated to engage in behavior defined by the sociologist as "deviant." Rather, the definition and content of deviant behavior are viewed as problematic, and the focus of inquiry shifts from the forms of behavior (modes of individual adaptation in Merton's terminology) to the "societal reactions" as deviant.[12] In contrast to Merton's formulation which focuses on forms of behavior as dependent variables (with structural pressures conceived to be the independent variables), we propose here to view the rates of deviant behavior as dependent variables. Thus, the explanation of rates of deviant behavior would be concerned specifically with the processes of rate construction.

The problem of the definition of "deviant behavior" is directly related to the shift in focus proposed here. The theoretical conception which guides us is that the *rates of deviant behavior* are produced by *the actions taken by persons in the social system* which define, classify, and record certain behaviors as deviant.[13] If a given form of behavior is not interpreted as deviant by such persons it would not appear as a unit in whatever set of rates we may attempt to explain (the statistics of local social welfare agencies, "crimes known to the police," Uniform Crime Reports, court records, etc.). The persons who define and activate the rate-producing processes may range from the neighborhood "busybody" to officials of law enforcement agencies.[14] From this point of view, *deviant behavior* is behavior which is organizationally defined, processed, and treated as "strange," "abnormal," "theft," "delinquent," etc., by the personnel in the social system which has produced the rate. By these definitions, a sociological theory of devience would focus on three interrelated problems of explanation: (1) How different forms of behavior come to be defined as deviant by various groups or organizations in the society, (2) how individuals manifesting such behaviors are organizationally processed to produce rates of deviant behavior among various segments of the population, and (3) how acts which are officially or unofficially defined as deviant are generated by such conditions as family organization, role inconsistencies or situational "pressures."

What are the consequences of these definitions for the question regarding the relevance of official statistics for sociological research? First, the focus on the processes by which rates are produced allows us to consider any set of statistics, "official" as well as "unofficial," to be relevant. The question of whether or not the statistics are "appropriately organized" is not one which is determined by reference to the correspondence between the sociologist's definition of deviant behavior and the organizational criteria used to compile the statistics. Rather the categories which organize a given set of statistics are taken as given—the "cultural definitions," to use Merton's term, of deviant behavior are *par excellence* the relevant definitions for research. The specification of the definitions explicitly or implicitly stated in the statistical categories is viewed as an empirical problem. Thus, the question to be asked is not about the "appropriateness" of the statistics, but about the definitions incorporated in the categories applied by the personnel of the rate-producing social system to identify, classify, and record behavior as deviant.

Second, a unit in a given rate of deviant behavior is not defined in terms of a given form of behavior or a "syndrome" of behavior. The behaviors which result in the classification of individuals in a given deviant category are *not necessarily* similar, i.e., the "objective" manifestation of the "same" forms of behavior may result in the classification of some individuals as deviant but not others. For example, with reference to the rates of delinquency reported by the police department, we would ask: What are the criteria that the police personnel use to identify and process a youth as "incorrigible," "sex offender," "vandal," etc.? The criteria of such categories are vague enough to include a wide range of behaviors which in turn may be produced by various "sources and contexts" with the social structure.[15]

Third, the definition of deviant behavior as behavior which is organizationally processed as deviant provides a different perspective on the problem of the "unreliability" of the official statistics. Insofar as we are primarily concerned with explaining rates rather than the forms of deviant behavior, such statistics may be accepted as a record of the number of those who have been differentiated as variously deviant at different levels of social control and treatment. The "successive layers of error" which may result from the failure of control agencies to record all instances of certain forms of behavior, or from the exclusion of cases from one set of statistics that are included in another, do not render such statistics "unreliable," unless they are assigned self-evident status. By the definition of deviance proposed here, such cases are not among those processed as deviant by the organizations which have produced the statistics and thus are not officially deviant. To reject these statistics as "unreliable" because they fail to record the "actual" rate of deviant behavior assumes that certain behavior is always deviant independent of social actions which define it as deviant.

Fourth, the conception of rates of deviant behavior as the product of the socially organized activities of social structures provides a method of specifying the "relevant structure" to be investigated. The rates are constructed from the statistics compiled by specifiable organizations, and those rates must be explained in terms of the deviant-processing activities of those organizations. Thus, rates can be viewed as indices of organizational processes rather than as indices of the incidence of certain forms of behavior. For example, variations in the rates of deviant behavior among a given group (e.g., Negroes) as reflected in the statistics of different organizations may be a product of the differing definitions of deviant behavior used by those organizations, differences in the processing of deviant behavior, differences in the ideological, political, and other organizational conditions which affect the rate-making processes.

III

We wish now to discuss briefly some recent work concerning adult and juvenile criminal acts which lends support to the thesis presented above.[16] Let us assume that an ideal system of law enforcement would lead to the apprehension of all persons who have committed criminal acts as defined by the statutes and adjudicated in the manner prescribed by those statutes. In the ideal case, there would be little room for administrative interpretation and discretion. The adjudication process would proceed on the basis of evidence deemed legally admissible and with the use of the adversary system to convict those who are guilty and exonerate those against whom there is insufficient evidence.[17] Criminologists have long recognized that the practiced and enforced system of criminal law, at all levels of the process, does not fulfill this ideal conception of criminal justice strictly governed by the definitions and prescriptions of statutes. Therefore, criminal statistics clearly cannot be assumed to reflect a system of criminal justice functioning as ideally conceived, and "labels assigned convicted defendants" are not to be viewed as "the statutory equivalents of their actual conduct."[18]

What such statistics do reflect, however, are the specifically organizational contingencies which condition the application of specific statutes to actual conduct through the interpretations, decisions, and actions of law enforcement personnel. The decisions and discretionary actions of persons who administer criminal justice have been documented by the American Bar Foundation study cited above. That study and other research[19] indicates the following:

1. There is considerable ambiguity in defining the nature of criminal conduct within the limits defined by the statutes. Categories of criminal conduct are the product of actual practices within these limits, and the decisions which must be made to provide the basis for choosing the laws which will receive the greatest attention.

2. The discretion allowed within the administration of criminal justice means that admissible evidence may give way to the prosecutor's power to determine whether or not to proceed, even in cases where there is adequate evidence to prosecute. The judge, as well as the police or the victim, also has discretion (e.g., sentencing), and some discretion is also extended to correctional institutions.

3. Most persons charged with criminal conduct plead guilty (from 80 to 90 per cent, according to the references cited by Newman) and jury trials are rare. Thus, the adversary aspect of the law is not always practiced because many of the lower income offenders cannot afford lawyers and often distrust public defenders. Criminal justice depends upon a large number of guilty pleas. Many of these cases would be acquitted if there were more trials.

4. Statistics are affected by such "accommodations in the conviction process." Some offenders are excluded because they are not processed even though known to be guilty (e.g., drug addicts, prostitutes and gamblers are often hired by the police or coerced by them to help apprehend other offenders), and the practices of relabeling offenses and reducing sentences because of insufficient evidence, "deals," and tricks (e.g., telling the defendant or his lawyer that because the offender "seems like a decent person" the charge will be reduced from a felony to a misdemeanor, when in fact the

prosecution finds there is insufficient evidence for either charge.) These accommodations may occur at the time of arrest, or during prior or subsequent investigation of crimes, filing of complaints, adjudication, sentencing and postsentencing relations with authorities, and so on.

The significance of the American Bar Foundation study goes beyond the documentation of the usual complaints about inadequate recording, inflated recording, and the like. More important, it underlines the way criminal statistics fail to reflect the decisions made and discretion used by law enforcement personnel and administrators, and the general accommodations that can and do occur. An offender's record, then, may never reflect the ambiguous decisions, administrative discretions, or accommodations of law enforcement personnel; a statistical account may thus seriously distort an offender's past activities.

The administration of justice vis-a-vis juveniles is even more discretionary than for adults due to the philosophy of the juvenile court law. The juvenile offender is not officially viewed as a criminal, but rather as an adolescent who is "misdirected," "disturbed," from a "poor environment," and the like. The legal concept of an adversary system is notably absent. The philosophy, however, is differentially interpreted, with police more likely to view juveniles as adult criminals, while probation officers and some judges view the offender within the intended meaning of the law. The early work of Paul Tappan on juvenile court practices[20] shows how a juvenile court judge, on the counsel of a social worker or other "treatment oriented" personnel, may dispose of a case in a manner which negates all previous characterizations of the offender by police, probation officer, school officials, and the like. The report of the more recent California Special Study Commission on Juvenile Justice[21] alludes vaguely to this inconsistency, and in some passages flatly states that many variations of organizational procedures and interpretations by personnel differentially influence the administration of juvenile justice in California. The use of existing stereotypes and imputations of social characteristics to juvenile defendants by law enforcement personnel routinely introduces nonlegal criteria and actions into the organizational procedures of the legal process and significantly influences the realization of judicial objectives.[22]

We wish to state explicitly that the interpretation of official statistics proposed here *does not* imply that the forms of behavior which the sociologist might define and categorize as deviant (e.g., Merton's modes of adaptation) have no factual basis or theoretical importance. Nor do we wish to imply that the question of how behaviors so defined are produced by the social structure is not a sociologically relevant question. The implication of our interpretation is rather that *with respect to the problem of rates of deviant behavior* the theoretical question is: what forms of behavior are organizationally defined as deviant, and how are they classified, recorded, and treated by persons in the society?

In our discussion, we have taken the view that official statistics, reflecting as they do the variety of organizational contingencies in the process by which deviants are differentiated from nondeviants, are sociologically relevant data. An individual who is processed as "convicted," for example, is sociologically differentiable from one who is "known to the police" as criminal—the former may legally be incarcerated, incapacitated, and socially ostracized; the latter remains "free." The fact that both may have "objectively" committed the same crime is of theoretical and empirical significance, but it does not alter the sociological difference between them. The *pattern* of such "errors" is among the facts that a sociological theory of deviance must explain, for they are indications of the organizationally defined processes by which individuals are differentiated as deviant.

Indeed, in modern societies where bureaucratically organized agencies are increasingly invested with social control functions, the activities of such agencies are centrally important "sources and contexts" which generate as well as maintain definitions of deviance and produce populations of deviants. Thus, rates of deviance constructed by the use of statistics routinely issued by these agencies are social facts *par excellence*. A further implication of this view is that if the sociologist is interested in how forms of *deviant* behavior are produced by social structures, the forms that must be explained are those which not only are defined as deviant by members of such structures but those which also activate the unofficial and/or "official" processes of social control. By directing attention to such processes, the behavior-producing and rate-producing processes may be investigated and compared within a single framework.

NOTES

[1] Robert K. Merton, *Social Theory and Social Structure*, revised, Glencoe, Ill.: The Free Press, 1957, Chapter 4.

[2] Edwin H. Sutherland and Donald R. Cressey, *Principles of Criminology*, fifth edition, New York: Macmillan, 1956, Chapter 4.

[3] Edwin M. Lemert, *Social Pathology*, New York: McGraw-Hill, 1951, esp. Chapters 1–4. See also, Sutherland and Cressey, *Principles of Criminology*, Chapters 12–13.

[4] The conception of the "rate-producing" processes as socially organized activities is taken from work by Harold Garfinkel, and is primarily an appli-

cation of what he has termed the "praxeological rule." See Harold Garfinkel, "Some Sociological Concepts and Methods for Psychiatrists," *Psychiatric Research Reports* 6 (October, 1956), pp. 181–195; Harold Garfinkel and Harry Brickman, "A Study of the Composition of the Clinic Patient Population of the Outpatient Department of the U.C.L.A. Neuropsychiatric Institute," unpublished manuscript.

[5]For a discussion of these problems, see Sophia M. Robison, *Can Delinquency Be Measured?*, New York: Columbia University Press, 1936. See also Sutherland and Cressey, *Principles of Criminology*, Chapter 2.

[6]Robert K. Merton, *Social Theory and Social Structure*, p. 147. Merton's comments on the theory of social structure and anomie may be found in Chapter 5 of that volume, and in "Social Conformity, Deviation, and Opportunity Structures: A Comment on the Contributions of Dubin and Cloward," *American Sociological Review*, 24 (April, 1959), pp. 177–189; See also his remarks in *New Perspectives for Research on Juvenile Delinquency*, H. Witmer and R. Kotinsky, eds., U.S. Government Printing Office, 1956.

[7]Merton, *Social Theory and Social Structure*, p. 134.

[8]Merton, *New Perspectives for Research on Juvenile Delinquency*, Witmer and Kotinsky, eds., p. 32.

[9]Merton, in *New Perspectves*, Witmer and Kotinsky, eds.

[10]For example, ". . . crude (and not necessarily reliable) crime statistics suggest . . ." etc., Merton, *Social Theory and Social Structure*, p. 147. In a more extensive comment on the limitations imposed on research by the use of official statistics, Merton states: "Its decisive limitation derives from a circumstance which regularly confronts sociologists seeking to devise measures of theoretical concepts by drawing upon an array of social data which *happen* to be recorded in the statistical series established by agencies of the society— namely, the circumstance that these data of social bookkeeping which happen to be on hand are not necessarily the data which best measure the concept. . . . Pragmatic considerations of this sort are of course no suitable alternative to theoretically derived indicators of the concept," p. 165.

[11]Merton proposes to define deviant behavior in terms of the "acceptance" or "rejection" of cultural goals and/or institutionalized means. Interpreting the two terms literally, a given form of behavior (adaptation) is to be considered deviant if it is oriented by some cultural goals (to be specified by the sociologists) and/or the institutionalized means (also to be specified) which govern conduct with respect to those goals. By this definition, appropriately organized data would require that behaviors be classified in the typology of "modes of individual adaptation." But what are the operational criteria by which "acceptance" or "rejection" of cultural goals and institutionalized means are to be inferred from observed behavior? How, for example, is the sociologist to distinguish between behavior which indicates "conformity" from "over-conformity" (which presumably would be classified as "ritualism"); or "retreatism" from "innovation"? Unless a set of rules for the classification of behavior as deviant can be derived from the theory, rates of deviant behavior cannot be constructed to test its validity.

[12]For a discussion of the concept of "societal reaction" see Lemert, *Social Pathology*, Chapter 4.

[13]For a preliminary research application of this formulation, see John I. Kitsuse, "Societal Reaction to Deviant Behavior: Problems of Theory and Method," *Social Problems*, 9 (Winter, 1962), pp. 247–56.

[14]We recognize, of course, that many individuals may be labeled "strange," "crooks," "crazy," etc., and ostracized by members of a community, yet be unknown to the police or any other official agency. Insofar as such individuals are labeled and treated as deviants, they constitute a population which must be explained in any theory of deviance. In this paper, however, we are primarily concerned with the theoretical relevance of official statistics for the study of deviance.

[15]In any empirical investigation of such criteria, it is necessary to distinguish between the formal (official) interpretive rules (as defined by a manual of procedures, constitution, and the like) which are to be employed by the personnel of the organizations in question, and the unofficial rules used by the personnel in their deviant-processing activities, e.g., differential treatment on the basis of social class, race, ethnicity, or varying conceptions of "deviant" behavior.

[16]The material in this section is taken from an unpublished paper by Cicourel entitled "Social Class, Family Structure and the Administration of Juvenile Justice," and is based on a study of the social organization of juvenile justice in two Southern California communities with populations of approximately 100,000 each.

[17]See Donald J. Newman, "The Effects of Accommodations in Justice Administration on Criminal Statistics," *Sociology and Social Research,* 46 (Jan., 1962), pp. 144–155; *Administration of Criminal Justice,* Chicago: American Bar Foundation, 1955, unpublished.

[18]Newman, "The Effects of Accommodations," pp. 145–146.

[19]See Newman, "The Effects of Accommodations," pp. 146–151, and the references cited.

[20]Paul Tappan, *Juvenile Delinquency,* New York: McGraw-Hill, 1949.

[21]Report of the *Governor's Special Study Commission on Juvenile Justice,* Parts I and II, Sacramento: California State Printing Office, 1960.

[22]To illustrate how organizational procedures and imputations can affect official statistics, we refer to a preliminary finding by Cicourel (cited in footnote 17) which shows that one of two communities studied (Community A) has both a slightly larger population and a higher adult crime rate. Yet this community had (as of November, 1962) 3,200 current cases of juveniles suspected or confirmed to be offenders. Community B, on the other hand, had approximately 8,000 current suspected or confirmed juvenile cases. Community A has two juvenile officers on its staff, while Community B has five juvenile officers.